ENFORCIN(

M000314896

2—

ENFORCING SILENCE

Academic Freedom, Palestine and
the Criticism of Israel

Edited by
DAVID LANDY, RONIT LENTIN AND
CONOR MCCARTHY

ZED

Enforcing Silence: Academic Freedom, Palestine and the Criticism of Israel
was first published in 2020 by Zed Books Ltd, The Foundry, 17 Oval Way,
London SE11 5RR, UK.

www.zedbooks.net

Copyright © David Landy, Ronit Lentin and Conor McCarthy 2020
Copyright in this Collection © Zed Books 2020

The right of David Landy, Ronit Lentin and Conor McCarthy to be identified
as the editors of this work has been asserted by them in accordance with the
Copyright, Designs and Patents Act, 1988

Typeset in Bulmer by Swales and Willis Ltd, Exeter, Devon
Index by ed.emery@thefreeuniversity.net
Cover design by Steve Marsden

Printed and bound by CPI Group (UK) Ltd, Croydon, CR0 4YY

All rights reserved. No part of this publication may be reproduced, stored
in a retrieval system or transmitted in any form or by any means, electronic,
mechanical, photocopying or otherwise, without the prior permission of Zed
Books Ltd.

A catalogue record for this book is available from the British Library

ISBN 978-1-78699-651-0 hb
ISBN 978-1-78699-650-3 pb
ISBN 978-1-78699-652-7 pdf
ISBN 978-1-78699-653-4 epub
ISBN 978-1-78699-654-1 mobi

MIX
Paper from
responsible sources
FSC® C013604

Contents

Figures

About the contributors

RABAB IBRAHIM ABDULHADI is Director and Senior Scholar in Arab and Muslim Ethnicities and Diasporas Studies and Associate Professor of Ethnic Studies/Race and Resistance Studies at San Francisco State University. A co-author of *Mobilizing Democracy: Changing US Policy in the Middle East* (1990) and over 70 articles, she co-edited American Quarterly's 'Forum on Palestine and American Studies' (2015) and *Arab and Arab American Feminisms: Gender, Violence and Belonging* (2011). She serves on the editorial board of the *Islamophobia Studies Journal*, and the boards of the World Congress of Middle East Studies and the Afro-Middle East Centre. She co-founded the California Scholars for Academic Freedom (http://cascholars4academicfreedom.word press.com/), the US Campaign for the Academic and Cultural Boycott of Israel (http://www.usacbi.org/), Feminists for Justice in/for Palestine, the Palestine Solidarity Committee, the Union of Palestinian Women's Associations in North America, and the US branch of the General Union of Palestinian Students. In 1985, she initiated and co-organized the 1985 national 26-city US tour on 'Israel and South Africa: The Apartheid Connection?'

HILARY AKED is a freelance writer and investigative researcher whose PhD thesis examined the UK Israel lobby and its responses to the Boycott, Divestment and Sanctions (BDS) movement. They are the author of the forthcoming book *Friends of Israel* (Verso, 2020), examining the UK Zionist movement, and co-author of three Public Interest Investigations reports, most recently *Islamophobia in Europe: How Governments Are Enabling the Far-Right 'Counter-Jihad' Movement* (Public 2019). They also contribute to *The Independent*, *Al Jazeera*, *Electronic Intifada*, and other outlets.

JEFF HANDMAKER teaches human rights and researches legal mobilization at the International Institute of Social Studies of Erasmus University Rotterdam. Among his publications are: 'Taking Academic Freedom Seriously: Exploring the Legal and Moral Underpinnings of BDS' (2015) and *Mobilising International Law for 'Global Justice'* (2019).

YARA HAWARI is an Honorary Research Fellow at the University of Exeter where she completed her PhD. She is also the Palestine Policy Fellow for Al Shabaka – the Palestine Policy Network.

JAMIL KHADER is Professor of English and Dean of Research at Bethlehem University, Palestine. He is the author and editor of two books and his numerous articles have appeared in various international journals and different collections. His political commentary has been featured in the *Philosophical Salon*, *Middle East Monitor*, *Mondoweiss*, *Truth-out*, *In These Times*, *Aljazeera* in English, *Jadaliyya*, *The Palestine Chronicle*, and others. He is currently working on a monograph on the significance of the concrete universality of the Palestinian struggle for freedom for rethinking international leftist politics.

DAVID LANDY is director of the Masters in Race, Ethnicity, Conflict in Trinity College Dublin and a former chair of the Ireland Palestine Solidarity Campaign. He is the author of *Jewish Identity and Palestinian Rights: Diaspora Jewish Opposition to Israel*

RONIT LENTIN is a retired Associate Professor of Sociology, Trinity College Dublin, and chair of Academics for Palestine. Her books include: *Women and the Politics of Military Confrontation: Palestinian and Israeli Gendered Narratives of Dislocation* (2002), *Thinking Palestine* (2008), *Co-Memory and Melancholia: Israelis Memorialising the Palestinian Nakba* (2010), and *Traces of Racial Exception: Racializing Israeli Settler Colonialism* (2018).

TALA MAKHOUL is an independent researcher. They have been presenting and publishing papers on political movements in the Arab world since 2017.

CONOR MCCARTHY is a lecturer in the School of English, Maynooth University. He is the editor of *The Revolutionary and Anti-Imperialist Writings of James Connolly 1893–1916* (2016), and author of *The Cambridge Introduction to Edward Said* (2010) and *Modernisation, Crisis and Culture in Ireland 1969–1992* (2000). He has published journal articles and book chapters on Edward Said and on Irish literature and intellectual politics.

SINEAD PEMBROKE works in Trinity College Dublin and holds a PhD in sociology from University College Dublin.

JOHN REYNOLDS teaches in the Law Department of the National University of Ireland, Maynooth. He teaches and writes about questions of international law as they relate to colonialism, race, and political economy. His book on *Empire, Emergency and International Law* (2017) was awarded the Kevin Boyle Book Prize for Outstanding Legal Scholarship.

NICK RIEMER is a senior lecturer in the English and Linguistics departments at the University of Sydney and a member of the Laboratoire d'histoire des théories linguistiques' at the Université Paris-Diderot. Active in the BDS campaign, he is currently preparing a study of the intellectual and institutional politics of the academic boycott.

C. HEIKE SCHOTTEN is Associate Professor of Political Science at the University of Massachusetts Boston and a member of the organizing collective for the US Campaign for Academic and Cultural Boycott of Israel (USABI). She is the author, most recently, of *Queer Terror: Life, Death, and Desire in the Settler Colony* (2018).

ARIANNE SHAHVISI is a Kurdish-British writer and academic, based in Brighton. She holds a doctorate in philosophy from the University of Cambridge, and is a lecturer in ethics at the Brighton and Sussex Medical School, where she conducts research across a range of topics in applied philosophy, with current projects focused on reproductive justice, feminist epistemology, migration, and global health ethics. Arianne serves as an editorial board member for *Kohl*, a bilingual gender studies journal focusing on the Middle East and North Africa region, and is science editor for literary magazine *The Offing*, which seeks out and supports work by those marginalized in literary spaces.

Foreword

Rabab Ibrahim Abdulhadi

When Ronit Lentin invited me on 22 March 2018 to contribute a chapter to a volume she and her colleagues David Landy and Conor McCarthy were co-editing on academic freedom and the academic boycott of Israel, I was excited. I immediately responded on the same day, affirming my interest and asking for the concept paper and more details on deadlines.

I was as eager to tell 'my story', and share how I experienced bullying, smearing, and harassment by the Israel lobby and its partners at San Francisco State University (SFSU) and on other university campuses. I did not see my story as my private property or a particular experience; it reflected and represented the collective stories of public intellectuals inside and outside the academy who sought to speak up for justice in and for Palestine.

It seemed to be a no brainer. I had known Ronit for a long time through her work as a staunch anti-Zionist Israeli feminist. Along with Simona Sharoni, Ella Shohat, Orly Lubin, Lea Pipman, Lea Tsemel, Felicia Langer, and many others, I saw Ronit as part of *my* community – a community that jointly builds a different future in Palestine to replace the Israeli settler colonial racist project that made it impossible for us to even physically meet on equal grounds unless we saw each other outside Palestine.

The importance of discussing these issues was very clear. To my knowledge, this is the first volume that addresses the relationship between academic freedom and institutional academic boycott. This relationship has had a major impact on my life in different aspects – as a Palestinian who experienced first-hand Israeli colonialism, racism, and occupation; as an activist in the student, feminist, and peace and justice movement; as a scholar who, like others, subscribed to the principles of BDS before the Palestinian 2005 BDS call; and finally, as a direct target of Zionist groups who sought to exact a massive punishment[1] against those of us who exercised our academic freedom by speaking up about justice in/for Palestine, including the call for an Academic and Cultural Boycott of Israel (ACBI) as a mechanism of accountability for publicly engaged intellectuals.

I do not recall a time in my life when I did not experience bans on freedom of speech. I grew up under Jordanian rule and Israeli military occupation. I remember Jordanian soldiers roaming the streets of my hometown, Nablus, listening for incriminating evidence to punish violators of the ban on Radio Cairo. I remember the grown-ups defying the ban, albeit privately, as my parents, aunts, and uncles listened to Jamal Abdel Nasser speeches and other broadcasts. That defiance in the 1950s and 1960s was an extension of rejecting the erasure of Palestinian experiences of displacement and dispossession since the Nakba in 1948.

Boycott was also an integral Palestinian strategy of resistance as it has been in other anti-colonial and anti-racist movements, such as South Africa, the United States, Chile, farm workers, etc. After 1948, Palestinian teachers boycotted the Israeli institutions of higher education and refused to participate in perpetuating a colonial education. In the West Bank, where I grew up, we boycotted Coca-Cola and Ford cars before 1967. After the 1967 occupation, I recall that normalization of Israel's rule was completely out of the question. My mother and her friends in the women's movement boycotted Israeli goods since they first appeared in the West Bank markets. No one I knew talked to, cooperated, or dialogued with Zionist individuals and groups though anti-Zionist Jews and Israelis were always seen as integral to the Palestinian resistance and liberation movement.

The refusal to normalize Israel's colonialism, racism, and occupation was a staple of Palestinian lived experience. This carried through the praxis of the General Union of Palestinian Students (GUPS) and other mass institutions of the PLO throughout the world, including the GUPS US chapter in which I was involved. A similar praxis characterized our approach in Palestinian feminist and solidarity circles. While every single convention we held between 1986 and 1995 included more than just a token Israeli and Jewish comrade, UPWA (Union of Palestinian Women's Associations in North America) resisted the normalization agenda that accompanied the 1987 Intifada.

We faced similar challenges of silencing Palestine in our work with the Palestine Solidarity Committee (PSC). Zionists on the New York City Board of Education habitually intervened to cancel a space we had already rented or to claim that a bureaucratic error made the space unavailable. The officials in the Board of Education would veto the rental agreements we signed with the custodians of the school. A glaring example was the auditorium of the Dr Martin Luther King, Jr. High School near the Lincoln Center. In the mid-1980s we reserved and paid a deposit for the auditorium for our annual 29 November commemoration of the International Day of Solidarity with the People of Palestine. To fight for the space and force the Zionists in the Board of Education to stop harassing us, Leticia Pena, a lawyer and a member of the National Executive Committee of PSC, called and promised to hold a press conference to expose their Zionist bias and violation of the contract if they did not back off. The Board of Education eventually did but not until they sent several undercover police officers to spy on us and harass our distinguished speakers.

Zionists in the peace and justice movement similarly denied us freedom of speech and excluded us from different platforms. For example, in the late 1980s/early 1990s, we had no choice but to boycott the Left Forum after the organizers demanded to review the list of books we were planning to display before agreeing to rent us a literature table. Likewise, leading organizers of several national protests against nuclear weapons, US intervention in Central America, and women's reproductive rights, refused to include speakers on Palestine. We argued for the relevance of Palestine, citing Israel's atomic bombs,[2] the arming of death squads in El Salvador and Guatemala and the Contras in Nicaragua,[3] and the large number of Palestinian women protesters who suffered miscarriages after breathing poisonous tear gas during the 1987 Intifada.[4] None of the arguments we made succeeded in breaking the silencing of Palestine until our expertise on regional history and politics was crucial to making sense of the 1991 US Gulf War on Iraq. Even then, demarcation lines of what we could speak about and what was completely off the table were drawn.

The problem was even worse in the academy than it was in the peace and justice movement or in mainstream circles of 'Middle East' politics. For starters, the academy is much more consistent, and has perfected the bureaucratic game of seeking to enforce a false dichotomy between the research agenda and research questions, on one hand, and the relationship scholars have with the subject matter and with the communities at the heart of that subject matter, on the other. The academy is also notorious for compartmentalizing research agendas and separating what it legitimizes as scholarship and what it defines as falling outside research and relegated to activism, with the latter denigrated and assigned a lesser value in the neoliberal academic 'market' than the former. Additionally, what 'cautious' academics present as genuine claims for 'neutrality', and 'lack of bias', and respect for the privacy of 'colleagues' views', only reifies the status quo, disciplines thought, and curtails critical thinking. The fear of losing the rewards administrators dangle before the eyes of academics they supervise forces the latter group to toe the line. Those who refuse such coercion are locked out of career stability and progression.

The neoliberal agenda uses 'concern for students' as a smokescreen to cover up the real motives to silence radical educators. For example, during my post-doc at the Center for the Study of Gender and Sexuality (CSGS) at New York University, the Sociology Department refused to cross-list my course on 'Gender, Identity and Society in the Middle East' that I had also taught at Yale as a grad student (and won the top award) under the pretext that my syllabus displayed bias. They pointed to information sheets I asked students to fill out which included the question, 'are you a feminist' with options for students to say, 'yes', 'no', 'I don't know', and explain their answers. Members of the same department also refused to participate in the faculty and student walkout in 2004 when US President Bush declared war on Iraq. While the walkout was largely symbolic, the faculty members who decided to cross the picket line justified their action through a conservative misunderstanding that the walkout would have been a reneging of the faculty's responsibilities to the students rather than their obligation to teach students in ways beyond the classroom.

Millennial political developments in the US and Palestine tested more than ever the university–community constructed boundaries, posing anew the question of how scholars respond to neoliberal academic changes that threaten their careers if they choose to speak up. This became especially acute in the aftermath of the 2001 World Trade Center bombings and the 2002 Israeli reinvasion of Palestinian cities, villages, and refugee camps. The Israel lobby seized the moment to draw on Islamophobic and 'war on terror' public and official discourses to discredit the Palestinian struggle. Meanwhile Israel was busy trying to destroy the infrastructure of Palestinian social fabric, especially education. Once again, the Israeli military closed down Palestinian schools and universities as a form of collective punishment. During that period, the Israeli military destroyed over one million records of Palestinian high school examinations.

Doing nothing in the face of violations to Palestinian academic freedom was not an option. When intellectuals in Palestine initiated ACBI as an organized and collective form of holding Israel and culpable Israeli academic institutions accountable, and called upon me, I did not hesitate to join. During my post-doc at NYU, I served as the unofficial faculty advisor to the Students for Justice in Palestine (SJP) who were planning an academic boycott inspired by Columbia University's example. As we see with other cases discussed in this volume, my activism in ACBI, speaking up against the US war on Iraq, Islamophobia, and the war on terror, was not cost-free. The tenure-track position that was to materialize upon my completion of the NYU post-doc never materialized. Though NYU endowment was at a record high, the university claimed that it had no funds to initiate a joint search in Gender and Sexuality and Middle East Studies for which I could apply.

SFSU repeated the same story almost verbatim in the aftermath of the 2008–2009 Israeli war on Gaza and the intensive lobbying by Zionist groups to silence Palestine. The immediate target was a planned lecture by Omar Barghouti, the co-founder of the BDS movement, on the second anniversary of the Palestinian Cultural

Mural honouring the late Professor Edward Said.[5] The long-term strategy of SFSU and its Zionist partners was to pre-empt any potential for organizing a BDS campaign on our campus. SFSU was exhibiting deeper commitments to the neoliberal agenda and courting corporate sponsors, including Zionist donors. In addition to hosting Barghouti and my participation in co-founding USACBI, I was also developing the academic program in Arab and Muslim Ethnicities and Diasporas (AMED) Studies that we saw as the latest chapter in decolonizing the curriculum, which started with the longest US student strike and what we refer to as 'the spirit of 68'.[6]

Immediately following Omar Barghouti's lecture, the SFSU president cancelled the searches for the two tenure-track faculty positions in AMED Studies and then proceeded to defund the two lines altogether, leaving me since 2010 as a one-person program with no staff, operating budget, or faculty. To make up for SFSU's hostility and lack of institutional support, we brought together a broad-based dedicated group of students, faculty, and activists from within and outside SFSU. Since then we have succeeded in institutionalizing AMED Studies in SFSU, with an academic minor, 22 courses, the Edward Said Scholarship, and collaborative agreement with An-Najah National University. However, defeating Zionist and neoliberal forces at SFSU only invited escalated attacks by the Israel lobby. This brings me to the reasons why I could not write the chapter I was so eager to contribute to this unique volume.

I received Ronit's email while I was in Nablus, Palestine. We had just concluded the second of two inaugural international conferences on 'Teaching Palestine: Pedagogical Praxis and the Indivisibility of Justice' at Birzeit University and An-Najah National University. We were elated that we were able to organize, hold, and conclude the two conferences on such a high note.

At the same time, we were concerned that Israel might stop Robin D. G. Kelley and me from entering Palestine. The two of us serve on the International Advisory Board of USACBI and Israel had started to more systematically stop and turn back other advocates of BDS, such as leaders of Jewish Voice for Peace and the Center for Constitutional Rights, in line with new Israeli legislation that seeks to prevent the Palestine solidarity movement from spreading further. Both Robin and I agreed that we would risk it and take our chances. We devised Plan B and Plan C for two alternative programs in Jordan and Lebanon if Israel prevented us from entering Palestine. Three young members of our delegation, a Palestinian and two African Americans, were stopped and interrogated by the Israeli military for several hours at the bridge (King Hussein according to Jordan and the world, and Allenby according to Israel). Eventually we were able to get on our way and reach our first destination in Ramallah on the eve of the Birzeit conference.

The next day, however, on Friday 23 March to be precise, I received an email from my university provost Jennifer Summit demanding that I take down the unofficial Facebook page of the AMED Studies[7] program on which a statement by Jews Against Zionism (JAZ) was shared by one of our community volunteers. SFSU anti-Zionist Jewish student activists founded JAZ to express their opposition to Zionism; and agreement with my criticism of our university president who had just welcomed Zionists to our social justice campus.[8] My right to academic freedom to criticize my university president is guaranteed to me not only by the US Constitution but also by the Collective Bargaining Agreement our faculty union, California Faculty Association, negotiated with our employer, California Faculty Association. Provost Summit threatened me with disciplinary measures and copied the university counsel on the email for reinforcement.

In what has now become a ritual and the norm rather than the exception in my academic career, I had no choice but to once again abandon my plans to write and instead compose my response to Provost Summit. She demanded a response by the next business day, having sent her an email on Friday night, and set Monday at noon as the deadline. The fact that she was on a 12-month contract compared to my 10-month academic contract and was not expected to work over the weekend (and received compensation when she did) did not matter. She had specifically mentioned 'disciplinary measures' and copied the university lawyer on the email for added emphasis. That I was on a university-approved trip on which the provost and other administrators (the dean, the president, and the chancellor) signed off also seemed irrelevant. Zionist ideologues demanded action and SFSU administrators were eager to comply. The Zionist tweets and other social media posts were circulating as I was making my way to Palestine.

These few examples show the intimate relationship between exercising one's academic freedom to speak up and the academic freedom to boycott. This intimate relationship also emerged in the ways in which SFSU administrators weaponized free speech to protect Zionist[9] and Nazi[10] hate speech while suppressing our academic freedom. This tendency is reflected at the highest levels of the US government.[11] White supremacist Richard Spencer perhaps captured it well when he stated, 'I am a white Zionist'[12] and applauded Israel's racist nation-state law.[13] In this era of neo-liberalism, the rise of the alt-right and the privileging of white supremacy, Islamophobia, and Zionism, administrators will find all sorts of ways to violate faculty members' rights, to silence critics. To enforce transparency, accountability, and engage in the intellectual project of producing critical and justice-centred knowledge, the relationship between the rights of individual faculty to speak up and the collective (and individual) right to not treat injustice as business as usual go hand in hand. This volume promises to excavate these connections and demonstrate the many ways opaque alliances of injustice work and what we need to do to undo them.

Notes

1 According to Brooke Goldstein, co-founder of the Lawfare project, that calls itself the legal arm of the pro-Israel community. Goldstein made this threat on a video to a Zionist audience in 2016. The video was deleted but not before Electronic Intifada saved it, https://electronic intifada.net/blogs/ali-abunimah/israel-lawfare-group-plans-massive-punishments-activists.

2 Mordechai Vanunu exposed that Israel had already built over 200 nuclear bombs at the Dimona nuclear power plant where he worked. He was sentenced to 18 years in prison in October 1988, https://www.theguardian.com/world/2018/mar/28/mordechai-vanunu-israel-spying-nuclear-1988.

3 Andrew Cockburn and Leslie Cockburn. *Dangerous Liaison: The Inside Story of the U.S.-Israeli Covert Relationship* (HarperCollins, 1992).

4 *Washington Post.* 'Israel's Use of Tear Gas Scrutinized'. 31 March 1988. https://www.washingtonpost.com/archive/politics/1988/05/31/israels-use-of-tear-gas-scrutinized/f44fdc56-d298-4324-82a6-e4ee400fc213/?utm_term=.0af18e5d8bff.

5 Palestine Legal. *The Palestine Exception to Freedom of Speech.* https://ccrjustice.org/sites/default/files/attach/2015/09/Palestine%20Exception%20Report%20Final.pdf.

6 See https://mondoweiss.net/2017/07/palestine-advocacy-indivisibility/.

7 https://www.facebook.com/AMEDStudies/.

8 https://www.facebook.com/search/top/?q=dear%20colleague%20Wong%20zionism&epa=SEARCH_BOX.

9 Kelly Rodriguez Murillo. 'Hate Speech Posters Cover SF State, Again'. *Golden Express*, 28 September 2017. http://goldengatexpress.org/2017/09/28/hate-speech-posters-cover-sf-state-again/.

10 Lorenzo Morrotti. 'Safety Concerns Lead to Event Cancellations in Wake of Self-proclaimed Nazi Student Revelations'. *Golden Express*, 31 October 2018. http://goldengatexpress.org/2018/10/31/safety-concerns-lead-to-course-event-cancelations-in-wake-self-proclaimed-nazi-student-revelations/.

11 Aaron Blake. 'Trump Tries to Re-write His Own History on Charlottesville and "Both Sides"'. *Washington Post*, 26 April 2019. https://www.washingtonpost.com/politics/2019/04/25/meet-trump-charlottesville-truthers/?utm_term=.401c264d4c23.

12 *Haaretz*. 'Richard Spencer Tells Israelis They "Should Respect" Him: "I'm a White Zionist"'. 16 August 2017. https://www.haaretz.com/israel-news/israeli-nation-state-law-backed-by-white-nationalist-richard-spencer-1.6295314.

13 *Haaretz*. 'Israel Nation-State Law Backed by White Nationalist Richard Spencer'. 22 July 2018. https://www.haaretz.com/israel-news/israeli-nation-state-law-backed-by-white-nationalist-richard-spencer-1.6295314.

Introduction: Palestine and academic freedom

David Landy, Ronit Lentin, and Conor McCarthy

In September 2017, the editors of this book co-organized an academic conference at Trinity College Dublin. The conference, entitled 'Freedom of Speech and Higher Education: The Case of the Academic Boycott of Israel', addressed the contentious topic of academic boycott and academic freedom and, inevitably, was subject to attacks from outside the university. We were aware that had we held an event which discussed academic freedom in general terms, we would have encountered no such problems. Academic freedom, like clean air or happy children, is something everybody supports. As such, it is a nearly meaningless aspiration in the abstract. It is when we approach the question as to what academic freedom means in specific concrete situations that the problems proliferate.

For the editors, the issue of academic freedom involves more than engaging in theoretical debate; it is centrally related to our work as Palestine solidarity activists as well as scholars in the field of Palestine and Israel studies. In organizing the conference and editing this book we were motivated by the actions of Israel and its supporters in seeking to shut down critical debate on Israel and Palestine in ways that move beyond the academy. Palestine was, then, not chosen by us as a random case study through which we could discuss the ramifications of the concept of academic freedom. Rather, our commitment to justice for Palestine as much as our work as academics led us to engage with the concept of academic freedom – its limits and its possibilities.

Academic freedom is not an absolute right. Virtually nobody, even those who identify as defenders of academic freedom, believes it should be so – Holocaust denial, for instance, should not be defended, nor paedophilia promoted. But whose and what speech is then covered by the concept of academic freedom and how does this struggle relate to Israel and Palestine? This is the central question with which this book wrestles.

There is an argument to be made that discussions surrounding academic freedom have become a form of special pleading. These discussions can be seen as ways to redefine the concept so that our opponents' arguments and freedom to speak lie outside it while ours, conveniently, lie within its jurisdiction. This cynical understanding views academic freedom as a tool that is deployed instrumentally, a shield or weapon that is taken up and discarded insofar as it is to one's advantage or not. In the context of Israel and Palestine, this is not an abstract understanding. Such arguments are a central aspect of the controversy surrounding the academic boycott of Israel, an important part of the international BDS (Boycott Divestment Sanctions) campaign. Does the academic boycott threaten academic freedom, or conversely, is the concept of academic freedom needed in order to defend those who call for boycott and, more widely, those who speak of Israel critically?

This book engages with these real-world conversations about academic freedom and seeks to move beyond gestures that demand it for ourselves and deny it to our opponents. The editors and the authors disagree among themselves, not simply over the instrumental value of academic freedom but also over its validity. Has academic freedom ever been more than a selection of pieties used to legitimate a hierarchical system which has always carefully governed who is allowed to speak and who has been silenced? Conversely, is it a freedom important in itself and used to protect other freedoms? The dividing line centres partly on a debate as to its ideological function and the means whereby it has been put to work. Such a debate asks whether the recourse to a liberal and perhaps elitist conception of rights, as encapsulated within the concept of academic freedom, is a valid means to secure social justice rights.

Seen in this way, this book is not a closing-in of the conversation on academic freedom to focus on one particular case study – Israel and Palestine – but rather seeks to open it up to encompass the wider issue of how powerful institutional actors seek to silence dissent and how best to respond to this process. In doing so, the book critically examines what academic freedom means in practical terms in neoliberal academic settings. We examine the institutional setting within which this discussion is played out, focusing on neoliberal bureaucracies, disciplinary control mechanisms, and precarity in academia. We then turn to the question of (neo)colonial universities, which is crucial in understanding how universities operate both inside and outside of Israel and Palestine. And finally we turn to the wider question of the value of academic freedom in advancing people's right to speak and act within universities.

In order to situate these individual chapters, this introduction opens with a discussion on academic freedom and how it relates to the issue of the academic boycott. Too often the conversation on academic freedom is conducted in idealist terms, unrelated to material situations where, as in Israel and Palestine, the freedom to teach and speak is restricted severely for Palestinians and critics of Israel, even as it is stridently demanded for mainstream Israeli academics. In such situations, we suggest, 'academic freedom' becomes a discourse designed to maintain situations of academic privilege. In the next section we examine this more closely, looking at the various means by which supporters of Israel have sought to restrict the abilities of its critics to speak, both within and outside universities. In this section we look at our own experiences in organizing the conference which gave birth to this book as it provides an example of how such pressures can be resisted. Finally, we outline the main arguments of the book and outline the sections and chapters.

Academic freedom, dissent, and the Israel/Palestine question

One aim of this book is to contribute to the fast-growing literature on the academic boycott component of the Boycott, Divestment, and Sanctions (BDS) campaign. The sheer success and intensity of activism, debate, and controversy on university campuses – particularly but not solely in the United States – has found issue in a proliferating array of scholarly publications and conferences. This section seeks to offer a working definition of academic freedom and of boycott, the twin poles between which the various chapters following will be found to move.

Steven Salaita, committee member of the United States Academic and Cultural Boycott of Israel (USACBI), outlines the main principles of the academic boycott of Israel:

> rejection of détente as a diplomatic manoeuvre at the level
> of the state, the prevalence of college campuses as sites of
> action, emphasis on the necessity of Palestinian voices, and
> disengagement from the orthodoxies of liberal Zionism
> (dialogue, coexistence, soul-searching, ethnocentrism,
> identification with state security apparatuses). (Salaita 2016, 31)

The Palestinian Campaign for the Academic and Cultural Boycott of Israel (PACBI), established in 2004, is the chief advocate for academic boycott and is a founding member of the Palestinian BDS National Committee (BNC).[1] PACBI is committed to academic freedom as defined by the UN Committee on Economic,

Social, and Cultural Rights (UNESCR).[2] While it rejects boycotts of *individual* academics, PACBI has been remarkably successful in getting academics and academic associations to participate in the *institutional* boycott of Israeli academics who represent the state or a complicit Israeli institution (such as deans, rectors, or presidents), or who are commissioned or recruited to participate in Israel's efforts to 'rebrand' itself. PACBI specifically

> urges academics, academic associations/unions, and academic ... institutions around the world ... to boycott and/or work towards the cancellation or annulment of events, activities, agreements, or projects involving Israeli academic institutions or that otherwise promote the normalization of Israel in the global academy, whitewash Israel's violations of international law and Palestinian rights, or violate the BDS guidelines.[3]

The BDS campaign in its overall form derives from the sense that conventional politics has failed Palestinian society, and that, insofar as the Oslo process as well as the bid to establish the Palestinian Authority as a state has installed security apparatuses in the occupied Palestinian territory while not adding to the security of the Palestinian population, and insofar as it has not prevented the expansion of settlement activity and the occupation, such state-level processes function as a fig leaf for further Israeli conquest. The BDS campaign switches the zone of action from this state-political realm to civil society. Academics are important actors in modern civil society, in that they provide education, research information, and critical discourse which is, or should be, put at the service of society as a whole. In Antonio Gramsci's famous terms, academics often function in a given society as 'traditional' intellectuals, elaborating an existing hegemony, but they also have strong potential to develop as 'organic' intellectuals, producing a new hegemony, or counter-hegemony, a new 'common sense' regarding the way that that society looks at itself. This functionality characterizes academics in the Occupied Palestinian Territories, in Israel, and internationally. This shared set of functions, in other words, is, if not 'universal', then certainly transnational. And it is this transnationality of academic function which gives the specifically academic boycott its particular relevance and power in the BDS campaign. BDS dissent, and the academic boycott movement within it, appeals over the heads of the elites who run and benefit from the international state system and the global capitalist system – the political and policy elites of the Palestine Authority but also of Israel and the wider world – to fellow civil society activists in all of those countries and regions.

Within the BDS movement the academic boycott has attained increasing success, as well as eliciting frequently fierce, and often unprincipled, reaction from Israel's 'friends' in the American and European academy. These poles of success and controversy are best illustrated by the vote at the annual meeting of the Association for American Studies in 2013 in favour of the academic boycott, and by Steven Salaita's loss of a tenured position he had just been offered at the University of Illinois at Urbana-Champaign in 2014.

The politics of universities, no matter how closeted, always sit in some dialectical, occasionally belated, relationship with the ideas and politics of the 'real world'. Of course, in this case, the politics of boycott has intruded directly into the realm of higher learning itself. There it encounters various conceptions of the role of the university, of the responsibilities and functions of pedagogy and research in both civil and political society, of the functions and responsibilities of scholars and intellectuals. This clash or encounter – between the politics of boycott and the university – has produced an ever-increasing flow of writing both academic and political (if one can actually separate the two).

The term 'academic freedom' itself is used freely but often imprecisely in these discussions. It is often conflated with freedom of speech as such, but it would be better understood as a subset of that wider category. And it is organized or legislated for in different ways in different jurisdictions. The most explicit and probably rigorous theorizations and codifications of academic freedom are those of the United States. In other Western democracies, academic freedom is often circumscribed by the fact that universities are state-funded institutions and so academics are civil servants, and are expected to maintain positions of neutrality and objectivity in their teaching, research, and writing. In the United States, the *locus classicus* enunciation of academic freedom is the '1940 Statement of Principles on Academic Freedom and Tenure', agreed between the American Association of University Professors and the Association of American Colleges (now the Association of American Colleges and Universities).[4] Academic freedom is generally held to cover institutional self-governance (including hiring and discipline), and to cover what is taught, how it is taught, what is researched and how, and how that research is written about. The most restrictive definition of academic freedom sees it simply as the freedom which academics need to perform their day-to-day academic work (Fish 2014). Other writers consider that the principle of academic freedom covers extramural statements, i.e. statements or actions which academics make or take beyond the strictly academic zone, and in the public sphere. Such arguments have several grounds: either that academics have a particular responsibility to engage in public debates, or simply that academics shouldn't be punished by their employer for their opinions, expressed away from the workplace. Either way, this expansive definition or concept runs the risk of being imprecise and hard to govern. It is no coincidence that most public debate concerning academic freedom centres on extramural utterances. For many, when an academic addresses a march, or appears on television to address a contentious political topic such as the question of Palestine, they have left the academic zone behind, and are no longer protected by legally codified academic freedom.

In *The Origins of Totalitarianism*, Hannah Arendt noted the exorbitance of theories of right which characterizes the post-1945 world. Since World War Two, we have seen a mushrooming of zones of human activity which are held to be governed by normative concepts of rights. Centrally, we have the United Nations Universal Declaration of Human Rights, and the panoply of humanitarian law (including the Geneva Conventions and the Hague Conventions) which are standards to which states may be held accountable internally and in their external relations. Arendt, writing in the wake of the Holocaust, notes the processes by which human beings can be gradually stripped of their rights. From this position, Arendt notes that a human being must have the right to have rights, as it were: that the codification of rights may be meaningless unless the material or institutional conditions are in place for those rights fully to be exercised (Arendt 2017, 383-390). This is a crucial qualification for many of the discussions of academic freedom and boycott which form the body of this volume.

For many academics keen to protest at the policies of the State of Israel, it seems clear that arguing for boycott may be an activity which itself deserves the protection of academic freedom. Conversely, for those academics opposed to the BDS campaign, it seems clear that boycott actually encroaches upon academic freedom. In other words, the situation can only be grasped as an antinomy of conflicting rights or freedoms. A classic abstraction of this situation may be found in Isaiah Berlin's essay 'Two Concepts of Liberty', written in 1958 (Berlin 2002, 166-217).

In this essay, Berlin discussed 'positive liberty' and 'negative liberty'. Positive liberty, for Berlin, is the self-mastery of the subject (a person or a people), and he derived the idea from Aristotle's concept of citizenship, where the citizen has the liberty of helping choose the form of governance of the city-state. Negative liberty, by contrast, is freedom from interference, and its proponents included major modern thinkers such as Locke, Montesquieu, Constant, Tocqueville, and Mill. Put in colloquial terms, we could say that positive liberty is 'freedom to' (act in a particular way), whereas negative liberty is 'freedom from' (interference, restraint, paternalism, manipulation, and so on).

Berlin's formulations may help us make some distinctions between thought about academic freedom and boycott, and allow us to understand the divagations of the American Association of University Professors (AAUP) in its attitudes to the academic boycott of Israeli universities. According to David Lloyd and Malini Schueller, the AAUP has failed to live up to its own guidelines with regard to academic freedom in Israel and in the Occupied Palestinian Territories. In its hostility to the academic boycott, the AAUP has made an exception of Israel in such a way as to run counter to the universalism which apparently subtends the Association's valorization of academic freedom (Lloyd and Schueller 2015). The Association can point to its history of 'censure' (a procedure suggested by Martha Nussbaum (2007) as an alternative to boycott) of oppressive governments. Yet, though it 'censured' apartheid South Africa and argued for divestment from that country, it will not even 'censure' Israel. The exceptional status of Israel in the AAUP's vision eliminates Palestinian rights from consideration. According to Lloyd and Schueller, the AAUP supports only a partial version of academic freedom, and pays no attention at all to the material underpinnings which enable the right to and the pursuit of that freedom.

So the AAUP has nothing to say in support of Palestinian academics, universities, and students, while it also denies itself the capacity to investigate or hold an opinion about a venture such as Ariel University located in the illegal West Bank settlement of Ariel. In Berlin's terms, the AAUP has failed to recognize that its approach enables Israeli 'positive liberty' in such a way as to erode Palestinian 'negative liberty'.

Palestinian scholar, Rima Najjar Kapitan (2015) makes a particularly important contribution to this debate, when she argues that 'academic freedom' is not some Platonic or transcendent ideal, but rather takes on real meaning in real situations and real institutions. Najjar Kapitan cogently separates 'academic freedom' from 'academic entitlement', noting that critics of the boycott assume it attacks academic freedom *tout court*. In doing so, they assume a 'selectively expansive understanding' of academic freedom. She means that Israeli scholars do not need or are not entitled to enforced academic co-operation in order to exercise their right to academic freedom. According to Najjar Kapitan's critique of Cary Nelson, former president of the AAUP, he 'broadens the definition of academic freedom to encompass anything that maximizes academic co-operation between Americans and Israelis, but restricts it when addressing Israeli actions that paralyze the educational system in the Occupied Territories' (Najjar Kapitan 2015, 146). In Berlin's terms, the academic freedom of Israeli or Israel-based academics is often conceived of by anti-BDS advocates as a kind of 'positive liberty', or, as Najjar Kapitan calls it, an entitlement. Meanwhile, the academic freedom of Palestinian academics in the Occupied Territories should be thought of as a kind of 'negative liberty' – a negative liberty, of course, which is very frequently breached. But the wider philosophical point, and the point that Najjar Kapitan is correctly making, is that a 'freedom' or a right, for one person or group of persons, can only extend so far as not to occlude the freedom or right of another person or group of persons. And very often, anti-BDS campaigners ignore the Palestinian right to academic freedom almost entirely. The effect of this, as Lloyd and Schueller point out, is that the protected academic freedom of Israeli scholars in the AAUP vision becomes a geographical or geopolitical advantage. But the point we must remember is that an Israeli or Israel-based academic's 'freedom' to teach, research, publish, debate is not predicated on an obligation of all that particular academic's potential interlocutors actually to listen to, respond to, co-operate with, publish, or fund that particular scholar. No scholar or group of scholars can demand, as of right, that they or their interlocutors engage with them. The American philosopher Judith Butler also contributes to this discussion in ways which reinforce Najjar Kapitan's arguments. Butler writes about the principle of rights and lucidly and shrewdly argues for the necessity of looking at the conditions of possibility for the exercise of a particular right for it to be fully understood. In this she follows Arendt (as cited earlier), who argued that a right has little meaning without instantiation in a shared world (Butler 2016). To summarize, Butler exposes the fallacy of talking only in abstract or idealist terms about academic freedom in Israel and Palestine, and shows the need to look at the often desperate compromises under which Palestinian academic freedom can be said to be 'exercised – if at all'. In this, she enriches philosophically Najjar Kapitan's point: that academic freedom must be seen in contextual terms, and that critics of the academic boycott such as Cary Nelson tend to think academic freedom in a vacuum. So Butler's argument – crucially that the right to academic freedom must be seen in relation to the right to an education – has the effect of bringing Israeli and Palestinian academic freedom into direct relation with each other. When one considers the extent of the militarization of the Israeli academy, one is drawn to the potential conclusion that Israeli academic freedom is ultimately exercised at the expense of Palestinian academic freedom. Hence again the relevance of Berlin's antinomy of negative and positive liberty, as a framework for thinking about academic freedom generally and also in the fraught context of Palestine and Israel.

Perhaps it is worth concluding this section with a rather more blunt statement of our position. Boycott is a tactic not a principle; it is non-violent; it has the potential to frustrate academic researchers, their careers and projects, and their institutions, but it can in no way be said to do serious practical damage to them; and its earlier usage should be an encouragement – it is true that the Nazis instigated a boycott of Jewish businesses in Germany in the 1930s, but boycott was also used by Jewish Americans against Henry Ford in the 1920s and against German goods in America, Britain, Palestine, Lithuania, and Poland in 1933. A boycott of British goods was organized by Gandhi in India. Boycott was deployed against South Africa in the apartheid era, and contributed considerably to the symbolic delegitimation of that racist regime. In the context of the failure and discrediting of the Middle East 'peace process' and the political elites (Palestinian, Israeli, American) involved in it, and of the unrelenting Israeli assault on Palestinian rights, land, economy, and life, boycott and BDS offer a firm but civilized form of pressure on Israel and of support for the Palestinians.

Indeed, it is impossible to disregard the fact that Israel has been on the colonizing offensive since its establishment in 1948, and that one of the targets of the substantially funded Israeli campaign against BDS and the 'delegitimization of Israel' is the academic field. The campaign focuses on academics, university campuses, and student groups such as Students for Justice in Palestine, founded in 1993 and currently numbering more than

80 chapters on US campuses.[5] The strategies employed by the State of Israel and its supporters include, *inter alia*, the mobilization of Israeli Studies scholars, who continue the long history of collusion by the Israeli academy in the colonization of Palestine (Lentin, this volume). It is this campaign against critics of Israel to which we next turn.

Interdicting critics of Israel

There is a small subgenre of Palestine solidarity and academic writing which we can call, following Gary Fine (1995), 'academic horror stories'. The term 'horror stories' is used by social movement scholars to refer to a genre of narratives told by movement activists in order to build up a sense of outrage and mobilize people towards action. In this case, the term refers to the many accounts of Zionist attacks on universities and academics. These accounts can either be in the form of individual academics recounting their experiences (e.g. Klein 2009; Pappe 2010; Peterson-Overton 2011; Robinson and Griffin 2017; Salaita 2015; Abdulhadi, this volume) or they can take the form of reports of how Israel supporters have threatened events and academia (Abraham 2014; *Arab Studies Quarterly* 2011; Drummond 2013).

While such stories are told to inform and mobilize movements, they can also demotivate and demobilize. They may serve to shift focus from the violence being done to Palestine to those who teach and write about it in academic arenas. There is a real risk that these stories can decentre the experiences of Palestinians and instead treat relatively privileged academics as the target of Zionist attacks; in doing so, such stories can serve to recapitulate forms of racial and class privilege which ostensibly they are challenging. In addition, there is a danger that in recounting a litany of oppressive experiences that academics face, these stories create the image of an all-powerful censorship machine, against which resistance is futile. Focusing on the power of censors and how they operate, talking of the risks involved with criticizing Israel leads to the question as to whether we are doing the censors' work for them and are therefore complicit in scaring critics into silence. To put the matter another way: how do we discuss the censorship machine without contributing to its effectivity? In answering this, it is important not to state that Zionist censors have succeeded in their task to interdict criticism of Israel. This is not simply because such a statement is disempowering, but also because it is false – academics clearly do criticize Israel, students increasingly mobilize against its treatment of Palestinians, and even timid academic bodies occasionally censure Israel. And thus in this book we seek to move beyond the horror stories. Firstly, we situate the threat to dissenting academics within wider Zionist practices that curtail freedom of speech – namely the use of Lawfare and accusations of antisemitism – and we examine specific issues within academia such as academic governance and precarity, which allow these threats to have such purchase. However, we finish by discussing the ways in which these pressures can be resisted using our own experiences in organizing the conference which led to this book.

Virtually everyone who has criticized Israel can attest to the fact that the accusation of antisemitism deployed as a silencing device is not confined to academics. Student activist and American Israel Public Affairs Committee (AIPAC) insider Raegan Davis (2019) writes that accusing pro-Palestine activists of antisemitism minimizes Islamophobia and racism but also real antisemitic crimes against Jews:

> Activists for Palestine, in growing numbers, are systematically being disenfranchised by the laws our government passes and defamed by pro-Israel advocates at the expense of their physical and emotional security. What does it mean that we as a society

would side with white nationalists and fascists in curtailing the First Amendment rights of pro-Palestine activists? ... What does it say about the world we live in that charges of antisemitism can 'cancel' leftists while real hate crimes are being carried out by the pro-Israel alt-right? How detached are we from the true suffering of Jewish people that we continuously use them as a stick with which to beat other marginalized individuals? And what does it say about AIPAC that this is exactly what they're aiming for?

The weaponizing of antisemitism against US critics of Israel was evidenced in April 2019 when Florida's upper legislative chamber unanimously passed a bill that classifies certain criticism of Israel as antisemitic. This bill drew sweeping condemnation from advocates for Palestine and free speech, who said the legislation violates the United States Constitution. It was passed just days after a US federal judge struck down a controversial anti-BDS law in Texas, saying it breached Americans' First Amendment right to free speech (Khalel 2019). Thus, we should not assume that such weaponization of antisemitism will always be successful.

Nobody would deny that real antisemitism continues to exist throughout the world as evidenced by the growing number of violent attacks on Jewish worshippers and of hate crimes against Jewish people (Aderet 2019). It is increasingly clear, as Winstanley (2019a) writes, that there is a continuity between antisemitism and Islamophobia, the current leading identifier of far-right groups all around the world. If Nazi propaganda constructed a global Jewish plot to control both Bolshevism and capitalism to foment Jew-hatred, which hasn't disappeared, then the current far right, of which neo-Nazis are only the most extreme part, has switched its focus from Jews to Muslims. However, the way that US and European politicians privilege antisemitism as the worst of all racial exclusions, well above Islamophobia, anti-migrant and anti-refugee racisms, and the current trend of weaponizing antisemitism to silence the freedom to criticize Israel, does nothing to prevent the ongoing racialization of real Jewish people. Indeed, antisemitism today has become a proxy for many politicians' commitment to antiracism, a move which serves to deny the persistent role of race and coloniality in securing white supremacy.[6]

This weaponization of antisemitism and its delinking from antiracist practices can be seen in the case of Temple University Media Studies professor and regular CNN commentator Marc Lamont Hill. As part of the 2018 International Day of Solidarity with the Palestinian People at the United Nations, Lamont Hill called on people 'to not just offer solidarity in words, but to commit to political action, grassroots action … that will give us what justice requires and that is a free Palestine from the river to the sea'. Within hours of his remarks, Lamont Hill was attacked by several pro-Israel US groups including the Anti-Defamation League (ADL) – a Jewish organization whose declared mission includes fighting antisemitism, combating hate, and standing up for Israel,[7] which accused him of advocating the destruction of the State of Israel.

Although Lamont Hill rejected the ADL's interpretation (Lamont Hill 2018), he was fired by CNN, with his university following suit in publicly censuring him, immediately declaring it was investigating what 'remedies' it was appropriate to apply to Lamont Hill. David Palumbo-Liu (2018) cites Temple President Richard Englert's statement that the university condemns hate speech and that Lamont Hill's comments do not reflect the university's beliefs (*The Temple News* 2018). Englert called the university a place of 'divergent points of view', implying academics' right to free speech. But he nonetheless seemed to accept *prima facie* that Lamont Hill's statements were antisemitic hate speech, even though there were no hearings or faculty discussions as to whether or not they met the criteria for either antisemitism or hate speech (Palumbo-Liu 2018). Discussing the implications of the Hill case for academic freedom, and more specifically, for the freedom to criticize Israel without being accused of antisemitism, Palumbo-Liu argues that Lamont Hill was punished unjustly and harshly:

> Patrick O'Connor, president of Temple's Board of Trustees, readily accepted the labels of hate speech and anti-Semitism, and stated that Hill's speech 'blackens our name unnecessarily' ... While O'Connor's statement leaves open the possibility of 'remedies' other than firing, it is nonetheless telling that he leads with the issue of the school's name ... But – and here is the most important thing to bear in mind – (university heads') job is not to punish professors for their extramural speech ... Thus, while the trustees can express their displeasure as much as they wish, the 'remedies' they are likely to consider would be a serious breach of their responsibilities. After all, they are trustees of a university, not (at least for now) a corporation.

Palumbo-Liu's analysis highlights several issues this book seeks to address. First, there is the increasing corporatization of universities which privileges donors' views above the liberty of academics to speak freely within or outside the university. This has been evident in the cases of several prominent pro-Palestine academics including Norman Finkelstein who was denied tenure at DePaul University, and Steven Salaita, who had his appointment to a tenured professorship revoked by the University of Illinois because of anti-Israel tweets he posted during Israel's assault on the Gaza Strip (Salaita 2015; see also Shahvisi and Schotten, this volume). While academic freedom appears to be publicly defended by university heads, when it comes to the freedom to criticize Israel or support the academic boycott of Israel, university managements, particularly in the United States, seem to succumb to the Israel lobby's pressure. Indeed, as Salaita (2016, 45) argues, 'even if they actually existed, and they do not, the violations of academic freedom falsely imagined of boycott, would be minuscule compared to the very real repression of academic freedom both Palestinians and their supporters in the United States must constantly navigate'.

Another *cause célèbre* in the US campus battle for the right to criticize Israel has been the case of Rabab Ibrahim Abdulhadi, Associate Professor of Ethnic Studies/Race and Resistance Studies in San Francisco State University (SFSU), and a pro-Palestine activist (who writes the foreword to this book). Her constant hounding illustrates not only the prevalence of the accusation of antisemitism but also the role of Lawfare or the use of legal means to silence critics of Israel. It has been the success of BDS and the academic boycott of Israel, and Abdulhadi's involvement with both, that led the Lawfare project (the self-described 'legal arm of the pro-Israel community') to pursue Abdulhadi by alleging antisemitism at SFSU (Spero 2019). The broader context is that while BDS seems to be winning in the court of public opinion, powerful supporters of Israel are using Lawfare to win through the formal court system (Dworkin 2015), targeting mostly pro-Palestine academics and student organizations on US campuses. This tactic is one where well-funded institutional actors threaten those who support Palestinian rights with legal actions and accusations of antisemitism (Handmaker, this volume). Abdulhadi won what became a milestone judgement against the Lawfare project, when in October 2018, federal judge William Orrick dismissed the case, effectively rejecting the Israel lobby's attempts to silence free speech on Palestine on US university campuses and to equate anti-Zionism with antisemitism. Significantly, Judge Orrick did not permit Lawfare to proceed with the lawsuit against SFSU, where Abdulhadi's acclaimed scholarship, teaching, and advocacy for Palestinian rights have been falsely smeared as antisemitic (Spero 2019).

The increasing surveillance of academics, accusations of antisemitism, and use of Lawfare are not confined to the United States. Indeed, the immediate motivation for the Trinity College Dublin conference was the treatment meted out to a previous conference held in the Republic of Ireland. 'International Law and the State of Israel' was originally scheduled for Southampton University but was cancelled and held in University College Cork (UCC) in March 2017. The Zionist campaign against this conference (Landy, this volume) brought home to us its growing threat to academic freedom, specifically the freedom to research, teach, and talk on Israel and Palestine without fear and without interference. We know the organizers of the UCC conference personally and offered them messages of support after they were attacked by supporters of Israel and defamed by online trolls. We saw how extremist Zionists turned the conference into an expensive circus, issuing threats and spewing hatred, demanding that it be shut down and disowned by the university, even by Cork City Council. We also noted how the UCC authorities responded – reluctantly allowing the conference to go ahead after the organizers had fulfilled an inventive variety of costly and restrictive demands made by these authorities. When discussing how academics have their livelihoods threatened and their freedom to speak and research curtailed, it is important to note that Palestinian academics, including 'foreign' academics teaching in Palestinian universities, have been attacked far more severely than those in the West (Lentin, this volume). And indeed in the West, it is Palestinian academics such as Salaita and Rabab Abdulhadi who have borne a large share of harassment and attack.

What affords these attacks some measure of success is the vulnerability and precarious working conditions of many academics.

Academic freedom is fundamentally the freedom to work within academia; it has long been recognized that without tenure or at least some level of job security, academic freedom simply does not exist – rather, what we have are various levels of academic privilege. There is a growing number of lecturers and researchers on short-term or piece rate contracts or even paid hourly for their work – an estimated three-quarters of US academics. Their experience is one of isolation, insecurity, pressure, exploitation, and fear of speaking out (Courtois and O'Keefe 2015), with their precarious working conditions making them the most vulnerable to outside pressure (Pembroke, this volume). It comes as no surprise that almost all the celebrated cases of threatened academic freedom involve precarious academic workers. While the media often frames the issue of academic freedom as one of left-wing purists seeking to shut down debate, in reality, academics mostly face pressure from the right.[8] Thus, in the case of Steven Salaita or previously Norman Finkelstein, it was powerful institutional actors in concordance with donors and right-wing ideologues who conspired to deny academic freedom (Moshman and Edler 2015).

Other attacks on academic freedom are more indirect than direct threats to people's jobs. One of the most insidious threats is the demand for 'balance'. At first glance, this demand seems innocuous. Who would disagree that academics need to consider all sides of a question, particularly one as contentious as that of Israel and Palestine? While this is clear, we would argue that this is not why outside actors demand balance from certain academics. The demand for balance can first be understood as a rhetorical device used to deny or obfuscate truths. This demand is not exclusive to teaching about Israel and Palestine; it is all too familiar to anyone who teaches evolution or who researches climate change. However, as Allen (2019) comments in the context of UK academia, 'The demand for "balance" is a favorite justification for curtailing academic debate when it comes to events on Palestine and a card that administrators disproportionately play against academics of color who support Palestinian rights'.

In the case of Israel, the demand works as a means of discounting the brutal practices of colonial control – the realities of occupation and racism needing constantly to be balanced by denials that such realities actually exist. This begs the question as to what balance means in an unbalanced situation. In a colonial state such as Israel, the call for 'balance', emanating as it does from one side, is an effort to disavow the colonial relationships between dispossessors and dispossessed, colonizer and colonized, containing the assumption that both sides are in some ways on an equal footing and need their narratives balanced. The claim of being balanced is also a denial of positionality undertaken in order to position oneself in a god's-eye position of interpretative control. Balance, in this view, is synonymous with objectivity.

In the academic context, we can argue whether 'balance' is ever possible or even desirable – we would argue that in the classroom one should teach critical thinking rather than 'balance', and in research one should pursue truth rather than 'balance'. Thus we can see the demand for balance as not simply the result of a faulty theoretical lens. It is rather a claim made by outside bodies in order to insert themselves into academic life so as to monitor and control the activities of academics. It is, above all, a one-sided demand – rarely, if ever is it asked of those in the well-funded field of Israel Studies where elision of Palestinian voices is the norm (Aked, this volume). Indeed an illuminating example of the relationship between Israeli policies and the Israeli academy is the special issue of the journal *Israel Studies* published in 2019 by the Association of Israel Studies (AIS), and titled 'Word Crimes: Reclaiming the Language of the Israeli–Palestinian Conflict'.

According to an open letter sent to the AIS by members of the Israeli group, Academia for Equality,[9] this special issue (volume 24, number 2), which castigates certain intellectual categories as 'word crimes', is not a starting point for discussion, but rather a call to arms:

> By describing terms as 'linguistic transgressions' and scholarship as lacking in 'sanity', the issue made clear that its aim was not to contribute to vigorous debate, but rather to police and shut down this debate. Passionate discussion on the adequacy of terminology and theoretical frameworks is the bread and butter of our profession, and should be welcomed, not 'criminalised'.

Thus, if we understand the demand for balance in academia within its colonial context, it is a means whereby the colonizer's voice is continually heard, is continually present and intruding into the conversation. The demand is deployed to try to ensure that those critical of colonialism are not allowed freely to think, associate, or develop their ideas without these powerful censorious voices constantly encroaching (Reynolds, this volume).

In organizing the conference at Trinity College Dublin, 'Freedom of Speech and Higher Education', we faced many of these issues. The demand for balance was the major way in which outside forces sought to derail the conference. We had decided in advance not to accept papers which argued pro- or anti-boycott positions as this was off-topic in a conference primarily discussing academic freedom. Despite this stricture being clearly stated, we received a slew of anti-boycott abstracts, most within a few days of each other. We were surprised at their sub-standard nature – had they not been rejected on grounds of irrelevancy, they would almost all have been rejected on that of quality. Later, we discovered why they were of such poor quality – most had been sent at the last minute in response to a secret call

by the Israeli Association of University Heads to pack the conference with anti-boycott papers (Hay 2017). This attempt by Israeli
universities to coordinate a political campaign to undermine the
conference was a testament to its relevance and indicates one way
in which Israeli academic institutions are used to attack perceived
enemies of the Israeli state. After the conference was held, in an
attempt to ensure the organizers received some level of institutional censure, the Israeli Association wrote to Trinity College
Dublin demanding that the authorities distance themselves from
it. The reason given was that the conference was unbalanced, not
only because these politically motivated papers were rejected,
but also because of those attending. The Association was
incensed that, according to its claims, most attendees supported
the international BDS campaign against Israel (Hay 2017). This
menacing tactic of collecting names of academics and pigeon-
holing them as enemies of the State of Israel has been a central
feature in attempts to curtail academic debate. As conference
organizers, we obviously had not conducted such a McCarthyite
headcount, although one would expect that there would be more
speakers supporting Palestinian rights at this conference than the
Israeli Association of University Heads would find acceptable. In
like manner, there would be more anti-Palestinian speakers at an
Israel Studies conference or more speakers supporting women's
rights at a gender studies conference. The demand for balance
was then both an effort to prevent ideas from being discussed
freely and an effort to prevent academics who are critical of Israel
from gathering and sharing ideas.

Despite this and other attacks, we do not want to overstate
the problems that were faced. There were some accusations
of antisemitism levelled against the TCD conference, several
hostile articles in the UK Jewish and Israeli press, intimidating comments by the Israeli embassy in Dublin as well as a few

attempts to derail it through Freedom of Information requests regarding conference details. But compared to other conferences on Palestine, these were minor annoyances and were easily dealt with. The relative mildness of the attacks was due to a number of reasons. First, the conference concerned academic freedom, and all but the most foolhardy supporters of Israel realized that openly attacking a conference on academic freedom was counterproductive. Second, as conference organizers, we decided to avoid social media and had neither a Twitter account nor a Facebook page to advertise the conference. We took this decision in order not to give Israel's paid and unpaid online trolls an identifiable target to attack (on this threat: Winstanley 2019b). We were concerned that – as with the conference in UCC – if an online mob gathered, this would raise security concerns with the administration in Trinity College and would lead to restrictions. This social media silence is not uncommon for academic events that discuss Israel critically; it was an irony raised at the conference that we had to censor ourselves in one arena in order to be granted freedom of speech in another. Thirdly, the organizers either had permanent jobs or were retired and so were not vulnerable to targeting. The final reason for the relative mildness of the attacks was that the university administration afforded the attackers no purchase, making no concessions prior to the conference, and not censuring it afterwards despite several strong requests to do so by Israeli universities.

The last point is crucial. With academic freedom written into Irish law in the 1997 Universities Act, and despite the problems faced by the UCC conference, the institutional context in Ireland may be especially favourable towards academic freedom. Trinity College Dublin, like many other universities, has an impressive official commitment to academic freedom, one that cites the problems of precarity, state control, and academic metrics.[10] In addition, a concatenation of institutional reasons may have been conducive in ensuring the university's support: one factor was that the provost of Trinity College Dublin, Patrick Prendergast, had spoken out strongly in favour of free speech earlier in 2017 when students protested the Israeli ambassador's presence on campus (McGreevy 2017). He may have felt it unwise to be seen to oppose it in this case. There were some small attempts at institutional interference – the University's Director of Public Affairs and Communications made some last minute panicked efforts to relocate the conference, but this was rebuffed (email correspondence).

This shows the value of understanding the institutional context of the university and also the possibility of working with and navigating through university structures. There is no need to labour the point; in some cases, attempts to work within administrative structures – no matter how painstaking – fail to avoid university censure (e.g. Drummond 2013). In other cases it has been equally worthwhile to organize academic events relatively independent of these structures. Either way, it is useful to bear in mind that universities sometimes feel the need to offer more than lip-service to academic freedom and that it is often productive to test the waters in this regard, rather than taking a purely oppositional stance. This is the line between realism and resignation that everyone dealing with powerful institutions needs to navigate.

Conclusion

Contributors to this volume explore the meanings and limits of academic freedom as it relates to the academic boycott of Israel and the narrowing of campus spaces for criticizing the Israeli colonization of Palestine in a variety of ways. Several contributors discuss aspects of the case of the Palestinian-American academic Steven Salaita, who was fired from his tenured position at the University of Illinois at Urbana-Champaign as a result of a series of tweets he posted in 2014 expressing his outrage at the Israeli assault on Gaza. The Salaita case has become a *cause célèbre* in the struggle to maintain the right to criticize the Israeli coloniza-tion of Palestine on campus and elsewhere. In a piece titled 'My Life as a Cautionary Tale', Salaita (2019) critically examines the limits of academic freedom, proposing that 'academic freedom is inhumane ... because it cannot provide the very thing it prom-ises: freedom'. Academic freedom, they write, can do little to alter the cultures of obedience that govern most universities, particu-larly those possessed by 'wealthy donors, legislative overseers, defence contracts, and opulent endowments'.

While academic freedom preserves democracy and embold-ens research, it also facilitates faculty governance and thus ought to be understood in relation to class, discipline, race, gender, and ideology. At base, Salaita argues, 'academic freedom entitles us ... to say or investigate things that might upset others with-out fear of retaliation', yet limits do exist. Take, for instance, the fact that while most of us would be unwilling to protect a Nazi's right to teach undergraduates, others believe that the principle of free speech overrides the harm done by the Nazi's presence. Yet, Salaita claims, while defenders of the absolutist view of academic freedom warn that 'limiting reactionary speech will inevitably lead to the repression of all speech, including from the left', allowing a civil liberty to dominate notions of freedom is problematic. The problem is that protecting speech equally and letting a marketplace of ideas sort the winners and losers never works where 'structural forces, often unseen, always beneficial to the elite, determine which ideas get a hearing' and which are considered dangerous.

Salaita, like the contributors to this volume, knows that speaking about Palestine is one of these 'dangerous ideas', like 'anything that conceptualizes racism or inequality as a systemic problem rather than an individual failing'. Indeed, in an academic environment that encourages obedience, academic freedom cannot prevent sexual violence, disrupt racial capitalism, hinder inequality, or deter genocide, and while Salaita does not attempt to convince us to dispose of academic freedom, he points out that the academic ruling elites monitor and control faculty and potential faculty's online presence, leading in their case to a situation where, 'I can't find a single university president who will affirm my right to extramural speech. I can't get an office job with any campus or corporation that has access to Google. I now drive a school bus'.

Salaita acknowledges their own complicity with the system during their 12 years in academia, and they are fully aware that 'civil liberties can offer recourse against governmental repression, but they're helpless against the capitalist impulse to eliminate disruptors'. Ultimately, academic freedom is not about individuals, not even precariously employed academics. It is about capitalist elite cultures of obedience, about racism, about colonialism: 'Academic freedom is critical to a functional university. But it shouldn't be an end in itself. It is only one instrument among many that can help us realize a world unlimited by the stagnant doctrines of pragmatism'.

Although Salaita's 2019 piece was written after we had mostly finished writing and editing this volume, its clarity helps us think about this book, which, we hope, makes a thought-provoking contribution to the ongoing debate regarding the multi-faceted links between the abstract concept of academic freedom and the limits set by Israel and its supporters on voicing our criticism of the Zionist colonization, occupation, siege, and oppression of the Palestinians.

The book proceeds from the particular to the general; from Part I, which discusses how university governance, precarity, and power affects the intersection of academic freedom and the struggle for civil justice, through Part II, which considers the role of colonialism in inflecting this intersection in the case of Israel and Palestine, and concluding with Part III, which offers a wider interrogation of the concept of academic freedom.

Part I, 'Universities and Academic Governance', asks what academic freedom means in specific institutional settings and begins with Hilary Aked's chapter, 'Whose University? Academic Freedom, Neoliberalism and the Rise of "Israel Studies"'. Aked examines the recent expansion of handsomely funded pro-grammes in Israel Studies in the United Kingdom, revealing how funders typically see themselves as contributing to the pushback against BDS. They argue that efforts by Zionist philanthropists to re-shape the academic landscape in a manner favourable to Israel is a corollary to censorship and suppression of critiques of Zionism in universities, and that we should understand Israel Studies as an attempt to re-legitimize Zionism in the face of what Israel terms the 'delegitimization' challenge. By tracing the roots of Israel Studies to disagreements within the Israeli academy, its emergence in the US and recent expansion in the UK, Aked's chapter suggests that Israel Studies faculty posts serve as academic 'facts on the ground' that undermine the movement for a boycott of Israel.

Not unlike Salaita, Nick Riemer is unconvinced of the value of relying on procedural 'academic freedom' arguments. Their chapter, 'Disciplinarity and the Boycott', links the suppression of debate on Palestine to the wider violation of academic freedom. They argue that this is innate in the way that academic life is struc-tured and parcelled out within distinct disciplines that are shaped by an exclusionary logic of practice. It follows that it is not sim-ply morally but tactically advantageous to link Palestine solidarity work to a wider democratization of university culture wherein the ability to think and act freely is not confined to elite actors.

In the same section, David Landy's chapter, 'The Academic Field Must Be Defended: Excluding Criticism of Israel from Campuses', considers the complexities and illiberalisms of those who purport to defend academic freedom, tackling the conundrum whereby purported 'defenders of academic freedom' attack, smear, or undermine practices of academic freedom in the name of that defence. Landy examines the variously flexible and para-academic arguments used to sustain this position, and why university administrators often accept the legitimacy of these arguments, made by politically motivated outside actors. Taking a somewhat different inflection from the other authors, they argue in favour of the value of working within university structures to defend academic freedom.

Using the specific case study of the American University of Beirut (AUB), Tala Makhoul's chapter, 'Lebanese and American Law at American Universities in Beirut: A Case of Legal Liminality in Neoliberal Times', teases out the legal, even constitutional, complexities which attend resistance to BDS in AUB. Offering an activist perspective on clashes within AUB on boycotting Israel, they use it as a case study to discuss how both neoliberalism and neocolonialism in universities in the Arab world are weakening anti-Zionist policies. The chapter argues that neocolonial ties with the US have driven university administrators to undermine Lebanese law (which enforces a boycott of Israel), and to promote normalization with Israel. In turn the deepening neoliberalization of the university has led to the depoliticization of student governance, making the growing links with Israel more difficult, though not impossible, to resist.

Concluding Part I, Sinead Pembroke's chapter, 'Precarious Work in Higher Education, Academic Freedom, and the Academic Boycott of Israel in Ireland', focuses on academic precarity, which, as Salaita (2019) argues, is often ignored by tenured academics, even those committed to academic freedom. Pembroke shows us how the increasingly managed neoliberal university, dependent on an ever-growing academic precariat of teachers and researchers on short-term contracts, acts to restrict the space for dissent of many kinds, including BDS. Taking Ireland as a case study, they discuss how relations of dependency, insecurity, and poverty are fostered by the increasing precarity of academic work, and how such factors undermine academic freedom of all kinds, not simply with relation to Israel and Palestine.

Part II, 'Colonial Erasure in Higher Education', puts the issue of colonialism and colonial discourse front and centre, when discussing academic freedom in the case of Israel and Palestine. It begins with John Reynolds's chapter, 'Colonial Apologism and the Politics of Academic Freedom'. In this chapter Reynolds provides a broad analysis of the ways academic freedom has operated in certain cases to defend work that distorts the legacy of historical colonialism and to support the *status quo* in spaces of ongoing colonization, of which Palestine is one. They conclude by arguing that whether we might think that anti-colonial challenges to racial and imperial discourses offer a more meaningful illumination of the substance and necessity of academic freedom as an ideal or not, we must be conscious of the structural context in which these are engaged. This is an argument most relevant both to the general discussion of academic freedom with regard to apologists for colonialism and to the specific mobilization of the academic freedom argument by Israel and its supporters to shut down spaces for debate and silence dissent.

Yara Hawari's chapter, 'The Academic Boycott and Beyond: Towards an Epistemological Strategy of Liberation and Decolonization', focuses on the need for the act of boycott to be situated in larger movements for Palestinian rights and Palestinian struggles. Suggesting that while aiming to protect knowledge production and the right of scholars to research, publish, and teach without hindrance, academic freedom also has obligations to uphold the liberty of others through recognizing the violations against such freedoms. Moreover, their discussion as to who gets silenced and replaced within academic arenas is important both in relation to the Palestinian struggle and more generally in the context of strategies of liberation and decolonization.

Ending Part II, Ronit Lentin's chapter, 'Colonial Academic Control in Palestine and Israel: Blueprint for Repression?' discusses how Israeli academia has always colluded in the ongoing colonization of Palestine, and delineates how this colonial programme of surveillance and control of both Palestinian and Israeli academics and students has adversely affected academic freedom in Palestine and in Israel. While Palestinians and some Israelis have fought back against this programme of control and surveillance, the chapter concludes by outlining how Israel's attempts to suppress dissent within academia are being exported abroad by arms of the Israeli state, including universities, and by Israel's Zionist supporters.

Part III, 'Interrogating Academic Freedom', discusses the limits and possibilities of academic freedom, as illustrated by, but not confined to, the situation of Israel and Palestine. It begins with Jeff Handmaker's chapter, 'Lawfare against Academics and the Potential of Legal Mobilization as Counterpower'. Handmaker argues that the realm of law has become a cockpit in anti-BDS control. At the core of their chapter is a pragmatic defence of 'legal mobilization' by Palestinian rights activists to advance their cause against attempts by Israel and its Zionist supporters to shut down free speech in academia. Handmaker argues that it is wrong to see Lawfare and legal mobilization as similar forms of legal instrumentalism, one used by 'our' side and the other by 'their' side. Legal mobilization, understood as the 'pragmatic use of law as a legitimate form of counterpower', offers a defence against the hegemonic use of law to silence dissent. This chapter contrasts interestingly with authors who are more sceptical as to whether the master's tools have any role in dismantling the master's house.

The section continues with a chapter by Jamil Khader, 'Rethinking Academic Palestinian Advocacy and Activism: Academic Freedom, Human Rights, and the Universality of the Emancipatory Struggle', in which Khader develops a new direction for thinking Palestinian human rights, inflected by the writings of Slavoj Žižek, deriving a new form of universalism from Žižek's philosophy with its Hegelian inheritance, to buttress the Palestinian claim to universal rights.

The two final chapters of Part III, and of the book, by C. Heike Schotten and Arianne Shahvisi, probably provide the most pertinent responses to Salaita's reflections on academic freedom and its discontents. Heike Schotten's chapter, 'Against Academic Freedom: "Terrorism", Settler Colonialism, and Palestinian Liberation', uses a Nietzschean mode of argument to daringly argue the usefulness of the very concept of academic freedom, which has been so crucial to the discussion of this book. Coming from the opposite direction to Khader's, and fully aware of the risks attendant on their strategy, Schotten argues, in a manner akin to Salaita's, that 'academic freedom', as a discursive marker, has become a weapon of the forces of neoliberal university administrations and, hence, needs to be abandoned by BDS campaigners.

Like the other contributors who examine the contexts of BDS dissent in diverse university locations, Arianne Shahvisi's final chapter prises open the discourse of 'civility', which was applied so fiercely to police the speech of Steven Salaita. In Salaita's case and in other, similar cases, the concept of 'civility' was deployed to limit academic freedom, yet was not defined or defended, leaving university administrators able to wield the concept to impose limitations which serve other interests. Providing one aspect of the silencing of what university administrations regard as 'dangerous' speech acts, Shahvisi describes how more rigorously defining the concept of civility might be helpful in understanding the objectives and limitations of academic speech.

Salaita (2019) asks 'whether my sharp criticism of Israel and subsequent recalcitrance – my unwillingness to grovel my way back into academe's good graces – was worth it', and answers:

> I wouldn't change anything, nor do I entertain regret. I endure the punishment not because I'm a sucker or a martyr – I have no illusions about the ruthlessness of capital, and I despise the lionization of public figures – but because I want the vision of freedom ubiquitous among the dispossessed to survive.

In conclusion, it is worth reiterating Salaita's claim that this is the only way to win: 'by defying the logic of recrimination, by depleting its power through unapologetic defiance'. For Salaita it meant being willing to drive a school bus, for others it means being willing to perform other menial tasks, even at the cost of giving up cushy academic positions, 'whatever allows us to feel intellectual freedom'.

We hope that the contributors to this volume, all academics still employed by, or retired from, neoliberal universities, have succeeded in teasing out the complexities of the notion of academic freedom and its uses and abuses by academia, and in making links between it and the freedom to criticize Israel and its colonization of Palestine, because, to quote Salaita again, we value: 'The one thing they can't extinguish: a fixation on equality, recorded in steady rhymes with an uncapped pen. In other words: freedom'.

Notes

1   https://bdsmovement.net/academic-boycott (accessed 24 October 2018).
2   https://ijrcenter.org/thematic-research-guides/economic-social-and-cultural-rights-2/ (accessed 15 September 2019).
3   https://bdsmovement.net/pacbi/academic-boycott-guidelines (accessed 15 September 2019).
4   https://www.aaup.org/report/1940-statement-principles-academic-freedom-and-tenure (accessed 11 September 2019).
5   https://www.adl.org/media/12176/download (accessed 1 May 2019).
6   See Alana Lentin (forthcoming).
7   https://www.adl.org/what-we-do (accessed 1 May 2019).
8   Though not always, as in the case of Rebecca Tuvel (Brubaker 2017).
9   https://medium.com/the-israel-studies-conversation/concerns-regarding-the-word-crimes-israel-studies-special-issue-29ee2b1eb85 (accessed 22 October 2019).
10   TCD Policy on Academic Freedom, https://www.tcd.ie/about/policies/academic-freedom.php#Introduction (accessed 20 June 2019).

References

Abraham, M. (2014), *Out of Bounds: Academic Freedom and the Question of Palestine*, New York: Bloomsbury Academic.
Aderet, O. (2019), 'Annual Antisemitism Report Finds Spike in Number of Jews Murdered Worldwide', *Haaretz*, 1 May, https://www.haaretz.co.il/news/world/1.7187184?lts=1556713489637 (accessed 1 May 2019).
Allen, L. (2019), 'Academic Freedom in the United Kingdom', *Academe* 105 (4), https://www.aaup.org/article/academic-freedom-united-kingdom (accessed 22 October 2019).
Arab Studies Quarterly 33 (3/4) (Summer/Fall 2011).
Arendt, H. (2017), *The Origins of Totalitarianism*, London: Penguin Books.
Berlin, I. (2002), *Liberty*, Oxford: Oxford University Press.
Brubaker, R. (2017), 'The Uproar over "Transracialism"', *The New York Times* 18 May.
Butler, J. (2016), 'Exercising Rights: Academic Freedom and Boycott Politics' in A. Bilgrami and J. R. Cole (eds), *Who's Afraid of Academic Freedom?* New York: Columbia University Press, pp. 293–315.
Courtois, A. and T. O'Keefe (2015), 'Precarity in the Ivory Cage: Neoliberalism and Casualisation of Work in the Irish Higher Education Sector', *Journal for Critical Education Policy Studies* 13 (1): 43–66.
Davis, R. (2019), 'I've Been inside AIPAC. Ilhan Omar Is Right', 11 February, https://medium.com/@raegandavis/the-way-we-talk-

about-palestine-is-downright-mccarthyist-181868eb6534 (accessed 30 April 2019).

Drummond, S. G. (2013), *Unthinkable Thoughts: Academic Freedom and the One-State Model for Israel and Palestine*, Vancouver, British Columbia: UBC Press.

Dworkin, J. (2015), 'Losing Public Opinion on BDS, Activists Turn to "Lawfare"', *Mondoweiss*, 22 May, https://mondoweiss.net/2015/05/lawfare-against-divestment/ (accessed 29 April 2019).

Fine, G. (1995), 'Public Narration and Group Culture: Discerning Discourse in Social Movements' in H. Johnston and B. Klandermans (eds), *Social Movements and Culture*, London: UCL Press, pp. 127–143.

Fish, S. (2014), *Versions of Academic Freedom: From Professionalism to Revolution*, Chicago, IL: University of Chicago Press.

Hay, S. (2017). 'Academic Boycott Conference in Ireland Rejects Anti-BDS Speakers', *Yediot Aharanot*, 13 September.

Khalel, S. (2019), '"Weaponising Anti-Semitism": Florida Senate Passes Bill Barring Israel Criticism', *Middle East Eye*, 29 April, https://www.middleeasteye.net/news/weaponising-anti-semitism-florida-senate-passes-bill-barring-israel-criticism (accessed 2 May 2019).

Klein, D. (2009), 'Why Is Norman Finkelstein Not Allowed to Teach?' *Works & Days* 26/27: 307–322.

Lamont Hill, M. (2018), 'Marc Lamont Hill: I Am Sorry My Word Choices Caused Harm: Opinion', *The Inquirer*, 1 December, https://www.philly.com/philly/opinion/commentary/marc-lamont-hill-temple-university-cnn-palestine-israel-united-nations-20181201.html (accessed 30 April 2019).

Lentin, A. (Forthcoming), *Why Race Still Matters*, Cambridge: Polity Press.

Lloyd, D. and M. Schueller (2015), 'The Israeli State of Exception and the Case for Academic Boycott' in A. Dawson and B. Mullen (eds), *Against Apartheid: The Case for Boycotting Israeli Universities*, Chicago, IL: Haymarket, pp. 65–72.

McGreevy, R. (2017), 'Trinity College Dublin Event Involving Israeli Ambassador Cancelled', *Irish Times*, 21 February.

Moshman, D. and F. Edler (2015), 'Civility and Academic Freedom after Salaita', *AAUP Journal of Academic Freedom* 6, https://www.aaup.org/sites/default/files/MoshmanEdler.pdf (accessed 30 November 2018).

Najjar Kapitan, R. (2015), 'Climbing Down from the Ivory Tower: Double Standards and the Use of Academic Boycotts to Achieve Social and Economic Justice' in A. Dawson and B. Mullen (eds), *Against Apartheid: The Case for Boycotting Israeli Universities*, Chicago, IL: Haymarket, pp. 37–44.

Nussbaum, M. (2007), 'Against Academic Boycotts', *Dissent* 54 (3): 30–36.

Palumbo-Liu, D. (2018), 'The Harsh and Unjust Punishment of Marc Lamont Hill', *The Nation*, https://www.thenation.com/article/marc-lamont-hill-academic-freedom/ (accessed 30 April 2019).

Pappe, I. (2010), *Out of the Frame: Academic Freedom in Israel*, London: Pluto.

Petersen-Overton, K. J. (2011), 'Academic Freedom and Palestine: A Personal Account', *Arab Studies Quarterly* 33: 256–267.

Robinson, W. and M. Griffin (eds) (2017), *We Will Not Be Silenced: The Academic Repression of Israel's Critics*, Chico, CA: AK Press.

Salaita, S. (2015), *Uncivil Rites: Palestine and the Limits of Academic Freedom*, Chicago, IL: Haymarket.

Salaita, S. (2016), *Inter/Nationalism: Decolonizing Native America and Palestine*, Minneapolis, MN: University of Minnesota Press.

Salaita, S. (2019), 'My Life as a Cautionary Tale: Probing the Limits of Academic Freedom', *The Chronicle Review*, 28 August, https://www.chronicle.com/interactives/08282019-salaita-academic-freedom (accessed 26 September 2019).

Spero, D. (2019), 'Palestinian Professor Sues SF State for Breach of Contract, Discrimination', *Mondoweiss*, 21 January, https://mondoweiss.net/2019/01/palestinian-professor-discrimination/?fbclid=IwAR0DUg3wZa-W4_N1fo9xqLak8s_Jel8XeKUdpzrUeaPV6TO-qRrPe6Liwzg (accessed 28 April 2019).

The Temple News (2018), 'Temple Administration, Advocacy Groups React to Marc Lamont Hill's Controversial UN Comments', 30 November, https://temple-news.com/cnn-drops-temple-professor-marc-lamont-hill-for-pro-palestine-u-n-speech/ (accessed 30 April 2019).

Winstanley, A. (2019a), 'The Self-declared Jewish State Is a Light unto the Islamophobes', *Middle East Monitor*, 25 April, https://www.middleeastmonitor.com/20190425-the-self-declared-jewish-state-is-a-light-unto-the-islamophobes/ (accessed 2 May 2019).

Winstanley, A. (2019b), 'Inside Israel's Million Dollar Troll Army', *Electronic Intifada*, 12 June, https://electronicintifada.net/content/inside-israels-million-dollar-troll-army/27566 (accessed 20 June 2019).

PART I | Universities and academic governance

ONE | Whose university? Academic freedom, neoliberalism, and the rise of 'Israel Studies'

Hilary Aked

Introduction

This chapter examines Zionist philanthropists' efforts to re-shape the contours of the academic landscape in a manner favourable to Israel by fostering the rise of 'Israel Studies'. It demonstrates that this drive is a corollary to censorship and suppression of critiques of Zionism in universities, arguing that we should understand Israel Studies as an attempt to re-legitimize Zionism in the face of the so-called 'delegitimization' challenge. By tracing the roots of the subject, its emergence in the US, and recent expansion in the UK, the chapter suggests that Israel Studies faculty posts serve as academic 'facts on the ground' which inherently undermine the movement for a boycott of Israel.

Critically, increased financial pressures on universities amidst intensifying neoliberalization in higher education appears to constitute the enabling context for the growth of Israel Studies. The chapter illustrates this by drawing on previously unreleased correspondence and other documents relating to the establishment of Israel Studies posts at several British universities, obtained using Freedom of Information requests – an under-used method of data-collection in academia (Walby and Larsen 2012).[1] These offer insights into the entrepreneurial role of academics, troubling narratives of academic 'objectivity' and neutrality often deployed by universities but shown here to be mythical. More importantly, they highlight the role of private donors on whom universities increasingly rely and whose political connections and motivations are analysed. In seeking to explain why elite echelons of the Zionist movement – theorized here as a social movement 'from above' – believe promoting Israel Studies to be an important facet of a wider strategy to respond to Israel's legitimacy crisis, the chapter suggests that consciously fostering 'epistemic communities' may be a means of using 'expert' knowledge to normalize, entrench, and sustain metropolitan support for Israel's settler-colonial project.

The chapter begins by tracing the roots of Israel Studies to internal struggles over Zionism within Israel/Palestine and introduces the connection between the subject's emergence and the increasing privatization of universities. The second section explains how Israel Studies dovetails with the Israeli government's official Brand Israel nation branding programme. It then documents the ties between the UK donors to Israel Studies and the Zionist movement, as well as donors' declared aims, arguing that the evidence suggests an attempt to instrumentalize academia in a pushback against the so-called 'delegitimization' of Israel. The third section presents detailed evidence on the influence exercised by entrepreneurial academics and, in particular, private donors in the establishment of Israel Studies posts at UK universities, in the context of the increasing reliance of higher education institutions on private funds. The fourth section explores the implications of this, arguing that professions of objectivity deployed by universities are misleading when, at the institutional level, wealthy philanthropists are considerably shaping the parameters of legitimate knowledge. Finally, the chapter points out that far from being unique, the Zionist movement's efforts to utilize academia to bolster Israeli state power are analogous to the 'Big Three' American foundations' funding of universities – both domestically and overseas – to protect and project US hegemony in the latter half of the twentieth century. Phenomena like these, the argument concludes, challenge the attenuated sense in which 'academic freedom' is often understood, including in debates about the boycott of Israel, and support the case for a more holistic concept which ultimately relates to struggles over the purpose of the university itself. Academia's continued incorporation of projects like Israel Studies into settler-colonial knowledge also means that initiatives to 'decolonize' universities are not merely about unpicking historical legacies but also require ongoing resistance.

Neoliberal universities, the Zionist movement, and the roots of Israel Studies

The Zionist movement is best conceptualized as a social movement 'from above', defined by Laurence Cox and Alf Nilsen as the 'collective agency of dominant groups' to defend, reproduce, or extend their hegemony (Cox and Nilsen 2014, 59).[2] Yet the continuum of activities pursued by different elements of the Zionist movement are comprehensible only in relation to the strategies of social movements contesting the hegemony of Israel and Zionism. In this respect, the most important transnational movement 'from below' – 'organized by subaltern social groups' and aiming to 'challenge the constraints' or 'defend aspects of an existing dominant structure' (Cox and Nilsen 2014, 63) – is the Palestinian-initiated Boycott, Divestment and Sanctions (BDS) movement. Critically for the purposes of understanding Israel Studies, note that 'mobilisations from above typically take the form of ideological offensives' (Cox and Nilsen 2014, 91).

Universities in the global North have long been a key site of concern for Israel's supporters. Trends in the academy are seen as prescient of the future direction of society as a whole and the Zionist movement fears that the 'leaders of tomorrow' are being educated in environments hostile to Israel, not least because of the growing strength of the BDS movement, of which the academic boycott is a key plank (Stand With Us 2017). Revealingly, one pro-Israel group has argued that trends in the academy brought about in large part by privatization bode well for Israel. In *A Burning Campus? Rethinking Israel Advocacy at America's Universities and Colleges*, a 2012 white paper published by US Israel-advocacy organization The David Project, universities are described as the arena in which 'the thinking of America's future political leadership is molded [sic]' and simultaneously 'the leading venue for anti-Israel activity' (The David Project 2012, 15). However, the proliferation of business schools and the 'weakening of humanities and social sciences' are welcomed as auguring well for defeating what is dubbed 'anti-Israelism' in academia. In contrast to humanities and social science disciplines – the recent diminishment of which is closely related to the corporate trajectory of university governance (Preston 2015) – The David Project argues that 'hard sciences point to new opportunities to promote Israel to receptive audiences' (The David Project 2012, 8). Meanwhile, some actors with close ties to the Zionist movement are seeking to directly exploit marketization trends in order to undermine Palestine solidarity and criticism of Israel in universities.

Yet to understand where Israel Studies comes from we must look at the activities of the Zionist movement within Israel/Palestine itself. The roots of the subject can be traced back to contestation within the Israeli academy, where the so-called 'post-Zionist' turn of the 1990s was shut down by what Ilan Pappe has called the 'triumph of neo-Zionism' (Pappe 2014, 256).[3] A conscious effort to shore up Zionist ideology within the Israeli academy itself was closely related to a wave of university privatization there. The country's first private higher education institution, the Interdisciplinary Centre (IDC) Herzliya and the privately funded Shalem College are key examples. Founded in 1994 and 2013 respectively, both were established with the explicit intention of producing committed Zionist thinkers, fit to be Israel's future leaders. At a time when post-Zionism was relatively widespread in Israeli universities, the IDC set out to 'change the academic agenda of the country' (Reichmann, n.d.). Meanwhile the rationale for the Shalem College was that 'Israel faces an internal threat stemming from the growing loss of conviction on the part of its young people regarding the justness of its founding and the legitimacy of its continued existence as a Jewish state' (Shalem Center, n.d.a). The college's *raison d'être* was to reverse this internal crisis of Zionism, since it held that,

> If this trend continues, Israel may well lose the fight – not to its enemies, but on account of negligence and sheer indifference. To ensure its survival and success, Israel needs not only a skilled military, a strong economic base, and highly trained technocrats. It also needs a cadre of visionaries (Shalem Center n.d.b).

Indeed, the Shalem College co-founder Yoram Hazony even declared: 'if my university is not established, Zionism will have no future', crystallizing the eminently political aims of his pedagogical project (Lanski and Berman 2007).

The connection of Israel Studies overseas to this schism in the Israeli academy over Zionism can be elucidated by examining how post-Zionism had expressed itself in Israeli sociology in the last decade of the twentieth century. One school of thought, the (post-/anti-Zionist) 'colonization perspective' – which took 'the Israeli–Arab binational set of relations as its vantage point' – argued that Israel could only be understood by way of reference to the Palestinians, so profoundly had their encounter shaped both societies (Ram 1999, 52; see also Lentin, this volume). By contrast, mainstream 'national sociology' took what Uri Ram calls a 'dualist approach'. Viewing Israel and Palestinians as separable entities, it simply 'drew the boundaries of "Israeli society" around the territorial and ethnic Jewish presence' (Ram 1999, 53). By privileging Jewishness and marginalizing Palestinians, the definition of Israel Studies offered by the Association for Israel Studies – 'the study of Israel, the Zionist movement, or the pre-state Jewish community in Palestine' (Association for Israel Studies n.d.) – clearly reflects this latter view. Thus, the framing of Israel Studies renders it a useful tool in a wider ideological offensive waged by the Zionist movement, especially since Israel's post-2000 crisis of legitimacy.

Brand Israel and the uses of Israel Studies: 'delegitimization' and re-legitimization

The first Israel Studies course in the US was founded in 1998 (Bard 2008). It therefore predates but neatly dovetails with the Israeli government's Brand Israel project. The key concept underlying this official national branding effort, launched in 2005 and managed by Ido Aharoni at the Ministry of Foreign Affairs, was moving 'beyond the conflict' (Ben-Ami 2005). It acknowledged that the Palestinian question could not be disappeared but aimed to 'broaden the conversation' about Israel so the country is not only viewed through the lens of state violence (Aharoni 2012). In this sense, Israel Studies – also seen to be concerned with 'broadening [the] scope of Israel-content courses *beyond the conflict* to areas of Israeli culture and society' (Koren and Einhorn 2010a, 19; my italics) – is entirely consonant with Israel's official propaganda aims as articulated and implemented in the Brand Israel project.

Given this compatibility, the idea of instrumentalizing Israel Studies to push back against so-called 'delegitimization' – a euphemism used by the Zionist movement to describe criticism

of Zionism – has long been articulated by key pro-Israel strategists. For example, the Tel Aviv think tank, the Reut Institute,
has argued that 'in the context of Reut's current work on how to
fight the delegitimacy of Israel, the suggestion to create chairs of
Israel Studies in leading UK universities could act as an important component of Israel's strategy' (White 2012). Similarly,
former American Israel Public Affairs Committee (AIPAC) staffer
Mitchell Bard in a paper for an Israeli Ministry of Foreign Affairs-
sponsored conference wrote that '[p]roviding the next generation
with a good education about Israel is vital for the future as well as
critical to countering present campus-based efforts to delegitimize
Israel', and advocated '[e]ncouraging more Israel Studies on campus as part of a broader rebranding' (Bard and Troy 2009, 11).

In light of such calls, it is pertinent to note that the private
donors who have been critical to engineering Israel Studies in
both the US and the UK are closely connected to Israel-advocacy
bodies and other Zionist movement organizations. Figure 1
shows all current Israel Studies posts at UK universities – notably
all founded since 2000 – together with the donors and amounts
given during the last known cycle of donations.[4] Figure 2 shows
that *all* of the funders of Israel Studies posts in the UK have strong
links to the Zionist movement.[5] It is important to note that the
organizations included in this diagram, which are Jewish communal bodies rather than explicitly Zionist ones, are included due
to strong empirical evidence of involvement in Zionist organizing, such as statements by leading figures that lobbying for Israel
is part of their mandate, as in the case of the Board of Deputies
(Arkush 2013) and the Jewish Leadership Council (Johnson
2014). Notably, one donor to Israel Studies at the University
of Sussex, the late Lord Weidenfeld – to whom Israeli Prime
Minister Benjamin Netanyahu paid tribute after his death – was
a lifelong Zionist and a former advisor to Israel's first president

Year	University	Post	Donor	Sum
2011	Oxford[1]	Stanley Lewis Professor of Israel Studies	Stanley & Zea Lewis Family Foundation (Michael Lewis) Pears Foundation (Trevor Pears)	£3 million over 3 years
2010[2]	Manchester	Pears Lecturer in Israel Studies	Pears Foundation (Trevor Pears)	£179,478 over 3 years
2011	Leeds	Pears Senior Lecturer in Israel and Middle East Studies	Pears Foundation (Trevor Pears)	£150,000 over 3 years
2011	School of Oriental and African Studies (SOAS), University of London	Pears Senior Research Fellow in Israel Studies[3]	Pears Foundation (Trevor Pears)	£480,000 (approx.) over 4 years
2012	Sussex	Yossi Harel Chair of Modern Israel Studies	R & S Cohen Foundation (Ronald Cohen) Atkin Foundation (Edward and Celia Atkin) Blavatnik Family Foundation (Leonard Blavatnik) Gerald Ronson Foundation (Gerald Ronson) Lord Weidenfeld (George Weidenfeld) Pears Foundation (Trevor Pears)	£650,000 over 4 years

[1] Previously at Oxford, an anonymous donor gave an unknown amount over approximately five years from 2002 and the post was called the Leone Ginzburg Fellow in Israel Studies.
[2] Pears also previously funded the post 2005-2006; 2006-2009.
[3] Pears also funds the European Association of Israel Studies (EAIS) which is headquartered at SOAS.

Figure 1 Donors to chairs of Israel Studies at UK universities

Source: University gift agreements obtained via Freedom of Information requests.

Chaim Weizmann (Dysch 2016). Although international donations are not included in Figure 2, two other Sussex donors,

Leonard Blavatnik and Gerald Ronson, have financially contributed to Netanyahu (Sadeh 2016). The Israel Studies donors are also considerably internally cohesive in other ways.[6]

In addition to these donors' strong links to the Zionist movement, political motivations have also been ascribed to them by Israel-advocacy bodies and some key donors have themselves been explicit about their reasons for fostering the subject. For example, one Israel-advocacy group – echoing the 'beyond the conflict' messaging of the Brand Israel project – states that teaching Israel 'in terms of the conflict' is reportedly 'exactly what they're [the donors to Israel Studies] fighting against' (Israel on Campus Coalition 2006, 22). In the US, Fred Lafer of the Taub Foundation – which has funded Israel Studies at New York University – affirmed this by unambiguously declaring that his aim was to counter the 'Arabic [sic] point of view' (Mearsheimer and Walt 2007, 181). In the UK, the former University of Oxford Israel Studies fellow Emmanuele Ottolenghi noted that the (originally anonymous) benefactor of his post had a firm 'commitment to Israel' (Ottolenghi 2005). Similarly, Lord Weidenfeld – who coordinated the group of donors to Israel Studies at Sussex University – welcomed the chair of Israel Studies at Oxford University by calling it 'vital in the fight against anti-Zionism' (Anonymous 2012) and 'conducive to fighting the boycott' (Rocker 2011). He even articulated the conscious political strategy guiding the process, stressing the importance of establishing Israel Studies in key universities, particularly 'those with an anti-Israel' presence (Anonymous 2012). Israel Studies posts have been funded at several UK universities where the Palestine solidarity movement has historically been very strong, notably the University of Sussex, the University of Manchester, and the School of Oriental and African Studies (SOAS), University of London, suggesting this strategy has been implemented with some success.

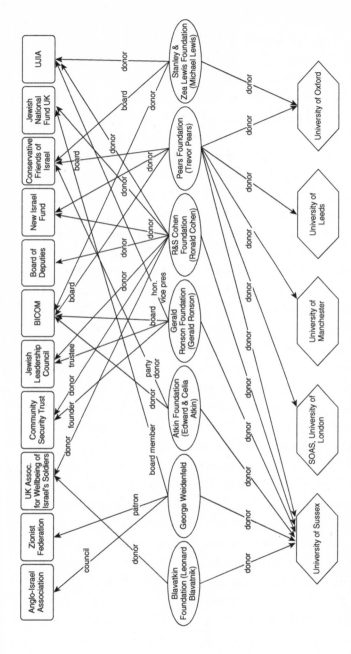

Figure 2 Zionist movement links of donors to Israel Studies posts at UK universities

Source: based on university gift agreements obtained under the Freedom of Information Act and profiles on Powerbase.info.

Given the evidence above – of the wish by Zionist movement strategists to instrumentalize Israel Studies, together with the donors' Zionist movement connections, their internal cohesiveness, and some of their stated aims – it seems reasonable to conclude that a key aim of these philanthropists in funding the expansion of Israel Studies in UK universities may be to push back against the so-called 'delegitimization' of Israel at universities and in wider society. From the donors' perspectives, Israel Studies appears to be viewed as a vehicle to centre Israel and de-centre Palestinians, assisting in a wider effort to 're-legitimize' Israel. A closer look at the top-down processes by which Israel Studies posts at UK universities were established, as well as the relationships between donors and university managers, provides insights into the driving forces behind decision-making at contemporary neoliberal universities and raises fundamental questions about the meaning of 'academic freedom'.

Supply and demand: donor influence and entrepreneurial academics

Even supporters of Israel Studies note that demand for the subject has been 'a response to supply', rather than vice versa (Koren and Fishman 2015). In other words, the rise of Israel Studies on both sides of the Atlantic has been a donor-led elite intervention, fostered via a 'top down process with private funding' (Shenkar 2010, 15) rather than a response to student demand. This stands in sharp contrast to bottom-up calls for more (public) funding to be funnelled into subjects like Black Studies, such as the 1968 campaign at San Francisco State College or the contemporary 'Why is My Curriculum White?' campaign in the UK and Australia.

How should we understand the relationship between universities and philanthropic foundations? As early as 1930, former London

School of Economics professor Harold Laski – incidentally an ardent Zionist (Jones 2015) – argued in an essay on the subject:

> A university principal who wants his institution to expand has no alternative except to see it expand in the directions of which one or other of the foundations happens to approve. There may be doubt, or even dissent among the teachers in the institution, but what possible chance has doubt or dissent against a possible gift of, say, a hundred thousand dollars? (Laski 1930, 170–171)

While this serves as a reminder that universities' dependence on private funding is not unique to the neoliberal era, marketization trends in recent years have intensified the situation. Arguably, Laski's observation is more pertinent today than ever before.

Correspondence obtained via a Freedom of Information (FOI) request illustrates this, as well as demonstrating the 'top-down process' through which Israel Studies has been brought into being. Staff at the University of Leeds raised concerns about a proposed Israel Studies post funded by the Pears Foundation in June 2011 and asked then Vice Chancellor Michael Arthur to suspend the appointment process pending wider consultation.[7] The Pears Foundation states explicitly that it seeks to 'support Israel' (albeit 'by being a critical friend')[8] and as Figure 2 shows, its head Trevor Pears has been linked to pro-Israel lobby groups including BICOM (Britain Israel Communications and Research Centre) and Conservative Friends of Israel. Bearing out Laski's prediction, Arthur (who is currently provost of University College London) was dismissive about the concerns raised in his initial response, calling the case for Pears being a 'pro-Zionist' organization 'flimsy'.[9]

However, in other ways, Laski's essay paints an overly deterministic picture. He suggests, for example, that 'it is merely the fact that a fund is within reach which permeates everything', and therefore implies that foundations exercise influence without needing to exert 'the slightest control ... or interference' (Laski 1930, 171). In the case of Israel Studies, this does not always hold true. Another document obtained via FOI demonstrates clearly that at least one donor to the University of Sussex, Lord Weidenfeld – the same donor who had explicitly acknowledged his political intentions – sought to influence the appointment process for the Israel Studies post he was co-funding. Correspondence

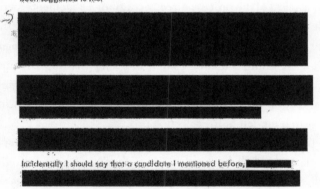

Figure 3 Letter from Lord Weidenfeld to University of Sussex Vice Chancellor Michael Farthing suggesting names of potential candidates for Israel Studies chair, 16 June 2011

Source: obtained by the author via Freedom of Information request.

shows that Weidenfeld wrote to then Sussex Vice Chancellor Michael Farthing in June 2011 with a list of names he suggested could potentially be candidates for the post.

Weidenfeld's letter mentions 'your kind suggestion [to] put forward names', implying that he was invited by Farthing to propose possible candidates. Other lines – 'my letter of 14 April in which I ... put forward names' and 'incidentally, I should say that a candidate I mentioned before, REDACTED ...' – reveal that this was not the first time the pair had discussed potentially suitable academics.[10] Since the university redacted the names supplied when it disclosed this document under the Freedom of Information Act, it is not possible to determine whether the current incumbent Professor David Tal was proposed by Weidenfeld. However, it is known that Farthing subsequently chaired the eight-person appointment committee. In addition, the Pears Foundation – which as Figure 1 showed, has contributed to every Israel Studies post in the UK – was offered the opportunity to suggest names for the external member of this committee.[11] These aspects of the process directly contradict statements made by the university, such as the claim that '[t]hose providing the funding for this chair have had no influence over the appointment process, including the composition of the appointing committee',[12] as well as Farthing's personal assurances to concerned alumni that the donors 'will have no influence on the outcome of the research funded or the selection process'.[13]

In two other cases at UK universities, donors knew which academics would fill the posts they were funding. Professor Colin Shindler's name was written into the 2011 deed of gift between the Pears Foundation and SOAS,[14] while the agreement between the Pears Foundation and the University of Manchester was renewed in 2009 on the understanding that the incumbent scholar, Dr Moshe Behar, would continue in the post.[15]

FOI documents also reveal the role played by entrepreneurial academics, several of whom eased processes along within their institutions (despite, in most cases, opposition from other staff and students). In 2011, for example, Shindler – who still holds the post of Professor of Israel Studies at SOAS – made a case in favour of the Pears Foundation donation (which funded his own job) to then SOAS vice chancellor, the late Professor Paul Webley. 'Israel–Palestine', Shindler wrote, 'is a "hot" subject and brings in lots of students. It therefore brings in fees and is financially viable'.[16] Given the earlier argument that Israel Studies is, for some, precisely about moving *away* from a focus on the Palestinian issue, this is an interesting pitch.

Similarly, Professor Christian Wiese from the University of Sussex wrote to then Sussex vice chancellor Michael Farthing in September 2010 expressing support for the Israel Studies proposal and declaring: 'I am convinced this is a golden opportunity which goes well beyond this single chair. Sussex is now on the radar of very potent donors'.[17] Donors' potency was also illustrated at Sussex when a disagreement over the naming of the post arose. Although Vice Chancellor Farthing initially advised that the university's policy was only to name posts after donors, he eventually agreed to name the post the Yossi Harel Chair of Modern Israel Studies after the father-in-law of one of the donors, Ronald Cohen. This happened after Professor Christian Wiese assured colleagues that only a 'staunch and ideological anti-Zionist' would object to a post named after Yossi Harel, a Haganah and Israel Defense Forces (IDF) intelligence unit officer who died in 2008.[18]

All these examples, including donors' attempts to influence shortlisted candidates and involvement in appointment processes, as well as on the deployment by academics of arguments about financial viability and donor potency, illuminate wider power dynamics. They illustrate that 'academic freedom' in marketized universities cannot be understood without reference to material issues of supply and demand – in this case, particularly supply – and that the resources of social movements from above enable them to seek to exploit this situation.

Performing objectivity, creating academic 'facts on the ground'

It is important to say that none of this need necessarily dent the scholarly credentials of the individual academics concerned. Yet both individuals and institutions involved in the growth of Israel Studies in the UK clearly harboured anxieties around the topic and laboured to 'perform objectivity' (Xu and Fine 2011, 596). A Q&A document produced by the University of Oxford's press office, for example, emphasized the supposed detachment of academic knowledge from the subject studied. In answer to the anticipated question 'What does Lord Weidenfeld mean when he talks about the new post at Oxford being "conducive to fighting the boycott"', the document suggested the following answer:

> It is not for us to comment on what he meant. What we can say is that this is an academic role, not a partisan role. Academics do not endorse (or indeed criticize) the subject of study simply by the act of studying it.[19]

Similarly, Professor Clive Jones's pitch for an (as yet unrealized) 'Leeds University Centre for Israel Studies (LUCIS)' declared that the centre would produce research relevant to those in media, government, business, and NGOs seeking 'objective expertise on Israel' and thus have uses 'beyond its academic utility'.[20] In both these cases, we see a disconnect between academic actors' profession of neutrality and the acknowledged goals of the external actors funding and promoting the subject, as discussed earlier.

Similarly, the American-Israel Co-operative Enterprise (AICE) – a key promoter of Israel Studies in the US, founded by aforementioned former AIPAC employee Mitchell Bard – also deploys avowals of apolitical academic neutrality. However, it does so in such a way as to inadvertently foreground the internal contradictions of Israel Studies and the political agenda of its supporters. AICE runs a visiting Israeli professor ('VIP') scheme to bring Israeli academics to North American campuses, and the organization's 'reasons for establishing the program' are described as 'anti-Israel propaganda activities' on campus (Koren and Einhorn 2010b, 4). Its selection process is described as follows:

> No political litmus test is applied, *but VIPs do need to accept the right of Israel to exist as a Jewish state* (Koren and Einhorn 2010b, 4; my italics).

Far from politically neutral, this criterion ensures what Lara Deeb and Jessica Winegar have referred to as 'compulsory Zionism' (Deeb and Winegar 2016, 18).

More broadly – while Israel Studies is certainly not mere propaganda – at the institutional level, wealthy philanthropic foundations funding the subject clearly have considerable impact on defining the parameters of 'legitimate and illegitimate knowledge' (Parmar 2012, 9) which ultimately filters into the public sphere. Professional scholars have agency and are not 'pawns on a chessboard' or 'the playthings of elites' (Parmar 2011, 199). However, private funding enables certain ideas to become more prominent, makes specific research areas more employable, and in the process helps to marginalize other ideas. Moreover, academics inevitably play a social and political role and therefore the spheres of 'Israel Studies', 'Israel education', and 'Israel advocacy' – which some present as sharply distinct (Horowitz 2010) – interact and overlap. The impact agenda in higher education means academics increasingly need to demonstrate that their research will have real-world influence ('beyond its academic utility', as Clive Jones puts it). Expertise is, in part, 'a strategic resource within contentious politics' (Xu and Fine 2011, 610); advocacy organizations can and do amplify certain knowledge produced by epistemic communities to create echo chambers in the public sphere (Morin 2014).

More concretely, the charter of the European Association of Israel Studies – based at SOAS and funded by the Pears Foundation – states that 'links' with Israeli universities 'will be encouraged'. Thus, funding the subject is also a practical way of creating academic 'facts on the ground' which inherently undermine the academic boycott movement in universities. Likewise, at least two of the foundations funding Israel Studies in the UK (the Pears Foundation and the Atkin Foundation) have simultaneously funded the Britain-Israel Research and Academic Exchange Partnership (BIRAX), a public-private partnership funded jointly by Zionist donors and the British and Israeli governments, explicitly intended as a response to calls for academic boycott (Aked 2016). Since its establishment, BIRAX has provided some £10 million for research collaborations between Israeli and UK universities. Similarly, the International Centre for the Study of Radicalisation at King's College London was originally conceived by key funder Henry Sweetbaum as a response to the BDS movement (*Pennsylvania Gazette* 2014) and is partnered with the IDC in Herzliya, Israel, thus institutionally pre-empting the possibility of an academic boycott.

Meanwhile, several of the Zionist groups to which Israel Studies donors are connected (as shown in Figure 2) also take an active interest in the contestation over Israel/Palestine in universities. This engagement has included silencing campaigns.

For example, both the Jewish Leadership Council (White 2015) and the Board of Deputies (Aked 2015) lobbied against an academic conference, 'International Law and the State of Israel: Legitimacy, Exceptionalism and Responsibility', which was scheduled to take place at Southampton University in 2015 but, following intense pressure, had to be relocated and rescheduled, eventually taking place in Ireland, at University College Cork, two years later (see Landy, this volume). In this sense, the promotion of Israel Studies can be situated as the corollary of more frequently discussed efforts to censor criticisms of Zionism and repress students' Palestine solidarity activism (Nadeau and Sears 2010; Abraham 2014), each one a facet of a multidimensional strategy to 'colonize the information environment' (Miller and Harkins 2010, 573). Israel Studies as an academic subject can never be completely separate from its funders or their political networks, agendas, and activities, so the performance of 'objectivity' is largely a myth closely tied to and sustaining an idea of 'academic freedom' which does not withstand scrutiny in the current landscape of higher education.

Elite organization, state power, and academic freedom

Efforts to shape the contours of academia to augment state power are nothing new. From the 1970s onwards, 'terrorism studies' emerged as a distinct field 'at the behest and with the active support of the state' (Miller and Mills 2010, 217), and its emphases have continued to be heavily influenced by government (Reid 1997, 91–106). In turn, states have also been indirectly supported through academia, for instance by third parties such as private foundations working to support US power on a global scale. Inderjeet Parmar notes that Gramsci emphasized 'the indispensability of private elite organizations for state legitimacy and power' (Parmar 2006, 13). Accordingly, Parmar has analysed the role of the 'Big Three' US foundations (Ford, Carnegie, and Rockefeller) in bolstering American hegemony, noting that domestically they 'pioneered area studies and IR [international relations] programs' in top universities, and, overseas, established institutions which produced 'cadres of academics imbued with knowledge ... orienting them towards a pro-American/Western approach to "modernization"' (Parmar 2012, 7). While playing a fundamental role in the rise of international relations as a subject, the foundations also targeted certain countries perceived as particularly prone to anti-Americanism (Parmar 2012, 7), just as Weidenfeld advocated establishing Israel Studies posts at universities 'with an anti-Israel' reputation. The Big Three foundations mobilized at critical junctures:

> Periods of anti-Americanism – such as during the Cold War and ... the Iraq war – led the major American philanthropies to launch private initiatives that dove-tailed in a semi-official division of labour with official state agencies' efforts to combat 'anti-Americanism'. (Parmar 2008, 29)

The emergence and expansion of Israel Studies, this chapter argues, should be understood as analogous to this phenomenon. Private foundations' fostering of Israel Studies may be termed 'philanthropy', but it also serves as a means of entrenching and normalizing metropolitan support for Israel's settler-colonial project, part of a wider strategy to defend Zionist hegemony at a time of legitimacy crisis for Israel.

All this constitutes a challenge to the attenuated sense in which 'academic freedom' is usually understood. The dynamics of state power and settler-colonialism intersect with and shape the battle for academic freedom within Israel and Palestine (Pappe 2010). For Palestinians, the realities of education under occupation are such that we need to begin to understand checkpoints and borders as academic freedom issues. Seen in this light, criticism of the movement to boycott Israeli universities on the grounds that this violates academic freedom appears deeply parochial. In Western academia, especially the US, cases of academics failing to secure jobs due to their stance on Palestine – sometimes with universities put under pressure by private donors – are well-documented. Scholars such as Norman Finkelstein (Abraham 2007) and Steven Salaita (Abunimah 2015) are the most high-profile. Yet the evidence above, especially pointing to direct interventions like Lord Weidenfeld's, reminds us that donors seek to influence who gets the job, as well as who does not. Censorship and the promotion of certain ideologies are two sides of the same coin and the increased reliance of the neoliberal university on private philanthropic donors offers opportunities for external influence of both kinds – influence which is certainly not unique to the Zionist movement, as Linsey McGoey's work (2015, 195) has demonstrated.

This makes it very important to understand academic freedom holistically, and to consider both sides of this equation. Classical liberalism tends to define freedom negatively; freedom *from* interference in individual activity is paramount. The UK's Prevent programme and state-led 'counter-extremism' agendas, for instance, have rightly come into the purview of liberal critiques for their deleterious influence on the free exchange of ideas in academia (not to mention a highly racialized impact on Muslim freedom of expression and equal participation in civil society). Censorship of Palestinian and pro-Palestinian voices in the British academy is increasingly affected by and justified with reference to countering 'extremism', making it vital to contextualize this phenomenon within the UK government's anti-terrorism Prevent programme.[21] However, there is also the question of who has the freedom *to* speak and to be heard. Thinking about academic freedom in positive terms, the question becomes: who has the opportunity and capacity to disseminate ideas in the first place? Who has the power to endow professorial chairs at universities (and who does not)? As Judith Butler notes, some rights are not 'asserted and then restrained' but 'have from the start no opportunity to be asserted' (Butler 2006, 11).

We must therefore put to bed the myth of academic freedom which holds that the university is a neutral space in which all voices in society compete on a level playing field. With the pressures of neoliberalism increasingly transforming universities, it is clearer than ever that there is a marketplace for ideas in higher education and, to a large extent, those with buying power can dominate the ideological environment, at least at the institutional level. Moreover, in light of recent movements and discussions concerned with 'decolonizing universities' (Bhambra, Nişancıoğlu and Gebrial 2018), the case of Israel Studies reminds us that such initiatives are not merely about unpicking historical legacies. Whether or not Israel Studies will have any substantial impact in dampening Palestine solidarity and BDS activism remains an open question, but the subject's growth exemplifies the way academia continues to be incorporated into settler-colonial knowledge projects and the ongoing need to challenge this phenomenon.

Notes

1 Investigative sociology is appropriate in 'settings where one is likely to find great discrepancies between frontstage and backstage activities' (Cassell 1988, 91). Though Freedom of Information as a tool can provide 'access to hidden documents' and thus reveal unseen or concealed phenomena (Williams 2012, 109), scholars have lagged behind journalists in exploiting the possibilities for data collection contained within this relatively recent legislation. This research demonstrates its efficacy.

2 This conceptualization is most helpful because the Zionist movement includes a wide range of actors engaged in a broad spectrum of

activities which cannot be encapsulated by the term 'lobbying' or the label 'lobby', popularized by Mearsheimer and Walt (2007). However, the dominant school of social movement thought is biased towards the examination of non-elites, whereas the framework of social movements from above and below allows us to conceptualize on the same level and analyse within one framework the 'collective agency of dominant and subaltern groups', in this case the Palestine liberation struggle and its attendant solidarity movement together with the Israeli state and transnational Zionist movement (Cox and Nilsen 2014, 61). This makes sense because they decisively shape each other's strategies and therefore 'have to be understood in relation to the conflictual encounter' (Cox and Nilsen 2014, 63).

3   The 'post-Zionist' turn was closely linked to the work of the so-called 'new historians', who used archival research to challenge the foundational Zionist myths of the Israeli state by pointing to evidence of deliberate and systematic ethnic cleansing during the 1948 Nakba. 'Neo-Zionism' was the re-assertion, in response, of a more 'nationalistic, racist and dogmatic' ideology (Pappe 2014, 249).

4   Further contracts may have been signed more recently than the agreements and figures upon which Figure 1 is based.

5   Not all the connections traced in Figure 2 remain extant, some refer to past ties which have now lapsed.

6   The internal connections between the donors are not mapped in Figure 2 but include Michael Lewis serving as chair of Weidenfeld's Institute for Strategic Dialogue think tank (Rocker 2011). This organization, in turn, holds joint events with Ronald Cohen's non-profit foundation, the Portland Trust, while Weidenfeld's publishing house produced a book showcasing Israel's scientific achievements, *Israel in the World*, commissioned by Trevor Pears. Copies of the book, according to the Reut Institute, were 'distributed by Israeli embassies' around the world (Reut 2010, 73).

7   'POLIS and the Pears Foundation', Email from Leeds University staff [REDACTED] to Michael Arthur, 23 June 2011, obtained via Freedom of Information request.

8   The Pears Family Charitable Foundation and School of Oriental and African Studies Deed of Gift (EAIS), 3, obtained via Freedom of Information request.

9   'Fwd: POLIS and the Pears Foundation', Email from Michael Arthur to Roger Gair, Michelle Calvert, and Jeremy Higham, 23 June 2011, obtained via Freedom of Information request.

10 Letter from Lord Weidenfeld to University of Sussex Vice Chancellor Michael Farthing, 16 June 2011, obtained via Freedom of Information request.

11   Email from Sussex University Director of Development Marina Pedreira Villarino to Charles Keidan of the Pears Foundation, 1 June 2011, obtained via Freedom of Information request.

12   Letter from Pro-Vice Chancellor Professor Chris Martin to REDACTED, 4 July 2012, obtained via Freedom of Information request.

13   Letter from Vice Chancellor Michael Farthing to Dr Harald Molgaard, 25 September 2013, obtained via Freedom of Information request.

14   The Pears Family Charitable Foundation and School of Oriental and African Studies Deed of Gift (SOAS posts), 3, obtained via Freedom of Information request.

15   Letter from Charles Keidan of the Pears Foundation to Prof. Phillip Alexander of the University of Manchester, 12 May 2009, obtained via Freedom of Information request.

16   Email to SOAS Vice Chancellor Paul Webley from Prof. Colin Shindler, 6 January 2011, obtained via Freedom of Information request.

17   Email to University of Sussex Vice Chancellor Michael Farthing from Prof. Christian Weiss, 22 September 2010, obtained via Freedom of Information request.

18   Email from Prof. Christian Wiese to Professor Chris Martin, Marina Pedreira Villarino, and Prof. Matthew Cragoe, 9 March 2011, obtained via Freedom of Information request.

19   University of Oxford press office media Q&A about Israel Studies post, 19 April 2011, obtained via Freedom of Information request.

20   Prof. Clive Jones's pitch for a Leeds University Centre for Israel Studies, n.d. (c. 2011), obtained via Freedom of Information request.

21   Prevent is the much-criticized UK Home Office programme aiming to 'safeguard people and communities from the threat of terrorism', part of the government's counter-terrorism strategy. It operates in the so-called pre-criminal space since its stated aim is to stop people becoming terrorists or supporting terrorism (https://www.ltai.info/what-is-prevent/, accessed 8 April 2019). In March 2019 a successful judicial review found the Prevent duty guide to universities unlawful in that it violates freedom of speech (Gayle 2019).

References

Abraham, M. (2007), 'The Case for Norman Finkelstein', *The Guardian*, 14 June, https://www.theguardian.com/commentisfree/2007/jun/14/abattleforacademicfreedom (accessed 3 April 2019).

Abraham, M. (2014), *Out of Bounds: Academic Freedom and the Question of Palestine*, London: Bloomsbury Publishing.

Abunimah, A. (2015), 'Steven Salaita Settles Lawsuit with Univ. of Illinois', *Electronic Intifada*, 12 November, https://electronicintifada.net/blogs/

ali-abunimah/steven-salaita-settles-lawsuit-univ-illinois (accessed 3 April 2019).

Aharoni, I. (2012), 'Nation Branding: Some Lessons from Israel', *Knowledge@Wharton*, University of Pennsylvania, 1 March, http://knowledge.wharton.upenn.edu/article/nation-branding-some-lessons-from-israel (accessed 28 March 2019).

Aked, H. (2015), 'So Much for Free Speech: Southampton University and the Pro-Israel Lobby', *Open Democracy*, 15 April, https://www.opendemocracy.net/ourkingdom/hilary-aked/so-much-for-free-speech-southampton-university-and-proisrael-lobby (accessed 13 March 2019).

Aked, H. (2016), 'Billionaire Donor Using British Council to Combat Israel Boycott', *Electronic Intifada*, 14 March, https://electronicintifada.net/content/billionaire-donor-using-british-council-combat-israel-boycott/15991 (accessed 3 April 2019).

Anonymous (2012), '"Vital" New Chair for Students', *Jewish Chronicle*, 2 March, https://www.thejc.com/news/uk-news/vital-new-chair-for-students-1.32020 (accessed 2 April 2019).

Arkush, J. (2013), 'British Jewry: Loud and Proud', *Jewish News*, 5 November, http://blogs.timesofisrael.com/british-jewry-loud-and-proud (accessed 29 March 2019).

Association for Israel Studies (n.d.), 'About Us', http://reg.co.il/ais/ais/about.ehtml (accessed 3 April 2019).

Bard, M. (2008), 'Introducing Israel Studies in U.S. Universities', *Jerusalem Center for Public Affairs*, 23 December, http://jcpa.org/article/introducing-israel-studies-in-u-s-universities (accessed 2 April 2019).

Bard, M. and G. Troy (2009), 'Delegitimization of Israel: "Boycotts, Divestment and Sanctions"', notes from working group at the Global Forum for Combatting Anti-Semitism in Jerusalem, 16–17 December.

Ben-Ami, Y. (2005), 'About Face', *Haaretz*, 20 September, https://www.haaretz.com/print-edition/features/about-face-1.170267 (accessed 3 April 2019).

Bhambra, G. K., K. Nişancıoğlu and D. Gebrial (2018), *Decolonising the University*, London: Pluto Press.

Butler, J. (2006), 'Israel/Palestine and the Paradoxes of Academic Freedom', *Radical Philosophy* 135 (January/February): 8–17.

Cassell, J. (1988), 'The Relationship of Observer to Observed When Studying Up' in R. Burgess (ed.), *Studies in Qualitative Methodology*, Vol. 1, London: Jai Press, pp. 89–108.

Cox, L. and A. G. Nilsen (2014), *We Make Our Own History: Marxism and Social Movements in the Twilight of Neoliberalism*, London: Pluto Press.

The David Project (2012), *A Burning Campus? Rethinking Israel Advocacy at America's Universities and Colleges*, Boston, MA: The David

Project, http://brandeiscenter.com/wp-content/uploads/2017/11/ngo/david
project.pdf (accessed 3 April 2019).

Deeb, L. and J. Winegar (2016), *Anthropology's Politics: Disciplining the Middle East*, Stanford, CA: Stanford University Press.

Dysch, M. (2016), 'Lord Weidenfeld Dies Aged 96', *Jewish Chronicle*, 20 January, https://www.thejc.com/news/uk-news/lord-weidenfeld-dies-aged-96-1.57764 (accessed 24 March 2019).

Gayle, D. (2019), 'UK Prevent Guidance to Universities Unlawful, Court Rules', *The Guardian*, 8 March, https://www.theguardian.com/uk-news/2019/mar/08/uks-prevent-guidance-to-universities-unlawful-court-rules (accessed 8 April 2019).

Horowitz, B. (2010), *Defining Israel Education*, iCentre, http://www.theicenter.org/sites/default/files/knowledge_base/bethamie%27s%20report.pdf (accessed 2 April 2019).

Israel on Campus Coalition (2006), *In Search of Israel Studies: A Survey of Israel Studies on American College Campuses*, Israel on Campus Coalition, https://web.archive.org/web/20130919031307/https://israelcc.org/docs/default-source/publications/in-search-of-israel-studies-(2007).pdf?sfvrsn=9 (accessed 3 April 2019).

Johnson, S. (2014), 'Simon Johnson: The JLC and Israel', Jewish Leadership Council, 1 May, http://www.thejlc.org/simon_johnson_the_jlc_and_israel (accessed 3 April 2019).

Jones, E. (2015), 'Zionism in Britain: A Neglected Chronicle', *Counterpunch*, 28 August, https://www.counterpunch.org/2015/08/28/zionism-in-britain-a-neglected-chronicle (accessed 26 March 2019).

Koren, A. and E. Einhorn (2010a), *Searching for the Study of Israel: A Report on the Teaching of Israel on U.S. College Campuses 2008–09*, Maurice and Marilyn Cohen Center for Modern Jewish Studies, Brandeis University.

Koren, A. and E. Einhorn (2010b), *Expanding the Study of Israel on Campus: The American–Israeli Cooperative Enterprise*, Maurice and Marilyn Cohen Center for Modern Jewish Studies, Brandeis University.

Koren, A. and S. Fishman (2015), *Israel Studies Report and Directory 2013–14 Report Update*, Maurice and Marilyn Cohen Center for Modern Jewish Studies, Brandeis University.

Lanski, N. and D. Berman (2007), 'Storm in a Neocon Teacup', *Haaretz*, 29 November, https://www.haaretz.com/israel-news/storm-in-a-neaocon-teapot-1.234226 (accessed 3 April 2019).

Laski, H. (1930), 'Foundations, Universities and Research', in *The Dangers of Obedience and Other Essays*, New York and London: Harper & Brothers.

McGoey, L. (2015), *No Such Thing as a Free Gift: The Gates Foundation and the Price of Philanthropy*, London: Verso.

Mearsheimer, J. and S. Walt (2007), *The Israel Lobby and U.S. Foreign Policy*, New York: Farrar, Straus & Giroux.

Miller, D. and C. Harkins (2010), 'Corporate Strategy and Corporate Capture: Food and Alcohol Industry and Lobbying and Public Health', *Critical Social Policy* 30 (4): 564-589.

Miller, D. and T. Mills (2010), 'Counterinsurgency and Terror Expertise: The Integration of Social Scientists into the War Effort', *Cambridge Review of International Affairs* 23 (2): 203-221.

Morin, J. F. (2014), 'Paradigm Shift in the Global IP Regime: The Agency of Academics', *Review of International Political Economy* 21 (2): 275-309.

Nadeau, M. and A. Sears (2010), 'The Palestine Test: Countering the Silencing Campaign', *Studies in Political Economy* 85 (April): 7-33.

Ottolenghi, E. (2005), 'The Isaiah Berlin Public Lectures in Middle East Dialogue: An Introductory Note', *Israel Studies* 10 (2): v-ix.

Pappe, I. (2010), *Out of Frame: The Struggle for Academic Freedom in Israel*, London: Pluto Press.

Pappe, I. (2014), *The Idea of Israel: A History of Power and Knowledge*, London: Verso.

Parmar, I. (2006), 'Conceptualizing the American State–Private Network during the Cold War' in H. Laville and H. Wilford (eds), *The US Government, Citizen Groups and the Cold War: The State–Private Network*, London: Routledge, pp. 13-27.

Parmar, I. (2008), 'Combatting Anti-Americanism: American Foundations and Public Diplomacy during the Cold War and the War on Terror' in R. Higgott and I. Malbašić (eds), *The Political Consequences of Anti-Americanism*, London: Routledge, pp. 29-43.

Parmar, I. (2011), 'American Hegemony, the Rockefeller Foundation, and the Rise of Academic International Relations in the United States' in N. Guilhot (ed.), *The Invention of International Relations Theory: Realism, the Rockefeller Foundation, and the 1954 Conference on Theory*, New York: Columbia University Press, pp. 182-209.

Parmar, I. (2012), *Foundations of the American Century: The Ford, Carnegie, and Rockefeller Foundations and the Rise of American Power*, Chichester: Columbia University Press.

Pennsylvania Gazette (2014), 'Radical Threats, Studied Solutions', *Pennsylvania Gazette*, 26 June, http://thepenngazette.com/radical-threats-studied-solutions (accessed 3 April 2019).

Preston, A. (2015), 'The War against Humanities at Britain's Universities', *The Guardian*, 29 March, https://www.theguardian.com/education/2015/mar/29/war-against-humanities-at-britains-universities (accessed 3 April 2019).

Ram, U. (1999), 'The Colonization Perspective in Israeli Sociology' in I. Pappe (ed.), *The Israel/Palestine Question*, London: Routledge, pp. 55–80.

Reichmann, U. (n.d.), 'President's Welcome', *The Interdisciplinary Center Herzliya*, http://web.archive.org/web/20010417230649/www.idc.ac.il/eng/content/about.asp (accessed 2 April 2019).

Reid, E. O. F. (1997), 'Evolution of a Body of Knowledge: An Analysis of Terrorism Research', *Information Processing and Management* 33 (1): 91–106.

Reut Institute (2010), *Building a Political Firewall against Israel's Delegitimization*, Tel Aviv: Reut Institute.

Rocker, S. (2011), 'Oxford's First Israel Chair', *Jewish Chronicle*, 14 April, https://www.thejc.com/news/the-diary/oxford-s-first-israel-chair-1.22474 (accessed 28 March 2019).

Sadeh, S. (2016), 'Benjamin Netanyahu's Billionaires Club', *Haaretz*, 18 June, https://www.haaretz.com/israel-news/.premium-1.724963 (accessed 28 March 2019).

Shalem Center (n.d.a), *Questions and Answers about Shalem College*, https://web.archive.org/web/20130116031619/http://danielgordis.org/sitefiles/wp-content/uploads/2012/01/Shalem-College-FAQs.pdf (accessed 3 April 2019).

Shalem Center (n.d.b), 'Shalem College Overview', https://web.archive.org/web/20120420010607/http://www.shalem.org.il/Mission-statements/Shalem-College-Overview.html (accessed 3 April 2019).

Shenkar, M. (2010), *The Politics of Normalization: Israel Studies in the Academy*, Unpublished doctoral dissertation, Ohio State University.

Stand With Us (2017), 'Important Announcement: University of Bath Rejects BDS, Distances School from Promoting BDS', Stand With Us, 10 April, http://standwithus.co.uk/2017/04/10/university-bath-rejects-bds (accessed 19 October 2018).

Walby, K. and M. Larsen (2012), 'Access to Information and Freedom of Information Requests: Neglected Means of Data Production in the Social Sciences', *Qualitative Inquiry* 18 (1): 31–42.

White, B. (2012), 'The Case for Israel (Studies): It's Not Hasbara. Honest', *Mondoweiss*, 21 June, https://mondoweiss.net/2012/06/the-case-for-israel-studies-its-not-hasbara-honest (accessed 3 April 2019).

White, B. (2015), 'Israel Lobby's Attack on Academic Freedom', *Al Jazeera*, 22 March, https://www.aljazeera.com/indepth/opinion/2015/03/israel-lobby-attack-academic-freedom-150322061358503.html (accessed 2 April 2019).

Williams, C. (2012), *Researching Power, Elites and Leadership*, London: Sage.

Xu, B. and G. A. Fine (2011), 'Honest Brokers: The Politics of Expertise in the "Who Lost China?" Debate', *Social Problems* 58 (4): 593–614.

TWO | Disciplinarity and the boycott

Nick Riemer

In her history of Boycott, Divestment and Sanctions (BDS) in US universities, Sunaina Maira comments on the importance of inter-disciplinary fields like critical ethnic, race, queer, and indigenous studies in stimulating pro-Palestine activity among academics. Discussing the American Studies Association's support for the boycott, Maira (2018, 57–58) says that it was precisely 'the interdisciplinarity of American studies that allowed for a basis for praxis and activism that is not generally possible in the more conservative disciplinary fields such as English, history or sociology'. Maira's claims throw attention onto the political affordances of the diverse institutional and epistemological structures in contemporary universities. Regardless of the general truth of her analysis – in some cases, the halo of radicalism that surrounds the most intellectually innovative fields risks excusing their members from concrete political activity like support for the boycott – Maira's conclusion about the US invites us to inquire into different disciplines' variable aptitudes as platforms for an emancipatory academic politics. On the positive side of this inquiry, there is much to be learnt, and then harnessed for the purposes of further activism, about exactly what – if anything – it might be in a field's makeup that can foster greater participation by its members in concrete progressive initiatives. In this chapter, by contrast, and taking my cue from Said's (1977, 24) call for research into 'the relationship between administrative ideas and intellectual discipline', I intend to focus on the complementary problem: the question of the ways in which traditional disciplinarity, along with the other intellectual 'enclosures' of contemporary academic life (Riemer, 2016), can block progressive academic politics by contributing to the reactionary administration of pro-Palestine and other emancipatory energies.

As crucial theatres of boycott politics, the humanities disciplines will be my particular focus.[1] I begin by considering a very general feature of the conditions of knowledge production in the humanities, which I label their 'discretionary' character. The relevance of this analysis to questions of silencing of campus Palestine solidarity will not immediately be obvious, but its value to our understanding of the reception of the boycott call in universities will, I hope, become clear. With this analysis established, I go on to explore the consequences of the humanities' discretionary character for how the suppression of academic activity in favour of Palestine is usually conceived, and suggest several ways in which the traditional construal – university administrators attacking Palestine supporters' academic freedom – might usefully be supplemented. I argue that in a university context in which 'academic freedom' is, in fact, a scarce and contested resource over which different institutional actors compete, Zionist attacks on it are likely to be perceived as just one exercise of power among the many to which academics have generally become habituated. The normalization of violations of academic freedom means that the case for Palestine in universities should be made first with reference to the scandal of Israeli apartheid, and only secondly on more 'procedural' academic freedom grounds. Finally, I show how these considerations demonstrate the deep solidarities that exist between progressive academics' Palestine work and wider efforts in support of the democratization and decolonization of higher education in the neoliberal era.

*

As Maira's observation suggests, the public utility of the older humanities disciplines, traditionally distinguished by their proud abstention from worldly affairs, is challenged by the very existence of newer, more overtly politicized fields. In the face of this challenge, traditional disciplines like English or philosophy are likely to fall back on claims of their *intrinsic* 'political' value. Rather than playing a role in solving any current social problems, the traditional humanities' relevance is supposed, in the mythology of liberal higher education, to lie in their particular contribution to universities' general civilizational mission: making the discoveries and disseminating the concepts that lay the groundwork for social progress; augmenting the sphere of expressive and artistic meaning; promoting sensitivity to human difference; and raising the standard of public deliberation by promoting more rigorous norms of debate and critique (see Collini 2017 for discussion and critique of clichés of this kind). That universities can hardly take all the credit for these impressive achievements, even on the occasions they actually eventuate, is typically glossed over, as is the fact that, rather than realizing these ideals, universities often work against them: the highly ambiguous nature of higher education's socio-political effects, including its real responsibility for the reproduction of exploitation and inequality, is conveniently ignored.

Higher education's destructive potential is rarely more obvious than in Israeli universities' facilitation of the ongoing ethnic cleansing of Palestine. Israeli universities, including their humanities departments, provide many of the material and ideological means by which Palestinians' 'academic freedom', like their civil liberties and human rights, are brutally crushed (see Pappe 2001, 2014; Taraki 2015; Riemer 2018). That is one of the many reasons for which Horkheimer's observation about the paradigmatic humanities discipline, philosophy, has lost none of its currency or its relevance to the humanities more widely: the theoretical harmony philosophy aims at, Horkheimer (1992, 182) memorably says, 'is given the lie on every hand by the cries of the miserable and disinherited'. In a world disfigured by protean exploitation and the galloping destruction of the natural and social environment, the claims of humanities disciplines' socially beneficial character seem increasingly bizarre, whether in Gaza, the West Bank, or elsewhere. The 'political relevance' of philosophy to Israelis, one might think, lies more in philosopher Asa Kasher's work on ethics for the Israel Defense Forces (IDF) – widely denounced as licensing multiple abuses (see e.g. Levy 2009; Halper 2010; Eastwood 2016; Lentin this volume) – than it does in any contribution it might make to Israeli public enlightenment. In the West, the humanities' claims of intrinsic social value are undermined by the enthusiastic defence of exploitation, colonialism, racism, and fascism regularly offered by some of its scholars, and bathetically accompany the slow throttling of the humanities' own prospects of ongoing institutional existence.[2] If it is to the humanities that we are supposed to look for social and political redemption, they need to up their game, if only to ensure their own survival of the current decades-long austerity spree which both they and their universities have, so far, done little to retard and much to abet. The humanities' record, in sum, is far from politically progressive – an abundantly obvious point, though one easily ignored by academics themselves.

Regardless of their intellectual content, one of the very obvious ways in which humanities disciplines structurally pose obstacles to progressive institutional politics is through the notion of disciplinarity itself and its role in restricting speech on contentious topics. Palestine- and BDS-supporters on campus are regularly criticized, especially when publishing on those themes, for exceeding the boundaries of their disciplinary competence and improperly using their academic authority in the service of a political agenda (Drummond 2013 contains much useful exemplification and discussion). A recent instance of such criticism was voiced by Jonathan Marks, in the context of the Association for Asian American Studies' pioneering 2013 boycott resolution: 'it is striking enough', Marks (2018) observed, 'that a scholarly association with no claim to expertise on the Middle East should have adopted a boycott resolution aimed at that region of the world'.

This criticism is validated and reinforced by a common interpretation of academic freedom, which understands that notion as strictly limited to the areas of a scholar's disciplinary 'expertise'. The American Association of University Professors' (AAUP) often-invoked 1940 definition of academic freedom, for instance, states that university teachers' classroom freedom is restricted to the discussion *of their subjects*.[3] Even though the AAUP enshrines protections for academics when they engage, as citizens, in speech outside their disciplines, it does so in a heavily qualified way: the AAUP's phrasing unmistakably tars public comment and political position-taking as inherently questionable ventures, and does nothing to prevent readers from reintroducing disciplinary expertise as an implicit precondition of the 'accuracy' in public comment that the text mandates.

Disciplinarity can serve in a straightforward way, then, to police pro-Palestine and other progressive advocacy on campus. But to describe this policing, as we might easily be tempted to do, as a political 'instrumentalization' of disciplinarity for reactionary purposes, inherently alien to the proper intellectual function of disciplinarity itself, would ignore the ways in which the concept does not necessarily serve the ends of knowledge or intellectual progress per se, but of institutional authority and, as a result, exclusion. Reflecting on the connections between disciplinarity and the boycott can, as I hope to show, issue in some useful conclusions about how best to argue for BDS with our humanities colleagues. In order to reach these conclusions, we need first to think about some deep properties of humanities disciplines. As we do this, questions of Palestine, Israel, and BDS will temporarily go into the background. I ask readers for their patience: the discussion will lead us directly to some concrete suggestions about how the case for the boycott should be prosecuted.

*

The ideology of interdisplinarity has made significant inroads in recent decades, but disciplines are still central structuring principles of many academics' working lives.[4] So it is not surprising that their exclusionary potential has been closely analysed in some respects, and in others mostly missed. On the one hand, traditional disciplines' role in perpetuating cultural and racist biases has received close scrutiny, and it is increasingly accepted that students should not, in Achille Mbembe's words, be 'asked to bow in deference before the statues of those who did not consider [them] as human and who deployed every single mean in their power to remind [them] of [their] supposed worthlessness' (Mbembe 2016, 32). Here, however, I would like to stress an obvious but often ignored fact: whatever a discipline's intellectual content, the very idea of disciplinarity plays an exclusionary role by limiting in advance the regions into which scholarly activity can legitimately venture. It is not just boycott opponents like Jonathan Marks admonishing academics to stay in their disciplines; it is many other academics too. Jacques Rancière's (2004, 22) analysis of the ideology of artisanal expertise has a clear equivalent in disciplinary knowledge in academia:

Now we know that a true shoemaker is not someone who
makes good shoes but someone who does not pass himself off
as anything other than a shoemaker. Indeed, ignorance of the
craft may even be better than expertise in it to guarantee the
monotechnics that alone constitutes the virtue of the artisan.
Idleness and incompetence are the disposition best suited to
ensuring what is singularly important, that the artisan does only
one thing, the thing that marks him off and puts him in his place.

Just as the shoemaker must only make shoes, so academics'
competence is called into question if they stray far beyond the
conventional borders of their discipline. We must stay quietly
put: for most disciplinary purposes – submission of articles to
the 'best' journals and publishers, proposals for undergraduate
courses, grant-applications, and so on – thought must be turned
back from regions colonized by others.

Within disciplines, knowledge is inseparable from the structure of institutional power, from students to recognized experts,
that governs it (see Drummond 2013, 258ff for a discussion in the
context of Israel–Palestine). Whether in a traditional disciplinary
area or an emerging one, claims of disciplinary expertise support
a logic of cumulativity that requires new entrants to a subject to
'show their allegiance to previous work', thereby guaranteeing the
ongoing influence of the researchers who initiated it (Lagasnerie
2011, 43). Disciplinary power is transmitted and regulated
through a set of multifaceted institution-bound practices which
go far beyond their strictly intellectual content: a given set of
words qualifies for academic purposes such as a thesis, essay, or
lecture only in the institutional context of a university programme;
express those same words somewhere else, and they lose much of
their disciplinary value. Intellectual content alone, that is, is not
a sufficient condition of disciplinary worth, but must be institutionally ratified to count for fully disciplinary purposes. Yet the

determinants of institutional ratification are far from depending on the work's purely intellectual qualities. As well as being bodies of knowledge, disciplines are instruments of careers, sites of competition between peers, and venues in which more general social antagonisms are played out. They are, therefore, intrinsically political, and politics – institutional, national, racial, sexual, electoral, etc. – is inescapable in the processes of ratification by which intellectual work is accredited for disciplinary purposes. Controversies over the legitimacy of 'Palestinian studies', 'Arab and Muslim Ethnicities and Diasporas', or 'Western Civilization' programmes are just the most obvious examples of a far wider situation: politics enters into the humanities at the most basic level (Brophy 2018; Spero 2019).

This particular receptivity of the humanities to politics is largely a result of their quintessentially discursive nature – the fact that value in them is determined, to a very large extent, in the course of textual interpretation.[5] Interpretative value-judgement is heavily *discretionary*, in that it necessitates the use of inference, contextualization, and other intrinsically hermeneutic operations, in a fundamentally free manner. This characteristic of the humanities is entirely general. With value assessed and students' and scholars' fate weighed in the black box of discretionary academic value-judgement, disciplinary considerations can easily function as the shibboleth or smokescreen through which the pursuit of political (self-)interest can enter and the stakes of social, ideological, and institutional reproduction can be concealed. On this micropolitical level, expressions of scholarly ideas can be understood as bids for disciplinary or other influence, moves in a game whose stakes are professional validation, institutional power, material reward, or, sometimes, public notoriety. Subjectively, this aspect of academic work is highly salient to humanities scholars. Its full

extent is revealed when we consider the bevy of questions likely
to spring to mind at the start of a new research project: *which
disciplinary players will I gratify or alienate by taking this position? What idea gives me the best chance of getting accepted in
such-and-such a journal? What is the most fashionable ('cutting-
edge') topic? Which theoretical framework or methodology will
position me best in the competition for disciplinary resources?*

In this discursive environment, very few checks are available
on the discretionary results of an academic's evaluations of others' work, especially those of an authoritative one, and none
that do not simply involve appeal to an equally discretionary
alternative authority. If, as the marker of undergraduate work,
I declare some essays good, others satisfactory, and others
inadequate, or, as the reviewer of several book proposals, find
some 'interesting' and others not, it is my declaration that performatively makes it so. No matter how fully and transparently
I justify my evaluations, they remain exactly that: the product
of my own private and to a large extent inscrutable reactions,
conditioned by the ensemble of subjective choices, associations, and biases that make up my disciplinary 'expertise'. The
discretionary and sometimes apparently arbitrary quality of
academic assessment is often highly salient to students in the
process of their socialization into disciplinary practices, and
it is experienced at first hand by humanities academics themselves whenever we submit ourselves to the lottery of funding
or job applications, or to peer review.

The very notions of disciplinarity and expertise, then, function
to sacralize individual discretion. The evaluation given to a piece
of work, positive or negative, is presented as a kind of professional
benediction on the part of the academic expert who dispenses it,
the anointing of the work with the balm of expert judgement. This
obscures the evaluation's fully discretionary character and the

status of the expert dispensing it not as an oracle channelling the supra-individual essence of their discipline, but as the very human maker of a subjective interpretation. Given that the evaluations made of academic work are directly correlated to wholly material rewards – the quality of the degree awarded to a student, the prospects of professional advancement for staff – disciplinary expertise in the humanities participates in one of the basic ploys of domination: what Maurice Godelier (2010, 24–25) describes in a different context as the dominant classes' need to present their exercise of power not as simple exploitation, but as a *service* rendered to the dominated. Within the overarching meritocratic ideology of higher education, the student who is rejected for a scholarship on the grounds that their essay is not the best, like the academic whose submission or grant- or tenure-application is refused, is assured that the reports in which these decisions are justified offer precious advice and opportunity for improvement. The fact that this is often true does not invalidate the point that in disciplinary evaluation, discrimination on intellectual grounds is harnessed to the task of the exclusion of the majority of applicants, no matter how worthwhile, from the distribution of material resources (scholarships, fellowships, publishing opportunities, jobs), at the same time as the excluded candidates are supposed to feel grateful for the 'opportunity to improve' that rejection provides – a circumstance that is, of course, far from limited to work in the humanities.

It is almost time to show the relevance of these considerations to the academic boycott. Before doing so, a conclusion: the humanities depend in their very nature on the inflation of personal judgement into disciplinary authority. Readers who feel that further empirical substantiation of this point is needed should refer to Michèle Lamont's (2009) study of the decisions of grant-funding panels, or Aaron Lawson's (2001) study of linguistics textbooks. This personal judgement is, one would like to believe, often exercised with scrupulous integrity and in a spirit of thorough-going 'impartiality'. Conscientious assessors of academic work control for their own most idiosyncratic preferences with the intention of acting merely as representatives of their discipline's broader community of interpretation, channelling biases understood not as personal but as representatives of an entire intellectual community. Clearly, however, an assessor cannot write their own individuality completely out of the picture. Far from it: no matter how dispassionately reached, their decisions remain the result of an exercise of judgement – the exercise, that is, of a private evaluation. A degree of intersubjective agreement is sometimes attainable by different assessors about *particular* positive or negative qualities in a piece of work, but agreement is often much harder to come by when different assessors are required to go beyond point-by-point reactions and synthesize their set of particular judgements into a general appreciation of the work's *overall* merit. Any humanities academic will have stories of the wildly different assessments of the same piece of work that come to light in examiners' meetings or in referee reports, often among assessors who are ready enough to broadly agree in their evaluation of particular details. Yet the holistic assessments of overall academic merit necessary to disciplinary evaluation are largely sheltered from real challenge. In contrast, no doubt, to the objective sciences, disciplinary authority in the humanities rests on the fundamental immunity from revision of these discretionary expert judgements – a circumstance that makes the humanities a particularly easy target of the audit and 'accountability' regimes to which contemporary higher education is subject.[6] The institutional workings of humanities fields would be overturned if the decisions of search committees, peer-reviewers, or grant-funders were systematically open to challenge and revision.

*

Disciplinarity therefore embeds an exclusionary logic at its centre. This intra-disciplinary exclusion has a familiar extra-disciplinary complement, amply on display in questions of the Middle East: one of the persistent themes of Chomsky's political writing has been the unjustified exclusion of the public from matters that would be straightforwardly accessible to them, were they not obfuscated by the mystifications of disciplinary 'expertise' (see e.g. Chomsky 1987). In questions of general importance where understanding of the details of particular political contexts is called for, it is not disciplinary accreditation that guarantees mastery of the necessary knowledge: mastery is, simply, its own criterion. The fact that members of the Association for Asian American Studies have no *disciplinary* expertise on questions relating to Palestine and Israel in no way disqualified them from making decisions about the boycott; what mattered was that they took the trouble to inform themselves of the facts, as anyone else able to take the time to do so could equally do.

The point of this discussion is to suggest that there is something missing in the characteristic description of the suppression of Palestine supporters' academic freedom as the work of 'university administrators who have been cowed by the [Israel] lobby' 'against faculty members and students' (as William I. Robinson and Maryam S. Griffin put it in the introduction to their important 2017 collection of testimonials by victims of campus repression). While entirely accurate and indeed necessary from the point of view of the struggle in universities, this description is incomplete in two ways. For one thing, it obscures the extent to which Zionist pressure can be *welcome* to university administrators, and not therefore constitute pressure in any real sense. This is partly because of the entrenched Zionist sympathies of many university authorities, who are often only too happy to gratify influential 'stakeholders' by disciplining staff who threaten their interests. But it is also a result of the utility of Zionist complaints as a tool of campus-level social control. BDS activism at my own institution, the University of Sydney, is a case in point: when Palestine-supporting colleagues are the objects of Zionist complaints, as we regularly are, the administration is supplied with ammunition against staff members who are typically also committed to a range of other activities which regularly bring them into conflict with university authorities: involvement in the trade union, public criticism of university managers, agitation among colleagues in order to stimulate collective resistance to the logics of the market university. In this context, Zionist complaints can offer university authorities just the pretext they need to make a move. If they do not achieve the outright dismissal of Palestine solidarity activists, then acting on Zionist complaints at least serves an intimidatory function, and sends a warning to any other staff who might be tempted by similar adventurousness. The added value supplied by the implicit or explicit accusation of antisemitism that often accompanies Zionist complaints allows university administrators to appear to be proceeding on principled grounds, and makes them less likely to be criticized within the institution for being motivated merely by the prospect of retaliation against their campus critics.

The second way in which the usual framing of anti-Palestinian repression on campus needs to be supplemented is in its overly dichotomized conception of the forces at work. This conception presents administrators' repression of academic Palestine sympathizers as an attack on the 'academic freedom' of the latter. BDS-supporting academics are understood as exercising a right intrinsic to their profession – the freedom to pursue ideas and their implications wherever they lead. Their being prevented from doing so by university administrators is therefore understood as a scandalous negation of academic freedom and, as such, seen as an existential threat to the norms that support academic work. This construal, on which administrators' repression of Palestine activism is taken to be wholly antithetical to the usual standards of academic professionalism, makes the very regularity of the administrative curtailing of academic freedom, whether on Palestine or on many other matters, deeply mysterious. In light of this, and of our analysis of disciplinary discretion, it needs revision.

As our discussion suggests, the disciplinary arena in which the academic victims of Zionist repression work, and with which the sphere of university 'administration' or 'management' is contrasted, is not one of undiluted 'freedom' – or, rather, it is one in which 'freedom' is constituted by lines of essentially unaccountable, intrinsically political discretion. As we have seen, academic work cannot be separated from the discretionary, micropolitical negotiation of institutional power. This discretionary negotiation is often seen as 'intellectual' or 'disciplinary' in nature, but what this amounts to in humanities disciplines, I have argued, is that it is inherently grounded in unaccountable personal judgement. This is a quality that it shares with administrators' decision to repress Palestine activism: rather than exemplifying wholly antithetical modes – on the one hand, the free exercise of disciplinary judgement and on the other, its repression – the antagonism between Palestine-supporting academics and the campus administrators who block them needs to be seen as playing out on the single continuum of discretionary institutional conduct. Unaccountable judgement is characteristic of this continuum as a whole, differing only in the modes and consequences of its exercise. As a result, the lines between the disciplinary exercise of 'academic freedom' for which Israel critics are repressed by university authorities, and the very discretionary, unaccountable exercise of institutional power by which university managers enact that repression, begin to blur uncomfortably: rather than doing fundamentally different things, the administrators who judge that pro-Palestine activism is to be repressed are in one respect behaving in essentially the same way as the humanities academics whose disciplinary action in favour of Palestine they are blocking: they are exercising unaccountable, discretionary judgement in their professional decisions. The difference, of course, is that Palestine supporters' discretion is being used to support social justice, whereas the administrators' is frustrating it. Recognizing differences between university managers' and Palestine supporters' discretion is easy, given that the two come into regular conflict. Recognizing the similarities between them in the way suggested here, however, is important if we want to develop an accurate account of the politics of BDS in universities.

My intention in making this suggestion is not to indulge in leftist one-upmanship, triumphantly revealing in the workings of traditional disciplinarity *yet another* previously hidden mechanism of domination. This is a familiar enough gambit, but a highly counterproductive one in a campaign which is trying to gain new adherents, and which therefore must not continually lessen the plausibility of victory by relentlessly pushing the conditions of its accomplishment back over an ever-receding horizon. We cannot tell our colleagues that, in order to support the boycott, they must also oppose disciplinarity. Far from any maximalist absurdity, my point is to draw four conclusions. (1) Because of the normalization of the discretionary exercise of power in the academic sphere, Zionist interest emerges as just one of the unaccountable lines of force by which academic space is structured and therefore should not be expected to be widely seen as highly exceptional or illegitimate. (2) Rather than a universal norm of academic work in principle equally possessed by all members of the 'academic community', 'academic freedom' should be understood as both a historically exceptional condition of intellectual activity, and as a scarce and contested resource over which different institutional actors compete, and which can be claimed in the interests of both Zionists and the Palestine solidarity movement. (3) The normalization of intellectually improper and arbitrary violations of academic freedom means that the case for Palestine in universities should be made first on the grounds of substantive considerations of the facts of Israeli anti-Palestinianism, and only secondly on the grounds of academic freedom. (4) The prospects of Palestine activism on campus go hand in hand with those of efforts to democratize all aspects of scholarly and educational activity. We will explore these conclusions in the rest of this chapter.

*

Discrimination is normal in academic work: the prevailing conditions of knowledge creation in the humanities are, we have seen, highly inegalitarian, and the discretion of academic authority is the mechanism through which inequality is enacted. Academics' habituation to the arbitrary and often discriminatory regimes of their profession can, surely, only raise their tolerance for the arbitrary discrimination which Palestinian academics and students suffer, both in the educational domain and outside it. In an institutional fabric woven together from a multiplicity of threads of discretionary interest, Zionism is just one more of the agendas jockeying for influence. And if, as is usually the case, most academics in Western universities are not doing anything against the injustices of their own professions, what motivation could they possibly have to risk exposing themselves in defence of Palestine or Palestine supporters?

There is, then, a sense in which 'academic freedom' is regularly and constitutively violated as part of the standing business of academia in the humanities. The freedom to conduct intellectual inquiry as one sees fit, and to be supported to do so, is not, apparently, highly prized by academics. Historically, indeed, academic freedom is a highly exceptional and recent norm of academic life, usually traced back to the principles of the modern German university as established by Humboldt (see Fuller 2009), and by no means continuously respected since (see, for example, Schrecker 1986). In current disciplinary and institutional conditions, the ability to work freely – the ability to exercise one's own intellectual discretion in the elaboration of ideas, following them where they lead, free of control by, but open to input from, the discretionary judgements of others – is often illegitimately limited by disciplinary and other norms. Since disciplines are constituted by competition for the scarce and contested resource of (actual) academic freedom, one scholar's enjoyment of academic freedom in the form of a grant or the offer of publication often means another's exclusion from it. Rather than a universal baseline of academic work equally possessed by all members of the 'academic community', complete 'academic freedom' is, in fact, currently reserved for a tiny clique of elite disciplinary players – those researchers whose 'star' status is sufficient to allow them to publish what they want, when they want, and for whom the usual processes of academic oversight like peer review are always constructive, never coercive or silencing. At the other extreme, the vast army of casual academics work in conditions of precarious employment that deprive them of the basic material security necessary for the 'free' pursuit of ideas.

This is not to say that 'academic freedom' isn't a value that should be defended. On the contrary, it is essential to assert the claim of 'negative' academic freedom – universities' and academics' right to be free from coercion by outside interests, whether the state, business lobbies, or Zionists. Nowhere is this more crucial than for Palestinians themselves, for whom academic freedom is threatened at the point of an IDF machine gun when it is not wholly obliterated by tanks, armoured bulldozers, or laser-guided bombs. But given Western academics' stunning acquiescence to the general lack of *positive* academic freedom in their workplaces – their lack of interest in doing anything to secure an egalitarian distribution of the resources that support academic work – it may be optimistic to believe that appeals to academic freedom pack the punch we would like. As incentives either to engage in the academic boycott – often presented as a way of promoting Palestinians' (positive) academic freedom – or to defend BDS proponents when they are under attack, academic freedom is not the most persuasive value to invoke. As other contributors to this volume also conclude, the case for Palestine in the academy should principally be made on the grounds of the facts of apartheid in Israel, rather than procedurally, out of respect for an overarching and abstract academic freedom. Academics should not just boycott, or defend boycotters, because doing so constitutes a defence of academic freedom, even though it certainly does that. The most powerful reason to boycott and to defend boycotters is to *end apartheid against Palestinians*, a particularly elementary and serious injustice, the resolution of which could significantly reset the bar in global rights activism. The possibility for Zionists to couch their hostility to BDS as itself motivated by respect for academic freedom, as of course they have continually done, and to claim the very assertion of Israeli crimes as a threat to their security on campus and hence to their own academic freedom, is another reason that that notion does not offer the political clarity needed to show what is actually at stake in the difference between boycott supporters and opponents.

Still, sceptics might reply, how likely are most Western academics to care about the freedom, academic or otherwise, of distant Palestinians? They have a point: despite the visibility of academic boycott efforts and the high price paid by some academics for their support for Palestinian rights, we should not expect that the academic profession will collectively be in the vanguard of the Palestine solidarity movement, for the same reasons that it is not in the vanguard of any other.[7] Nevertheless, many academics not currently participating in the boycott are, of course, sensitive to the political responsibilities that their profession should entail, and far from deaf to appeals to justice. As I have illustrated elsewhere (Riemer 2017), even political boycotts are not, as a simple matter of fact, as exceptional in academia as the Zionist opponents of BDS would like us to believe; there is, as a result, every reason to think that the momentum for the rights-based academic boycott of Israel will increase. The speed with which it does, however, is in part a function of the extent to which expectations of equality are normalized in the academy. As I have shown, they are currently anything but normal, at least as far as concerns the conditions under which intellectual work is done. This suggests that the more democratic the overall temper of the university, the less exceptional and arbitrary the call for action in favour of Palestinian freedoms will seem.

As people concerned with knowledge, academics have an obligation to democratize it. More knowers means more knowledge: the surest guarantee of increasing the overall 'stock' of knowledge, as it were, is to foster the intellectual growth, and hence the knowledge-generating capacities, of as many people as possible. A disciplinary culture in which this principle was better understood and more often applied would be substantially more conducive to Palestine solidarity activity. As a matter of fact, those in universities calling for Palestine solidarity are not infrequently also those calling most loudly for the democratization of higher education, including through its release from the managerial stranglehold around it. The considerations I have been exploring here suggest that this is not a strategic coincidence. There is a very concrete advantage if the struggle for Palestine goes hand in hand with the struggle for greater campus democracy: in democratizing academic workspaces and minimizing as much as possible the exclusionary operations of discretionary authority, we slowly undermine the dispositions that contribute to normalizing general, arbitrary inequality, and render Palestinians' oppression, the silencing of their supporters, and Palestinians' de facto exemption from the universality of human rights, increasingly anomalous.

Discretion is intrinsic to the knowledge generated by the humanities, disciplines in which creativity and individual sensibility necessarily play a large part. It would therefore be neither possible nor desirable to eliminate it entirely: in even the most egalitarian academic culture, individual discretion will need to be applied to create and evaluate intellectual work, and the originality of individual scholars will continue to be prized – appropriately so – as a virtue. Rather than abolishing discretion, then, the goal of a progressive academic politics should be to minimize its inegalitarian uses and to socialize access to its exercise. The opportunities to exercise discretion – the opportunities to think rigorously *as oneself* and to be respected in doing so – should not be confined to a small clique of powerful disciplinary and institutional players. There are any number of fronts on which efforts can be made to distribute the opportunities for discretion more equally: most fundamentally, by arguing that education – all education – is a right which students should not have to pay to enjoy, and which should be equally available to everyone, whether they are in Palestine, Australia, or the UK.

Within universities, priorities might include issues like ending the power of unaccountable managers and granting a real role to students in decisions about how the university should be run; stopping the serious exploitation constituted by structural reliance on precarious and casualized labour; and democratizing the financial and other resources needed to do advanced work. Within individual disciplines, the effort to restrain exclusionary and generalize the right to non-exclusionary discretion might take the form of the wholesale rethinking of peer review and other assessment processes, greater transparency about the considerations behind disciplinarily significant decisions, promotion of universal access to disciplinary fora through open access publishing and an end to exorbitant conference registration fees, and more affirmative action in favour of minority and disadvantaged scholars and those in the global South, including Palestinians. These reforms and many others, all desirable in themselves, would slowly foster an environment in which an expectation of justice was the norm, not the exception, and where expressions of solidarity with Palestinians or with other victims of settler-colonialism like indigenous Australians or Americans, would seem far less unnatural.

None of these reforms can happen overnight, obviously. But the very act of urging them in the same breath as urging justice for Palestinians would be a fruitful recontextualization of the latter demand, which would be less likely to come across as utopian, sectarian, mischievous, or a simple display of leftist exhibitionism, and more likely to be seen as naturally bound up with a politics of exception-less social justice that actually has consequences. We will most effectively campaign against Israel's violent, militarized attack on Palestinians' academic freedom if we do not consent so easily to the normalized violations of our own. If Maira is right and the newer interdisciplinary areas *are*, as a general rule, more inclined to activism, it may be because the disciplinary structures that entrench exclusionary discretion have not yet solidified, and the democratic values which the academic boycott aspires to support are consequently less unreal. In that case, as well as decolonizing the humanities, *de-disciplinizing* them – transforming the exclusionary discretion of hierarchical 'disciplines' into the more egalitarian discretion of flatter, more open 'fields' – might be one logical step we could take to create a more favourable environment in which claims for justice for Palestinians can be pressed.

Notes

1 It is entirely possible that some of the features attributed to the humanities in this chapter characterize other academic fields as well. The discussion here is limited to the humanities in order to avoid committing me to claims which I do not have enough experience to substantiate. For some interesting discussion of BDS' lack of traction among scientists, see Michael Harris, 'Scientists and BDS, in France and in the US', http://www.aurdip.org/scientists-and-bds-in-france-and.html.

2 See for instance Bruce Gilley's and Nigel Biggar's notorious recent rehabilitations of colonialism (Gilley 2018; Biggar 2017). Aspects of the long history of academic flirtations with fascism are charted by Wolin (2004) and Sternhell (2012).

3 See https://www.aaup.org/report/1940-statement-principles-academic-freedom-and-tenure.

4 For a useful account of the sociology of disciplines, see Chapter 4 of Martin (1998).

5 The most useful account of this is still, in my opinion, the one offered by Gadamer (2004).

6 Thanks to David Landy for suggesting this point to me.

7 We should not be misled here by the centrality of university campuses as sites of BDS activity: numerically, and quite possibly also in terms of their impact in the public sphere. It is *students' non-academic* activities such as Israeli Apartheid Week actions, divestment motions in unions, and disruption of Israeli officials' campus visits that have been the dominant form in which BDS activity on campus has been manifested.

References

Biggar, N. (2017), 'Don't Feel Guilty about Our Colonial History: Apologising for Empire Is Now Compulsory but Shame Can Stop Us Tackling the World's Problems', *The Times*, 30 November, https://www.thetimes.co.uk/article/don-t-feel-guilty-about-our-colonial-history-ghvstdhmj (accessed 3 October 2019)

Brophy, D. (2018), 'Australians Must Reject a Nationalist Push into Our Universities', *New York Times*, 29 October, https://www.nytimes.

com/2018/10/29/opinion/australians-must-reject-a-nationalist-push-into-our-universities.html (accessed 5 April 2019).

Chomsky, N. (1987 [1969]), 'Objectivity and Liberal Scholarship' in J. Peck (ed.), *The Chomsky Reader*, New York: Random House, pp. 83–120.

Collini, Stefan (2017), *Speaking of Universities*, London: Verso.

Drummond, S. (2013), *Unthinkable Thoughts: Academic Freedom and the One-State Model for Israel and Palestine*, Toronto: UBC Press.

Eastwood, J. (2016), '"Meaningful Service": Pedagogy at Israeli Pre-military Academies and the Ethics of Militarism', *European Journal of International Relations* 22 (3): 671–695.

Fuller, S. (2009), 'The Genealogy of Judgement: Towards a Deep History of Academic Freedom', *British Journal of Educational Studies* 57 (2): 164–177.

Gadamer, H.-G. (2004 [1960]), *Truth and Method* (2nd ed.) (J. Weinsheimer and D. G. Marshall, trans), London: Continuum.

Gilley, B. (2018), 'The Case for Colonialism', *Academic Questions* 31 (2): 167–185.

Godelier, M. (2010), *L'idéel et le matériel. Pensée, économies, sociétés*, Paris: Flammarion.

Halper, J. (2010), 'The Second Battle of Gaza: Israel's Undermining of International Law', *MR Online*, 26 February, https://mronline. org/2010/02/26/the-second-battle-of-gaza-israels-undermining-of-international-law/ (accessed 5 April 2019).

Horkheimer, M. (1992), *Eclipse of Reason*, New York: Continuum.

Lagasnerie, G. de (2011), *Logique de la création: sur l'université, la vie intellectuelle et les conditions de l'innovation*, Paris: Fayard.

Lamont, M. (2009), *How Professors Think: Inside the Curious World of Academic Judgement*, Cambridge, MA: Harvard University Press.

Lawson, A. (2001), 'Ideology and Indoctrination: The Framing of Language in Twentieth-Century Introductions to Linguistics', *Language Sciences* 23 (1): 1–14.

Levy, G. (2009), 'It's All Kosher for Kasher', *Haaretz*, 4 October, https://www.haaretz.com/1.5395171 (accessed 5 April 2019).

Maira, S. (2018), *Boycott! The Academy and Justice for Palestine*, Oakland, CA: University of California Press.

Marks, J. (2018), 'How BDS Is Undermining Academic Freedom', *Mosaic*, 18 April, https://mosaicmagazine.com/observation/2018/04/how-bds-is-undermining-academic-freedom/ (accessed 21 February 2019).

Martin, B. (1998), *Tied Knowledge in Higher Education*, https://www.bmartin.cc/pubs/98tk/tk04.html (accessed 21 February 2019).

Mbembe, A. (2016), 'Decolonizing the University: New Directions', *Arts and Humanities in Higher Education* 15 (1): 29–45.

Pappe, I. (2001), 'The Tantura Case in Israel: The Katz Research and Trial', *Journal of Palestine Studies* 30 (3): 19–39.

Pappe, I. (2014), *The Idea of Israel*, London: Verso.

Rancière, J. (2004), *The Philosopher and His Poor* (J. Drury, C. Auster and A. Parker, trans), Durham, NC: Duke University Press.

Riemer, N. (2016), 'Academics, the Humanities and the Enclosure of Knowledge: The Worm in the Fruit', *Australian Universities' Review* 58 (2): 33–41, https://issuu.com/nteu/docs/aur_58-02/35 (accessed 21 February 2019).

Riemer, N. (2017), 'A Question of Academic Freedom', *Jacobin*, 31 July, https://www.jacobinmag.com/2017/07/bds-boycott-divest-sanctions-palestine-israel-academic-universities (accessed 21 February 2019).

Riemer, N. (2018), 'The Attack on Palestinian Universities', *Jacobin*, 30 December, https://www.jacobinmag.com/2018/12/palestinian-univer sities-higher-eduction-israeli-violence (accessed 5 April 2019).

Robinson W. I. and M. S. Griffin (eds) (2017), *We Will Not Be Silenced: The Academic Repression of Israel's Critics*, Chico, CA: AK Press.

Said, E. (1977), *Orientalism*, Harmondsworth: Penguin.

Schrecker, E. (1986), *No Ivory Tower: McCarthyism and the Universities*, New York: Oxford University Press.

Spero, D. (2019), 'Palestinian Professor Sues SF State for Breach of Contract, Discrimination', *Mondoweiss*, 21 January, https://mondoweiss.net/2019/01/palestinian-professor-discrimination/ (accessed 5 April 2019).

Sternhell, Z. (2012), *Ni droite ni gauche: l'idéologie fasciste en France* (4th ed.), Paris: Gallimard.

Taraki, L. (2015), 'The Complicity of the Israeli Academy in the Structures of Domination and State Violence' in A. Dawson and B. Mullen (eds), *Against Apartheid: The Case for Boycotting Israeli Universities*, Chicago, IL: Haymarket, pp. 21–30.

Wolin, R. (2004), *The Seduction of Unreason: The Intellectual Romance with Fascism from Nietzsche to Postmodernism*, Princeton, NJ: Princeton University Press.

THREE | The academic field must be defended: excluding criticism of Israel from campuses

David Landy

> This conference is an outright attack on everything academic
> work is about. Many are already protesting in the hope that
> UCC [University College Cork] can be persuaded to recognize
> the threat to scholarship that such a conference poses for
> academic teachers and researchers everywhere. (MacEoin 2017)
> University College Cork in support and in the spirit of
> academic freedom is facilitating this event on its campus but is
> neither a sponsor nor promoter. ('International Law and the
> State of Israel' Conference Programme 2017)

This chapter tries to solve an important conundrum: how do people deny the academic freedom of others when they passionately demand academic freedom as a fundamental right? Understanding this conundrum is, I argue, crucial for those seeking either to speak critically of Israel within universities or to defend the rights of academics to criticize Israel.

Most supporters of Israel cast themselves as defenders of academic freedom due to their campaign work against the academic boycott of Israel: a main tenet of this campaign is that the boycott attacks academic free speech (e.g. Nussbaum 2007; Nelson and Brahm 2015). Leaving aside the truth of this argument, it means that those who attack the boycott identify as free speech defenders. This should not be dismissed as a cynical debating tool for opponents of the academic boycott, a means of framing the situation while at the same time not really believing in the value of free speech. In contentious politics, participants are inhabited by the discourses they wield – the identity of being a defender of free speech is sincerely felt, especially because one portrays one's opponents as being enemies of such freedoms (Steinberg 1999). This identity is buttressed by the prevalent discourse on the right, with which Zionists increasingly identify, of supporting free speech against 'the intolerant left' (Nagle 2017). Thus I would argue that Zionist self-identity as free-speech warriors isn't a false one and also isn't inconsequential.

And yet supporters of Israel consistently try to deny academics the right to discuss Israel critically, by attacking these critics directly, by seeking to curtail their right to speech and employment as academics, and most dramatically by trying to shut down conferences where it is feared Israel will be criticized. Before examining the subject of the chapter – the discursive strategies of those seeking to shut down academic conferences – I should explain why this is important.

It could be argued that the rhetoric of those seeking to exclude criticism of Israel from college campuses is of little interest, and that examining this is missing the main point. That point would be that what matters is not what they say but what they do: how they deploy an arsenal of personal 'price tag' attacks, donor pressure, and threats of disruption to make it unattractive for universities or academics to consider investigating Israel critically. Yet power needs consent as well as coercion. If opponents of Israel-critical thought did nothing but engage in bullying, university administrators would tend to stand up to them. Their arguments matter and it is precisely by examining the discursive strategies of 'defenders-of-free-speech-arguing-against-free-speech' that we can explain why such arguments have been so successful in swaying college administrators.

This chapter takes as a case study the campaign against the 'International Law and the State of Israel: Legitimacy,

Responsibility and Exceptionalism' conference, originally scheduled for Southampton University in 2015 and again in 2016, and
finally held in University College Cork in 2017. It investigates the
paradox of how those who sincerely believed they were defending
freedom of speech managed to attack it. It is based on official conference material, media articles, and consultations with organizers
and participants. The chapter argues that Zionists productively
overcome this paradox by discursively placing criticism of Israel
outside the academic field. This enables them to present their
attempted censorship as a defence of the integrity of the academic
field and thus a defence of academic freedom. This rhetoric also
gives them multiple points of attack on critics of Israel and helps
them label criticism of Israel as not worthy of discussion due to
the fact that it is insufficiently 'academic'. Finally, this line of
attack also helps explain why university administrators so often
cave in to these attacks. It is because they are successful, to a certain extent, in terming criticism of Israel as non-academic, a form
of thought which by right ought to be excluded from academia.

Academic field

Before turning to the case study, it is firstly useful to examine the
concept of academic field. Pierre Bourdieu argued that social life
is structured in a series of semi-autonomous fields of practice – for
instance, the fields of art, of education, and of politics. Each field
has its own rules, practices, and forms of field capital, and we can
view social life in terms of struggle over relatively autonomous field-
dependent capital between the various agents that make up a field.
The positions that people within a field of practice take depends on
where they stand and the power relations within these hierarchically
structured fields (Bourdieu and Wacquant 1992, 99). Universities
can be seen as structured by the power relations between two forms

of capital – academic capital, deriving from the bureaucratic hierarchies of the university, and scholastic or intellectual capital, which relates to recognition by peers of scholarly activity.

It seems obvious to say, but the importance of the struggle over field-specific capital indicates that underlying the struggle between agents in the field is a fundamental agreement regarding the value of this capital. This agreement indicates that all actors are interested in maintaining the autonomy of their field of practice. We can understand academic autonomy as the idea that universities should be governed by their own 'rules of the game', the specific demands of academia, understood as a pursuit of the truth, detached from outside interests. In reality, the academic field is far from autonomous. It is a heteronomous field permeated by rules set by outside forces. Thus it does not only answer to an internal logic of academic rigour, but also to the demands made by external actors and their fields – bureaucratic, political, and economic. The degree to which academic autonomy ever existed can be questioned – indeed it is argued that the concept was first advanced to legitimize the nationalist political projects of universities in the nineteenth century (Baier and Gengnagel 2018). However, what is certain is that the academic field has grown less autonomous over the past few decades and is increasingly oriented towards the concerns of the economic field and structured by the logic of bureaucracy (Bourdieu 1993; Maton 2005).

This heteronomy has not diminished the usefulness of the claim of academic autonomy for actors within the field. If anything, the reverse is true and the cultivation of academic autonomy is still held to be a crucial task, one which validates the academic credentials of the individual academic (Nash 2019). The claim to academic autonomy can then be seen as a form of position-taking within the field, allowing self-legitimization and enabling successful claimants to 'impose their interests on the field' (Baier and

Gengnagel 2018, 68). By the same token, signalling that opposing agents are in fact not autonomous academics, but rather are bringing outside discourses into the field serves to delegitimize and discredit them. This is a game – labelling other academics as too responsive to bureaucratic concerns, too enmeshed in politics and so on – with which academics are all too familiar.

A final point: while I refer to strategies, agents do not exist outside these strategies. Again following Bourdieu, these strategies should be understood as existing on a dispositional level, with actors deeply invested in the idea of academic autonomy. When I speak of people wielding concepts such as protecting academic integrity, they do not do so cynically. If they did, they would not be able to wield these concepts so well.

The conference

So how was the discourse of protecting academic integrity deployed by those attacking the 'International Law and the State of Israel' conference (henceforth 'International Law' conference)? Firstly, we have to ask why the conference was attacked. There is, as Mazen Masri said, something about conferences that makes them flashpoints for controversy:

> When focused on a specific question or topic, conferences
> indicate that this question or topic is an important one in which
> many people take interest. Because of the discourse-creating/
> reinforcing potential, conferences could be seen as a more
> serious challenge to widely held beliefs and therefore can be
> expected to face more resistance. (Masri 2011, 4)

In other words, it is conferences' power to challenge previously dominant forms of knowledge, to upset the pre-existing balance of discourse which makes them such a target for those wishing to defend the status quo.

While most conferences last several days, the 'International Law' conference could be thought of as an event that lasted three years. Originally scheduled for Southampton in April 2015, it was postponed till 2016 and then cancelled at short notice by university administrators. Both times the administrators referred to security concerns due to possible protests. In 2016, the conference wasn't formally cancelled but rather, organizers were told they had to pay over £24,000 in security costs for it to go ahead (Winstanley 2016). Nevertheless, as discussed later, there is good reason to believe that these concerns were spurious, and only used to give the university an excuse to cancel. The conference was certainly controversial – there was an online petition signed by several thousand people against it and it was condemned by right-wing and Jewish newspapers as well as by prominent Conservative Party politicians. In addition, Jewish communal organizations and the Israeli government lobbied the university to cancel it (Abunimah 2015).

In response to this decision by the University of Southampton, the organizers relocated the conference to University College Cork (UCC), booking rooms for the conference in late 2016 and scheduling it for 31 March – 2 April 2017. There the same groups (Zionist Federation, Board of Deputies of British Jews) that caused it to be cancelled in Southampton started putting pressure on UCC to do the same (Harpin 2017a). The reaction of the UCC administration was similar to that of Southampton – claiming security concerns, disruption to students, and failure of the conference organizers to notify administration of the conference, it tried to prevent the conference from going ahead, demanding that the conference organizers postpone the conference and pay extra security costs (McCahill 2017).

However, following a backlash against the university administration over these demands, a compromise was reached. The extra security costs which organizers estimated to be nearly €15,000, were paid (personal communication). By jointly hosting the conference between UCC and Cork City Hall, the conference organizers ensured that the conference took place. The university authorities were still keen to disclaim the conference. They issued a statement that although it was happening in UCC and organized by UCC professors, 'it is not a university-sponsored or promoted event', a disclaimer that, remarkably, college administrators forced the conference organizers to put on their literature and website (UCC 2017; personal communication).

The conference, it should be noted, also garnered supporters, with prominent figures, professional associations, and internationally recognized academics voicing their support ('International Law' conference 2017). Normally, a university would be delighted to host a conference endorsed by luminaries such as Judith Butler, Noam Chomsky, and Archbishop Desmond Tutu, so one must ask why the conference was so dangerous for UCC to associate with. Or more correctly, why did supporters of Israel seek to make it dangerous for the university to associate with this conference? The answer lies partly in the topic, partly in the roster of speakers. As the Organizers' Statement described the conference:

> It aims to generate a debate on legitimacy, exceptionalism and responsibility under international law as provoked by the nature of the Israeli state. It will also examine how international law could be deployed, expanded, and even re-imagined, in order to achieve peace and reconciliation based on justice ('International Law' conference 2016).

In other words, the aim was to examine the nature of the Israeli state under an activist conception of international law, or as supporters of Israel understood this, to debate the legal legitimacy of the State of Israel and to attack 'Israel's right to exist' (Harpin

2017a). Their dislike for the conference was compounded by the list of speakers – many of the most prominent Israel-critical academics were speaking at the conference. Speakers like Ilan Pappe, Ghada Karmi, Joel Kovel, Virginia Tilley, Yakov Rabkin, Haim Bresheeth, and Richard Falk serve as Zionist hate figures due both to their political positions and to their academic work. It would be fair to say that any conference they attended – irrespective of content – would be subject to protests.

Regarding how these events are protested, one can speak of Zionist intervention methods which have solidified over the past decade.[1] Zionists will demand the event be cancelled or failing that, dis-embedded from its academic environment, and they will try to ensure that the conference and individual organizers pay a 'price tag' in the form of extra costs, personal harassment, and reputational damage. The term, 'price tag attacks' was originally used for Israeli settlers taking revenge – exacting a 'price' – on Palestinians in response to state attempts to discipline settlement expansion. Such actions also serve to intimidate Palestinians in the occupied Palestinian territory. In what can be seen as an extension of practices of colonial control, the influential Israeli think tank, the Reut Institute, called for price tag attacks on critics of Israel – meaning that these critics should be forced to suffer for any criticism of Israel they make (Reut Institute 2010). This can be seen as part of a more general Israeli campaign to 'delegitimize the delegitimizers', which is sanctioned by the Israeli government (Peled 2013). In relation to academic conferences, these price tag attacks are conducted through four means: legal actions/lawfare, private lobbying, journalistic attacks, and social media mobbing which, to a certain extent, will continue beyond the conference. This means that Zionist tactics as experienced by critics of Israel consist of various forms of bullying. While it is understandable and important to highlight this bullying, it is also important not to discount the arguments deployed by those seeking to shut down academic conferences.

Defending free speech and defending balance

The main lines of attack on the 'International Law' conference are summarized in the following extract from David Collier, a blogger who wrote obsessively about the conference and its participants over the course of three years, and who attended and videoed the conference in Cork. He wrote of the conference speakers:

> They have the right to be activists, they have the right to be wrong, they have the right to gather together many hate-minded, vicious and sinister people to create fiction, spread lies, distort history and attempt to pass on whatever nasty disease they have all caught. They just should not be permitted to do this as if it were a legitimate academic exercise. (Collier 2017)

There are several aspects to this quotation. First, there is the claim that there is no attempt to prevent free speech, 'just' that it should not happen in universities. In Collier's previous open letter to the University of Southampton this point is emphasized where he declares that 'my opposition to this conference is neither political nor one on a principle of silencing opinion, rather it is one of academic quality and misrepresentation' (Collier 2015). Second, there is the characterization of those involved as activists, not really academics. Third, there is the attack on their moral character – those who attend the conference are 'hate-minded, vicious and sinister people'. This extreme language is important, as it enmeshes those spoken of within a rhetoric of political invective. Finally, the quotation as a whole is a performative utterance, a piece of rhetoric that is also an action, one that places academics under scrutiny. It declares this to the world at large as well as to the academics themselves.

This line – that one is not attacking free speech but rather defending academic speech – was reiterated time and again by those attacking the conference. As stated in the press release of the Board of Deputies of British Jews, celebrating Southampton's cancellation of the conference:

> This conference was never about academic freedom. It represented the opposite of free speech. It was to be an international gathering of anti-Zionists who were using the cover of a distinguished university to promote their view that there should never have been a Jewish state ... Such events have no place at a reputable British university. (Board of Deputies, quoted in Firsht 2015b)

This is but one of the multiple times that those seeking to ban the conference spoke up for academic freedom. No doubt some of these declarations were disingenuous – routine phrases needed to legitimize attacks on free speech. However, it is not pure hypocrisy. Behind it is an understanding of academic discourse as being above partisan position-taking and moreover that such position-taking represents the antithesis of academic speech. This understanding requires the speakers to sincerely believe that their own political opinions are not really politics as such but more the stuff of common sense, whereas the opinions of their opponents not only represent partisan politics but an unacceptable version of them. While this is a common practice in colonial situations, where misrecognition is a key element of control practices, an understanding of academic discourse as non-partisan goes beyond colonial contexts. Those seeking to protect the university from Israel-critical thought and other critiques can draw on a perhaps nostalgic but – in academic circles – very powerful belief in academic research as the dispassionate search for scientific and universal truths, uninfluenced by politics or economics. In a situation of declining academic autonomy, such a claim appears increasingly ungrounded. However, it is precisely the growing heteronomy of the academic field which makes the idea of field autonomy – the campus as a space free from the problems of the world – so attractive to many within the field and so difficult to argue against.

This can be connected with the idea, popular in conservative circles, of the university as a pillar of society, rather than a site for disruptive ideas. It was revealing that one of the main things the opponents of the conference in Cork did was to try to move the conference off-campus. Again, this was not an isolated experience; in Southampton, in Dublin, and previously in the 'Mapping Models' conference in Toronto the exact same tactic was tried. While this can be seen as a price tag attack, it was also an expression of the belief that Israel-critical ideas should not have – in the most literal terms possible – any place on college campuses. This aim to keep campuses free from being polluted by such thinking can be connected with wider conservative attempts to proscribe gender or critical race studies departments and other manifestations of modern thought (e.g. MacDonald 2018).

The reason given for the conference being un-academic was primarily that it was unbalanced. Worries about lack of balance permeated across the Zionist spectrum, from the most vitriolic letter writer and blogger to the Israeli embassy in Ireland expressing concerns that organizers were promoting an 'unbalanced agenda within academic institutions, that seeks to demonize and delegitimize Israel' (Khan 2017). There are two parts to the claim regarding lack of balance – both allowing for points of entry to attack the academic credentials of the events. The first part is that those who are taking part are not 'balanced academics' in any sense of the word – that they are mentally unbalanced and even evil, and that their work is not the balanced work that academics should carry out. They are characterized as activists who, by seeking legitimation from the academy, are polluting it with their political views. There was a constant attack on the academic credentials of participants, with pro-Israel commentators describing them as 'low-grade academics and self-described activists' (Murray 2015).[2] The aim is to try to place participants outside the academic field both rhetorically and performatively. This purpose is to be achieved rhetorically by questioning the validity of their academic credentials, and performatively by indicating that they are under observation by non-academics and thus caught up in their discursive field. Needless to say, every single academic involved in such conferences cannot be called a non-academic or an antisemite – so certain participants are singled out for vilification, the vehemence of these attacks also serving to remove the conference from the academic field and turn it into a circus. In the case of this conference it was primarily Richard Falk, professor emeritus of international law at Princeton University and former UN Special Rapporteur on Palestinian human rights, who was accused time and again of antisemitism, and whose presence at the conference was held as good reason for decent people not to participate (Harpin 2017b).

The claim that certain academics are at best, not academics, and at worst, evil racists is supplemented by the second part of the accusation of lack of balance – that the group of speakers is unbalanced. By this it is meant that there are not sufficient numbers of pro-Israel speakers to balance the anti-Israel ones. This allows supporters of Israel to set an unusual and reductive criterion of academic goodness – linking it to the degree of support for Israel. This was done most specifically by David Collier who offered three criteria for academic goodness – have the academics ever used the word 'apartheid' when discussing Israel, have they ever used the word 'genocide' when discussing Israel, have they ever stated their support for BDS (Collier 2017)? This rhetorical strategy does more than simply 'prove' that the collectivity of academics is unbalanced or the event is unbalanced. It claims the normativity of 'balance' on Israel/Palestine as a standard for judging academic production. Balance in this case is the demand to treat Israel as if it were a democratic Western nation, not engaged in colonizing Palestine. Failure to do so is taken as proof that the academic discourse is not only unbalanced and unfair but by being so, is un-academic.

The problematic nature of the demand for balance can be seen more clearly when examining the 2009 'Mapping Models' conference in York University, Toronto. The conference proposed discussing the one-state and two-state models for Israel/Palestine and as a result was placed under severe bureaucratic restrictions and surveillance by the university administration (Drummond 2013; Masri 2011). The organizers were forced to fend off demands for personnel balance made for explicitly public relations reasons by the university administration. These included requests to dismiss the only Palestinian member of the organizing committee, to appoint an explicit Zionist member, to have a pro-Israel politician as a keynote speaker, and to invite supporters of the two-state model to address the conference (Drummond 2013). University administration made these egregious demands, which ironically would have undermined the conference as an autonomous academic event, because they accepted the claim made by Canadian Zionist organizations that the conference was unbalanced between supporters of one-state and two-state models. Specifically, it was unbalanced against the then dominant two-state model – Mazen Masri, whose Palestinianness was held to unbalance the conference, was correct in remarking that had the conference been unbalanced in favour of the two-state solution, there would have been no controversy (Masri 2011, 18–19).[3] Seen from the vantage point of the present, where the two-state model is increasingly seen as impractical and there is growing discussion of alternatives, this refers back to the idea that conferences sometimes seek to unbalance previously dominant knowledges. They are sometimes necessarily unbalanced.

One can speak of the discourse of balance – correctly understood as not being unbalanced against dominant forms of power/knowledge – as the introduction of non-academic standards to judge academic work. However, the matter is more complicated; there is an internal conflict between possessors of academic capital who tend to be concerned about balance and the public perception of academic professionalism, and those who possess scholastic capital and seek to further their own lines of enquiry, irrespective of 'balance'. Because of this, balance can be and often has been portrayed as an academic virtue which needs to be protected. In this regard, 'balance' serves the same function as 'civility' in US universities, which administrators increasingly demand from both academics and students (see Shahvisi, this volume). While the demand is framed in terms of civility being a precondition for academic discussion, in reality the demand is used to supress contentious speech and silence dissent, thereby creating a corporate university that will not offend donors (Moshman and Edler 2015). Thus it is an internal demand, although one that can be exploited by those outside the field to impose their logics on academia.

Surveillance and invective

'If you're racist, the world should know', so goes the tagline for Canary Mission, an anonymous website that smears Palestine solidarity activists as racists, concentrating on academics and students. The aim is to create a blacklist and frighten pro-Palestinian speakers into silence. However, the tactic of surveillance goes beyond this one website. It is a constant element of Zionist attempts to counter criticism of Israel, one which can be linked to the intense regime of surveillance within Israel/Palestine. Surveillance, as Zureik (2016) notes, is a necessary tool of colonial control, one that creates fear, imposes classificatory systems, and represses the hopes and aspirations of the surveilled, as well as being used for the more mundane task of identifying targets for the colonial state to attack. It is also a tactic increasingly used in universities to repress dissident speech and thought, especially in the UK where the anti-terrorism Prevent programme has created a culture and architecture of surveillance on campuses (Allen 2019).

The use of surveillance was common among critics of the 'International Law' conference, and indeed critics of all such conferences. In this case, lists of conference speakers with their out-of-context views were created by the indefatigable David Collier and distributed around the internet. Such lists were not only created to attack the participants, but also to silence and scare off other academics. One can talk of such lists working as a virtual panopticon, to put all academics on notice that they will be observed and attacked should they criticize Israel. At times in conferences, the surveillance is also carried out by the academic bureaucracy. In the case of the 'Mapping Models' conference, as the organizers did not accede to the administration's demands for balance, they were made subject to further sanction in the form of an investigation of the conference by a lawyer appointed by the university administration (Drummond 2013, 204–223).

This creation of a zone of surveillance, which delineates critics of Israel as existing in a separate space from other academics, can be linked to the extraordinary language used by opponents of the 'International Law' conference. There was – putting it mildly – no mincing of words, with commentators falling over themselves in using invective to describe the 'anti-Israel hate-fest', 'rally of hate', 'freak show', and so on. The use of invective, I would argue, serves as a means of dis-embedding the conference from academia.

Vitriol was used extensively in print media – in newspaper reports, critics regularly called the conference (which, it should be noted, had not been yet held) a racist, antisemitic affair. But the invective mainly occurred through attacks on Twitter and other social media platforms. Engagement online has proven to be a minefield for academics to navigate since social media has created a collapse of context and register – the intermeshing of orality and literacy-based communication styles easily leads to slippage of academic personas and of academics no longer sounding like academics (Stewart 2016). While individual academics find it possible to negotiate the hyper-personal and casual style of social media, it is more difficult for events like conferences to do so. This problem was amplified by the response to the conference on Twitter, a site notorious for its culture of defamation.

Twitter traffic on the Cork conference was extreme, personalized, and hate-filled. Of the various accounts, https://twitter.com/CorkConference, a parody account, was perhaps the most extreme and certainly the most extensive with over 1,800 posts, many of them incomprehensible, brimming with vicious invective. The tweets contained extreme homophobia, sexism, class hatred, Islamophobia, and other forms of racism. For instance,

> Irish Jews ALWAYS carry the Irish Flag Jew haters NEVER DO Notice the Pro Palestine Jew haters rarely have Irish surnames?
> We've dropped our ticket prices so that full time, unemployed, living off the State they hate-Social Justice Warriors can attend. #Wankers.

There was also antisemitism, sometimes combined with Islamophobia. This was expressed by fake tweets, purportedly coming from the real conference:

We demand an end to JEW/Zionist/Jew investment in CORK.
When is the Beat The Jew Banquet. I could eat two camels!

One can speculate on the psychology of Zionists who seem to find delight in 'parodying' antisemitism. At times there was no attempt to hide the antisemitism – when attacking the conference participants who were Jewish. However, leaving aside the psychological issues behind such rhetoric, this online activism has political effects and can be seen as part of the more conventional price tag attacks on opponents of Israel – they create personal anxiety and reputational damage. But they also work to enmesh academics in other discursive fields and create the impression of critics of Israel as controversial figures engaging in arenas far from common academia.

Conclusion

This chapter has argued that supporters of Israel follow well-established methods when trying to shut down academic conferences they dislike. The argument they use will be that the conference is not a 'real' academic conference and so by attacking it, they are not attacking academic freedom – far from it, they are defending the university by protecting academic speech and the necessary civility on campus that enables reasoned discussion. The reason given for the claim that the conference is not really academic and therefore shouldn't be accorded institutional recognition is primarily because it is not balanced in terms of speakers or content; the speakers themselves are 'unbalanced' and un-academic, and the gathering of speakers is unbalanced against those supporting the status quo in Israel/Palestine. An ancillary way of demonstrating that it is not part of academic discourse is to try and enmesh it in other discursive fields – thus the falsity of sensationalist accusations, the incivility of Twitter controversies is not, under these terms, a problem that opponents of the conference need to address. Rather it is a tactic to make the conference part of a shitshow.

There is no effort to engage with Israel-critical academics as academics, since they are not seen that way. What matters is shutting down the conference. The most successful way, as we have seen, is undermining it through bureaucratic means. In the UK and Ireland, as noted earlier, health and safety concerns are used; the possibility is raised that there will be pro-Israel protests and/or Palestinian counter-protests that will endanger the safety of students and academics. The interchange in Southampton between university authorities and the Board of Deputies of British Jews is revealing in this regard. As reported in the *Jewish Chronicle* the meeting went as follows:

> Board of Deputies president Vivian Wineman said: 'When we had a meeting with the university vice-chancellor they said they would review it on health and safety terms.
> 'The two lines of attack possible were legal and health and safety and they were leaning on that one'. (Firsht 2015a)

Health and safety as 'lines of attack'. One can similarly dismiss the security concerns raised by the university authorities in Cork, where there had been no Zionist political activity, no chance of protest, and where the Special Branch – the Irish political police – informed the university that there was no risk (personal communication). However, the question is why the university authorities sought these pretexts. I argue that it is not simply because of threats from supporters of Israel, but because, to a certain extent, university authorities accepted their position that in some way, the conference's academic credentials were somewhat suspect.

If one talks about the effect of these attacks, it is important to note that the conference went ahead in Cork and was judged by attendees to be a success. Indeed, the shutdown of the Southampton conference was something of an anomaly. However, the Cork conference went ahead with a large security bill and was surrounded by an aura of poisonous attacks and threats from supporters of Israel. This can be considered a partial success for the Israel lobby – a 'price tag' attack on the conference and on discussing Israel critically. But perhaps the bigger price tag was in spreading the idea that criticism of Israel exists outside the academic sphere. This is an idea that can and should be challenged. I would argue that to do so, one needs to understand how Zionist ideologues manage to convince university authorities that there is validity to their position. For there is a vast gulf between these ideologues who truly believe that Israel-critical thought represents – in whatever form it exists – illicit thought, and conservative academics or administrators seeking to preserve the autonomy of the university. Rather than obscuring this gap by acting as if both are operating in the same field of practice, it would be useful to reveal not only the ideological purposes of those seeking to shut down academic speech, but how their actions threaten academic autonomy and are attacks both on critics of Israel and the university as a whole.

Notes

1 The tactics used were, for instance, remarkably similar to those used to protest the 2009 'Mapping Models' conference in Toronto as well as the 'Academic Freedom' conference the editors of this volume organized in Trinity College Dublin (TCD) in 2017 (see introduction for details).

2 This tactic of attacking academic credentials can also be seen in Cary Nelson's attempted trashing of Steven Salaita's academic record after the latter was refused tenure (Nelson 2015).

3 The York conference was not the only one to be attacked this way. In 2012 in the US, Zionist organizations protested against a student-led conference in Harvard University on the one-state solution, and Senator Scott Brown demanded that the university shut it down as it represented a form of 'dangerous thinking' which did not belong in the university (Bierman 2012).

References

Abunimah, A. (2015), 'Univ. of Southampton Cancels Conference after Government, Israel Lobby Pressure', *Electronic Intifada*, 31 March, https://electronicintifada.net/blogs/ali-abunimah/univ-southampton-cancels-conference-after-government-israel-lobby-pressure (accessed 15 January 2019).

Allen, L. (2019), 'Academic Freedom in the United Kingdom', *Academe* 105(4), https://www.aaup.org/article/academic-freedom-united-kingdom (accessed 22 October 2019).

Baier, C. and V. Gengnagel (2018), 'Academic Autonomy beyond the Nation-State', *österreichische Zeitschrift für Soziologie* 43(1): 65–92.

Bierman, N. (2012), 'Scott Brown Calls on Harvard to Cancel "One State" Conference', *Boston Globe*, 2 March, https://www.bostonglobe.com/news/politics/2012/03/02/harvard/Fg6zeyvcyr2vnVc7sit6sM/story.html (accessed 30 January 2019).

Bourdieu, P. (1993), *Sociology in Question*, London: Sage.

Bourdieu, P. and L. Wacquant (1992), *An Invitation to Reflexive Sociology*, Cambridge: Polity Press.

Collier, D. (2015), 'An Open Letter to the University of Southampton', http://david-collier.com/open-letter-university-southampton/ (accessed 12 January 2019).

Collier, D. (2017), 'Corked: Ben Dor's Anti-Israel "Circus of Hate" Comes to UCC in Ireland', http://david-collier.com/ben-dors-circus-hate/ (accessed 12 January 2019).

Drummond, S. G. (2013), *Unthinkable Thoughts: Academic Freedom and the One-State Model for Israel and Palestine*, Vancouver: UBC Press.

Firsht, N. (2015a), 'Southampton University Confirms It Is Considering Cancelling Anti-Israel Conference', *Jewish Chronicle*, 31 March, https://www.thejc.com/news/uk-news/southampton-university-confirms-it-is-considering-cancelling-anti-israel-conference-1.65916 (accessed 13 January 2019).

Firsht, N. (2015b), 'Southampton University Cancels Anti-Israel Conference over "Safety Concerns"', *Jewish Chronicle*, 2 April, https://www.thejc.com/news/uk-news/southampton-university-cancels-anti-israel-conference-over-safety-concerns-1.65932 (accessed 13 January 2019).

Harpin, L. (2017a), 'Community Organisations Condemn Irish University Decision to Host Anti-Zionist Conference', *Jewish Chronicle*, 5 January, https://www.thejc.com/news/uk-news/conference-to-ask-should-israel-exist-1.430118 (accessed 13 January 2019).

Harpin, L. (2017b), 'Pro-Israel Speaker Pulls Out of Conference over Presence of Richard Falk', *Jewish Chronicle*, 21 March, https://www.thejc.com/news/uk-news/pro-israel-speaker-pulls-out-of-conference-over-presence-of-richard-falk-1.434719 (accessed 13 January 2019).

International Law conference (2016), 'Organizers' Statement – Dec 2016', https://israelpalestinelaw.wordpress.com/ (accessed 19 January 2019).

International Law conference (2017), 'Endorsements', https:// israelpalestinelaw.wordpress.com/endorsements/ (accessed 21 January 2019).

Khan, Z. (2017), 'Israel Conference to Go Ahead in Cork', *Trinity News*, 13 March, http://trinitynews.ie/2017/03/israel-conference-to-go-ahead-in-cork/ (accessed 22 June 2019).

MacDonald, H. (2018), *The Diversity Delusion: How Race and Gender Pandering Corrupt the University and Undermine Our Culture*, New York: St. Martin's Press.

MacEoin, D. (2017), 'UnCorked: Ireland's Pseudo-Academic Anti-Israel Hate-Fest', Gatestone Institute, 7 January, https://www.gatestoneinstitute.org/9701/ireland-conference-israel (accessed 12 January 2019).

Masri, M. (2011), 'A Tale of Two Conferences: On Power, Identity, and Academic Freedom', AAUP Journal of Academic Freedom 2: 1–28.

Maton, K. (2005), 'A Question of Autonomy: Bourdieu's Field Approach and Higher Education Policy', *Journal of Education Policy* 20 (6): 687–704.

McCahill, C. (2017), 'UCC Involved in Row with Israeli Embassy over Conference', *University Express*, 28 January, https://uccexpress.ie/ucc-involved-in-row-with-israeli-embassy-over-conference/ (accessed 18 January 2019).

Moshman, D. and F. Edler (2015), 'Civility and Academic Freedom after Salaita', *AAUP Journal of Academic Freedom* 6, https://www.aaup.org/sites/default/files/MoshmanEdler.pdf (accessed 30 November 2018).

Murray, D. (2015), 'This Is No Debate but a Rally of Hate Directed at Israel', *Daily Express*, 13 March, https://www.express.co.uk/comment/expresscomment/563569/Cambridge-University-s-debates-over-Israel-State (accessed 4 December 2018).

Nagle, A. (2017), *Kill All Normies: Online Culture Wars from 4chan and Tumblr to Trump and the Alt-right*, London: Zero.

Nash, K. (2019), 'Neo-liberalisation, Universities and the Values of Bureaucracy', *The Sociological Review* 67 (1): 178–193.

Nelson, C. (2015), 'Steven Salaita's Scholarly Record and the Problem of His Appointment', *AAUP Journal of Academic Freedom* 6, https://www.aaup.org/sites/default/files/Nelson.pdf (accessed 30 November 2018).

Nelson, C. and G. N. Brahm (eds) (2015), *The Case against Academic Boycotts of Israel*, Detroit, MI: Wayne State University Press.

Nussbaum, M. (2007), 'Against Academic Boycotts', *Dissent* 54 (3): 30–36.

Peled, D. (2013), 'Delegitimizing the Delegitimizers', *Jewish Quarterly* 57 (1): 32–33.

Reut Institute (2010), 'The Delegitimization Challenge: Creating a Political Firewall', http://reut-institute.org/en/Publication.aspx?PublicationId=3769 (accessed 27 November 2018).

Steinberg, M. (1999), 'The Talk and Back Talk of Collective Action: A Dialogic Analysis of Repertoires of Discourse among Nineteenth-Century English Cotton Spinners', *The American Journal of Sociology* 105 (3): 736–780.

Stewart, B. (2016), 'Collapsed Publics: Orality, Literacy, and Vulnerability in Academic Twitter', *Journal of Applied Social Theory* 1 (1): 61–86, https://socialtheoryapplied.com/journal/jast/article/view/33 (accessed 5 January 2019).

UCC (2017), 'Statement: Proposed Conference on Israel', https://www.ucc.ie/en/news/archive/2017/statement-proposed-conference-on-israel-.html (accessed 21 January 2018).

Winstanley, A. (2016), 'Southampton University Bans "Controversial" Israel Conference Again', *Electronic Intifada*, 16 March, https://electronicintifada.net/blogs/asa-winstanley/southampton-university-bans-controversial-israel-conference-again (accessed 15 January 2019).

Zureik, E. (2016), *Israel's Colonial Project in Palestine: Brutal Pursuit*, London and New York: Routledge.

FOUR | Lebanese and American law at American universities in Beirut: a case of legal liminality in neoliberal times

Tala Makhoul

Introduction

In the past decade, there has been a burgeoning attempt by the ruling classes in the Middle East to foster open diplomatic, economic, and military relationships between the 'Zionist state' and Arab governments. The Gulf monarchies, which have not formalized relations with the 'Zionist state', openly bolster their informal relationships with leading representatives of the state, while other Arab states like Egypt and Jordan continue to honour the terms of their treaties with it. The move towards normalization reflects a growing disconnect between the ruling classes and Arab civil society, which is overwhelmingly anti-Zionist in nature.

Ali Abunimah notes that 'growing cracks' in American public support for Israel are most evident on university campuses, where anti-Zionist activity is more prominent than in other arenas of public life (Abunimah 2014, 169). Universities in the Arab world closely follow this trend; campuses are one of the few public venues where Arabs, especially Arab youth, are explicit about their anti-Zionism. In May 2018, a collective of Qatari youth called 'Qatar Youth Opposed to Normalization' (QAYON) at the Northwestern satellite campus in Doha protested the presence of prominent Zionist propagandist Alan Dershowitz on their campus, claiming that 'Zionists are not welcome here' (QAYON 2018). At my alma mater, the American University of Beirut (AUB), there have been several mobilizations against administrative breaches of Boycott, Divestment, and Sanctions (BDS) in the past decade. The latest, which took place in October 2018, protested a talk given by an American scholar affiliated with the Hebrew University of Jerusalem (among other Israeli institutions). These are just two of many examples of pro-Palestine activism and solidarity on American university campuses across the Arab world.

University students, both on campuses across the Arab region and abroad, have been stripped of decision-making power by their respective university administrations. This is indicative of a global neoliberal turn in academe, whereby the university is increasingly invested in profiteering and the circulation of capital, often among the upper circles of the administration. Universities in the Middle East are not immune to this trend, and the situation is worse at American universities in the Arab world. Presidents of these universities speak only of promoting 'uniquely American' (quoted in Hermez and Sukarieh 2015) values in the region. These 'uniquely American' values are given benign-sounding names like 'academic freedom' and 'tolerance'. These labels obscure one of the main purposes of American universities in the Arab world: to soften hostile attitudes to US foreign policy. This includes neutralizing opposition to the US's unconditional commitment to Israel. These values, much like the devaluation of graduate student and adjunct faculty labour, the proliferation of profit-oriented goods and services on university campuses (like mushrooming ATMs on university campuses), the provision of university services by private subcontractors (like cafeteria vendors and housekeeping companies), and the silencing of dissent are all symptoms of the broader neoliberal turn on American university campuses in the Arab world.

While Arab governments in Egypt, Jordan, and others have had open diplomatic relations with Israel for decades, others remain committed to an Arab boycott of the Zionist entity.[1] Lebanon is one of the few Arab states that remains staunchly committed to the economic, social, and cultural boycott of Israel, at least in a legal capacity. The boycott law has been enshrined in Lebanese law since 1955 and is still upheld today. Empirically speaking, what makes the case for boycott at American universities in the Arab world so complex is the dual legal commitment these universities have. On the one hand, they must follow the laws and regulations of the United States to continue receiving federal funding. On the other, they must follow the laws of their host country. In the Arab world this often (but not always) means that formal relations with Israeli universities, corporations, or scholars are strictly prohibited. Sami Hermez and Mayssoun Sukarieh, in their discussion of the case of academic boycott at AUB, note that 'all the key questions that inevitably arise in conflicts over academic freedom in the global north – knowledge for what, and freedom for whom and from whom – take on another dimension in neocolonial contexts (like AUB) in the global south' (Hermez and Sukarieh 2015). This is definitely true in the case of AUB and other American universities in the Arab world.

In this chapter, I examine the issues surrounding the boycott of the 'Zionist state', academic and otherwise, at the American University of Beirut (AUB) and the Lebanese American University (LAU), with a brief look at other American universities in Lebanon. My examination primarily relies on a close reading and analysis of laws surrounding the boycott of Israel in Lebanon and the US, university policies affirming compliance with the laws of both countries, and administrative, faculty, and student statements surrounding the issue of BDS and academic boycott at AUB. I also incorporate personal anecdotes from my time as a Palestine solidarity activist at AUB in an attempt to understand the repeated failure to elicit an explicit position on BDS or academic boycott from the AUB administration. The failure of our repeated attempts (in which

I was involved between 2015 and 2018) cannot be seen in isolation from the legal liminal space in which AUB, and other universities like it, exist. In this chapter, I hope to add to the work of Sami Hermez, Mayssoun Sukarieh, and others who have explored what it means to undertake BDS activism in close proximity to Palestine.

The legal predicament at AUB

The following is stated in AUB's 'USAID Grant Compliance Policy',

> AUB must adhere to all applicable U.S. federal and state laws, rules and regulations applicable to it in the operation of the University Scholarship program ... AUB must also comply with the laws of Lebanon, the country in which it operates. (AUB President's Office 2017)

While some may argue that this is only applicable to the University Scholarship programme enabled by the United States Agency for International Development (USAID), AUB's 'Policy on Compliance with the US Economic Sanctions Program' reaffirms that 'as a US educational institution, AUB also recognizes that it must comply with all applicable laws of the United States as well as the laws of Lebanon, the country in which it operates' (AUB President's Office 2017). This indicates that the policies ratified by the AUB administration repeatedly acknowledge a commitment to upholding their legal commitments in both Lebanon and the US.

In March 2017, the New York Senate passed three education bills: the first bill amended a pre-existing education law to add BDS and other boycotts of American-allied nations to a clause prohibiting student organizations that 'participate in hate speech' from receiving public funding. The clause, at the time of writing, explicitly defines boycotts of American-allied nations as hate speech. The second bill

> prohibits any college from using state aid to fund an academic entity, to provide funds for membership in an academic entity, or fund travel or lodging for any employee to attend any meeting of such academic entity if that academic entity has undertaken an official action boycotting certain countries or their higher education institutions.

The third bill 'prohibits state contracting with, and state investment in, persons and businesses that promote or engage in activities to boycott American-allied nations' (quoted in Redden 2017). While the three bills attempt to maintain an air of neutrality through the inclusion of other 'American-allied nations', Governor Andrew Cuomo's executive order no. 157, which was signed a few months after the passage of the three education bills, explicitly denounces 'any activity intended to inflict economic harm on Israel or persons doing business with Israel' (Cuomo 2016). In other words, while the bills are consciously written as applying to all American-allied nations, it is clear that they are a pointed response to the success of BDS activism on several university campuses throughout the US.

As an organization registered in the state of New York, the passage of those three education bills, along with Cuomo's executive order, are undoubtedly a complication for AUB, which strives to comply with 'all applicable [American] laws', including education laws. Indeed, AUB was forced to pay a hefty fine of 700,000 USD for 'fail[ing] to take reasonable steps to ensure against providing material support to entities on the [US] Treasury Department's prohibited list' (Kim et al. 2011, quoted in Reuters, Dobuzinskis 2017). AUB had hosted a series of free media workshops between

2007 and 2009, and representatives from Al Manar, Al Nour, and other Hezbollah-affiliated media outlets had taken part among a larger group of journalists, and now they had to pay the price. Undoubtedly, the US federal government interpreted this as a breach of AUB's policy of compliance with US economic sanctions,[2] discussed above.

The American regulations to which AUB is beholden are directly at odds with Lebanese law. Lebanon does not recognize the State of Israel; indeed, the two countries are still formally at war. In 1955, the government of Lebanon passed a law forbidding any direct relations with Israel. Lebanon is also home to one of the oldest organized grassroots efforts to boycott the State of Israel. Activists in these circles diligently ensure that the boycott law is enforced at every turn by notifying the government whenever notable individuals or organizations violate it. One recent effort by the Lebanese public to mobilize the law culminated in the ban of *Wonder Woman* film screenings across Lebanon. The lead, Gal Gadot, was a former soldier in the Israel Defence Forces (IDF), where she served as a physical trainer. Furthermore, she explicitly supports the IDF, as evidenced by her online activity during the 2014 Israeli aggression against Gaza, where she called for the IDF to 'free Gaza from Hamas'. Another recent example was the mobilization against Lebanese director Ziad Doueiri, who filmed *The Attack* in Israel, with Israeli actors, in 2013. Doueiri's detention (and prompt release) spotlights the Lebanese state's inconsistency in its enforcement of the 1955 boycott law, while civil society's mobilization against him indicates that the Lebanese public has no love for the State of Israel. The IDF occupied the south of Lebanon for decades, and briefly occupied Beirut in 1982. In 2006, Israel instigated another war against Lebanon that killed thousands of civilians and internally displaced many more. Thus, it comes as no surprise that the Lebanese public is heavily invested in ensuring the implementation of the boycott law; their safety and security is at stake, not to mention the safety and security of the thousands of Palestinian and Syrian refugees in their midst.

Academic boycott at AUB?

At AUB, an American university that receives congressional funding and is classified as a 'tax-exempt corporation', navigating this public sentiment among students, faculty, and staff is incredibly complicated. On the one hand, many believe that the punishment of BDS activism at AUB is absurd, considering the 1955 Lebanese boycott law – it would make no sense to punish students and faculty for following Lebanese law. At the same time, a brief glance at the discourse expressed by administrators at AUB illustrates how the administration 'invoke[s the principle of academic freedom] in order to stifle or shut down protests launched against a series of administrative decisions serving, intentionally or not, to counteract the academic boycott of Israel' (Hermez and Sukarieh 2015). Further, the administration has responded to most of the petitions and actions concerning BDS on campus by deflecting from the demand that AUB take clear steps to honour Palestinian civil society's call for boycott, divestment, and sanctions by pointing towards scholarships given to Palestinian students and other such distractions.[3]

Hermez and Sukarieh (2015) document these administrative decisions, which took place under former AUB President Peter Dorman. In 2011 and 2012, the university attempted to grant both James Wolfensohn and Donna Shalala honorary doctorates. Wolfensohn is notorious for his links with an Israeli think tank and Israeli businesses, and Shalala is an avid supporter of partnerships with Israeli universities and an ardent opponent of BDS. The response from the campus community was to circulate petitions opposing these administrative decisions, successfully forcing the administration to rescind the honorary doctorates. As noted by Hermez and Sukarieh, the administration defended its position in both instances, claiming that 'AUB is deeply committed to upholding the essential values' of academic freedom. In 2011, Dorman spoke about the university's commitment to academic freedom at the graduation commencement, contradicting his earlier email to the university community where he claimed that faculty were 'deliberately slanted to serve narrow interests regardless of facts' and 'fundamentally dishonest' (quoted in Hermez and Sukarieh 2015).

The inauguration of AUB's first president with Lebanese heritage did not fundamentally reverse this use of academic freedom in public and defamation in private to obfuscate demands for justice. Under President Fadlo Khuri, the decisions emerging from AUB's administrative offices have been the same, and even worse in some cases. A few months after Khuri's inauguration, the provost's office unilaterally dissolved a search committee following its recommendation of Dr Steven Salaita for the director position at the Center for American Studies and Research (CASAR), citing 'procedural irregularities'. The administration failed to corroborate this claim with an investigation, leading students at the centre – who were now left without a programme director – to circulate a petition expressing their concern about the state of academic freedom at AUB and demanding the reversal of the decision and the reinstatement of the search committee. Khuri responded with an email calling the petition a 'malicious distortion of the facts involved in this case' (Fadlo Khuri, internal communication to the AUB community, 14 April 2016).

In October 2016 students organized a sit-in outside the on-campus Nestlé Tollhouse Coffee Shop. The cafe is no stranger to such protests; it has been contentious among students since it opened, with the debate culminating in a petition by 'AUB Students Against Nestlé', demanding that AUB divest from Nestlé and other companies complicit with the Israeli occupation. At the sit-in that took place on 5 October 2016, the dean of student affairs, dispatched to shut down the protest, claimed that 'Zionists [aren't violent] when they build settlements', implying that the students' blockade of the cafe, in contrast, was violent.

Much like Dorman's claims about the faculty and students who circulated petitions regarding Wolfensohn and Shalala, the administration's response was to attack the character of those invested in justice for Palestine, and, more importantly in this case, refuse to take a stance on the question of BDS and the academic boycott at AUB. There has still been no official acknowledgement of pro-Palestine activists' demand that AUB divest from complicit multinationals such as Nestlé and Hewlett Packard.

So far, I have discussed AUB's overt engagements with multinationals which are complicit in the colonization of Palestine. When it comes to the academic boycott of Israeli institutions, both individual scholars and departments at AUB have been more covert in their engagement with Israeli academe. Overt engagement with Israeli universities and scholars is prohibited under the 1955 Lebanese boycott law. This means that some form of academic boycott is state-imposed regardless of whether the call to boycott is officially ratified by any AUB authority. However, this has not stopped the AUB administration and some faculty members from contentious collaborations with either Israeli scholars or those complicit with the occupation. The most recent examples of this happened in the autumn semester of the 2018–2019 academic year. On 3 September 2018, the administration and the Chemistry Department invited the 2016 Chemistry Nobel Laureate Sir Fraser Stoddart to deliver a lecture on campus. Stoddart had delivered a lecture in Israel in celebration of the 70th anniversary of 'Israeli independence' a few months previously, congratulating the entity on their 'spectacular output' (Boycott Campaign in Lebanon 2018). As Lisa Taraki (2015) notes,

> the emphasis on scientific innovation and advances in technological know-how is part of Israel's decades-long quest for legitimacy and acceptance by the rest of the world; it is meant to secure a place for Israel in the ranks of the enlightened Western academy.

The celebration of Israel's scientific output is yet another means of legitimizing Israel's existence, and Stoddard's participation in perpetuating and celebrating this output denotes complicity with the crimes committed by the State of Israel.

Less than two months after that, the Philosophy Department hosted Dr Jeff McMahan to deliver a lecture entitled 'Rethinking the Ethics of War'. McMahan is an advisor at the Hebrew University of Jerusalem, which is one of the major Israeli universities that work with the Israeli arms industry (Taraki 2015). McMahan seems to believe that the Israeli state is an inherently neutral entity. In a radio interview on the ethics of the Israeli war against Gaza, he states that 'Israel [has no] conceivable interest in harming or killing innocent people ... it works very much to their disadvantage when their missiles kill children, for example' (McMahan 2008, 4).[4] By claiming that the State of Israel has no interest in killing Palestinian children he elided the fact that Israel is a settler colony with its own logic of elimination (Wolfe 2006).

Pro-Palestine activist students at the university emailed the organizers of the event, demanding that they respect the academic boycott of Israel at AUB. In their email, they cited McMahan's affiliation with the Hebrew University of Jerusalem as a primary cause for their opposition to his presence on campus. The organizers responded dismissively, inviting the students to attend the talk and 'voice all the objections [they] want to voice' (email correspondence between student clubs and Haydar 2018).[5] The event generated public outcry, culminating in one of the most visible student protests against normalization with Israeli academics and collaborators in the past decade at AUB. Nine student clubs released a collective statement denouncing McMahan's lecture and his presence on campus, and reaffirmed their 'support for the academic boycott of Israeli institutions and [their opposition] to all efforts to normalize the Zionist occupation of Palestine' ('AUB Students Against Normalization with the Zionist Entity' 2018). Faculty United, a chapter of the American Association of University Professors (AAUP) at AUB, also called on the AUB administration to

> take all appropriate steps to comply with Lebanese legislation in relation to the Zionist state of Israel, similar to the active compliance program it implements with regards to US sanctions [including] refraining from participation in any form of academic and cultural cooperation, collaboration or joint projects with Israeli institutions, including their affiliates and active collaborators. (AUB Faculty United 2018).[6]

As Hermez and Sukarieh (2015) note, 'state-imposed Arab boycott[s have] provided legal protection as one line of defense against the normalization of Israel's ongoing violations of international law against the Palestinian people'. The Faculty United statement explicitly uses this as a tactic to condemn the AUB administration and the organizers of the McMahan lecture on legal grounds.

Following student outcry in response to the McMahan invitation, the Office of Communications at AUB circulated a statement which claimed:

AUB is a community of scholars and educators that is *proud to uphold free speech and debate*, and to be a place where sincere ideas of all kinds are voiced and examined in a rigorous, safe, scientific and humanistic setting. AUB follows the laws of Lebanon and *adopts the principles of liberal education developed in the United States*, the country where the university is registered. These principles enshrine the right of students to protest peacefully on matters of importance, but not to *disrupt the freedom* of other members of the community to engage in legitimate academic inquiry and discussion without hindrance or intimidation. AUB does not support 'normalization' as that would contravene Lebanese law and flagrantly contradict the university's standing as the top higher education institution in Lebanon and the Arab world. (AUB Office of Communications 2018; emphasis added)

While this example is milder than the earlier examples of administrative responses to pro-Palestine student and faculty critiques, it reiterates many of the same points made by administrators including the president and the dean in 2016, as well as former president Peter Dorman. All administrators have reiterated the university's commitment to academic freedom, while framing the student and faculty critics as disruptive and illiberal. As Hermez and Sukarieh note, any attempt by US university administrations to promote 'uniquely American' values such as academic freedom and mutual respect for people of diverse backgrounds inadvertently or deliberately implies that 'such values do not exist where these universities are operating' (Hermez and Sukarieh 2015). Notably, the above statement reiterates its commitment to Lebanese law and American principles; however, as shown by the case of the 700,000 USD fine mentioned above, AUB is bound by more than just 'American principles'. It is also bound by US law, as evidenced by their continuing lack of acknowledgement of BDS or the academic boycott of Israel.

This feeble response is even more interesting when the statements of dissident students and faculty are taken into account. On the one hand, the students' statement stresses a commitment to the academic boycott of Israel and the refusal to normalize the Zionist occupation of Palestine. At the same time, the faculty statement (AUB Faculty United 2018) reminds the administration that normalization is against Lebanese law, and that AUB is just as beholden to Lebanese law as it is to US law.

Embedded in the faculty's statement is an implicit accusation that the AUB administration places a higher value on US law than Lebanese law; the statement from the Office of Communications attempts to counter that accusation by reaffirming AUB's commitment to Lebanese law. Further, the statement from the administration directly addresses the issue of normalization, directly quoted from the collective statement from students, by again reaffirming its commitment to Lebanese law. However, the administration, yet again, fails to address the students' demand that AUB adhere to the academic boycott of Israel, embodied by the calls of both the Palestinian Campaign for the Academic and Cultural Boycott of Israel (PACBI) and the US Campaign for the Academic and Cultural Boycott of Israel (USACBI). These repeated failures by the administration to take an explicit stance on BDS and academic boycott are not accidental. They are attempts to avoid direct repercussions from both the US federal government and the state of New York. Whether this is deliberate or not is beside the point; the point is that the use of 'academic freedom' distorts their primary motivation and results in the vilification of Palestine solidarity student activists. At the same time, the administration's use of academic freedom as the primary reasoning for refusing to take an explicit stance on the issue gives these student activists a bit of leeway. While the administration can tacitly vilify them and police their behaviour on campus, they cannot overtly or explicitly stop students from professing their belief that AUB, as a university *in Lebanon*, should take an explicitly positive stance on BDS.

Activists' dilemma: the neoliberalization of AUB

In the context of the AUB administration's silence on the issue of BDS and academic boycott, it is harder for student activists to set clear goals and organize around them. While it is clear that the AUB administration would not benefit from officially ratifying the call for boycott of, divestment from, and sanctions against Israeli organizations, institutions, collaborators, and affiliates, this has never been explicitly stated. Instead of affirming that it is anti-BDS, the administration gestures to academic freedom to obfuscate and derail the issue. Faculty members like the organizers of the McMahan lecture further derail the issue by claiming that AUB would be unable to collaborate with Harvard and MIT if they had to boycott every institution with stakes in the Zionist entity (Haydar, personal communication 2018). This *tu quoque* logical fallacy, by derailing the issue, makes it harder for students and sympathetic faculty to organize. Thus student activists invested in the boycott, myself included during my time at AUB, have no clear roadmap showing where or how to begin agitating for a ratification and formal commitment to BDS and the academic boycott. The duality of AUB's legal status is at the crux of this ambiguity; had AUB not been governed by both Lebanese and US law, then an explicit affirmation or denunciation would be an attainable goal.

What exacerbates matters at AUB is the fact that autonomous student governance is practically non-existent. The university boasts about autonomous student governance, but in reality the 'student government' – the University Student Faculty Committee (USFC) – is a collective of 19 elected students and six faculty members, one representing each faculty. There is no mechanism that gives the 19 elected students any real voting power; instead, the students give nominal suggestions to administrative policy-makers which may or may not be taken into account. There is also no mechanism that allows the student government to hold the administration accountable for any action it may take to the detriment of the students. Instead, the USFC is envisioned as largely apolitical, encouraging students to 'get involved' and volunteer to organize events that generate profits for AUB, like the annual AUB Outdoors (which is marketed as an on-campus Coachella) or other benign, apolitical events around campus.[7] In other words, the students do not have the power to ratify binding resolutions on BDS, the academic boycott, or any other truly important political matter that binds the university to the outside world. The deadlock in student governance, coupled with the legal duality existent at AUB, is what makes BDS advocacy so challenging on this campus.

The neoliberalization of AUB – following the global trend – has contributed to the de-politicization of student governance at the university. There are three student blocs at AUB. The platforms of these blocs range from policies that impact the day-to-day lives of students (such as book borrowing policies and increasing student study spaces on campus) to broader policies on tuition, administrative transparency, and student events. These groups are mostly unconcerned with geopolitics or related issues,[8] such as the divestment from companies complicit with Israeli coloniza-tion of Palestine.

The de-politicization of student government is tied to AUB's neoliberalization. I am using Harvey's definition of neoliberal-ism as a 'set of political economic practices that proposes that human well-being can be best advanced by liberating individ-ual entrepreneurial freedoms and skills within an institutional framework' (Harvey 2005, 3). Sealey-Huggins and Pusey (2013, 83) rightly claim that the neoliberalization of higher education in the UK is linked to the 'depoliticized' condition of contemporary social life, which 'results in a consensus that takes capitalist liberal democracy for granted as *the* legitimate form of social and political organization'. While they are using higher education in the UK as a case study, this claim can explain the de-politicization of student governance at AUB. Rather than lose themselves in ideological battles, candidates and elected representatives focus on 'expert management and administration' (Žižek, cited in Sealey-Huggins and Pusey 2013, 83). Even if elected student representatives decide to take on ideological battles within the USFC, they would be blocked by the heavy faculty presence and administrative influence surrounding them.

A note on LAU and other American universities in Lebanon

The Lebanese American University (LAU) is another prominent American university in Lebanon that is also registered in the state of New York. The preamble of LAU's constitution states that 'this constitution is in full conformity with the Charter granted by the Board of Regents of the University of the State of New York and the Education Law of both the State of New York and the Republic of Lebanon' (LAU 2018). The constitution further affirms that the university's purpose is to provide higher education 'under the conditions acceptable to the culture and needs of the area while ensuring the Christian and liberal arts character of the University in accordance with the heritage of its Presbyterian founders' (LAU 2018). The Christian, Presbyterian heritage cited in the constitution is an almost explicit reference to 'American principles', evident in the affirmation of the university's commitment to 'non-discrimination'. Indeed, LAU's 'Discrimination, Harassment, and

Sexual Misconduct Prevention Policy' affirms LAU's commitment to preserving and encouraging academic freedom (LAU 2018). This caveat is included to stress that preventing discrimination, harassment, and sexual misconduct 'should by no means be construed as inhibiting free speech, freedom of association, or the free communication of ideas'. This is a fascinating point, one which highlights the importance of adherence to 'American values' and honouring LAU's Christian, Presbyterian heritage.

As far as I am aware, there has been no organized effort to elicit an administrative ratification of BDS or the academic boycott at LAU. However, based on the similarity of the cases of LAU and AUB vis-à-vis legal duality, there is no reason to assume that any organized effort to instigate boycott, divestment, and sanctions at LAU (or other American universities in Lebanon) would not be met with the same ambiguity from the administration. This is not to say that the situations at AUB and LAU are one and the same; while LAU is a 10-minute walk away from AUB, the histories and legacies of the two universities are quite different. However, the legal case for both universities with regard to BDS and the academic boycott are remarkably similar. Indeed, both AUB and LAU could use the fact that boycott is state-imposed to claim that an explicit statement formally ratifying the principles of BDS is unnecessary, considering that both universities are indeed bound by the Lebanese 1955 boycott law.

There are three other American universities in Lebanon: the American University of Culture and Education (AUCE), the American University of Science and Technology (AUST), and the American University of Technology (AUT). Interestingly, the policies on AUST's website affirm a commitment of 'respect for the laws of Lebanon and of [sic] the social, cultural, economic, political, and religious aspects that define Lebanon' (AUST n.d.). The others do not have an archive of university policies, and indeed all do not seem to receive congressional funding, to be chartered in the US like AUB and LAU, or to have missionary roots like them. Whether or not they are beholden to the laws of a foreign state as well as to Lebanese law is a potential avenue of investigation. I am inclined to believe, however, that they are in a much different position than both AUB and LAU.

Conclusion

In this chapter I have attempted to map out the specific challenges facing proponents of BDS and the academic boycott at American higher education institutions in the Arab world. While I mainly focused on AUB, the case with which I am most familiar, pro-Palestine solidarity activists could face similar challenges in other American universities in Lebanon (such as LAU) and perhaps even worse challenges at other American universities in the Arab world, especially satellite campuses in the Gulf states.

This chapter inadvertently paints a rather hopeless picture for the case of the academic boycott in American campuses in the Arab world. It is true that matters are becoming more complicated for pro-Palestine solidarity activists in the Arab world, especially with the – fairly recent – aggressive turn towards normalizing relations with Israel in the Gulf states. However, I take solace in the growing number of university campuses across the globe on which divestment resolutions have passed, knowing that these resolutions are the culmination of years of organized activism and strife. I take comfort in the fact that students at AUB and other American campuses in the Arab world have refused to sit idly by as their university campuses become more complicit in normalizing the Zionist occupation of Palestine, despite the threat of real, material repercussions. As Steven Salaita (2015) notes, recrimination against supporters of Palestine is an unfortunate reality; however, any recrimination by a university administration is dwarfed by the horrors of the Israeli occupation, horrors that Palestinians have to live with every day.

Notes

1 Unfortunately, the number of nations fully committed to the boycott is dwindling. Gulf Arab states are increasingly focused on developing covert relationships with the Zionist entity rooted in their shared animosity towards Iran. These geopolitical dynamics are worth noting, but an in-depth exploration is beyond the scope of this paper.

2 Interestingly, Version 1 of this policy was published a few days before AUB settled the issue with the US government (for 700,000 USD). Undoubtedly, AUB was still bound by a policy of compliance with sanctions despite not having an explicit policy about it on their website (or else the US government would not have been able to issue a fine).

3 Scholarships are particularly important for economically disenfranchised students – especially Palestinian students from refugee backgrounds – and this point is not meant to dismiss those who benefit from them but rather to note that it is not enough for AUB to offer financial assistance to Palestinian refugees while also maintaining contracts with multinationals that contribute to their need to seek refuge in a foreign country.

4 McMahan is also a self-admitted opponent of the academic boycott of Israel; he states in an opinion piece written in response to students demanding that his invitation to AUB be revoked, that 'justice for the Palestinians will not be achieved through force but only through mutual understanding and reconciliation, which require discussion that is open and respectful on both sides' (McMahan 2019).

5 Obtained with permission to use from student activists in the Red Oak Club – AUB.

6 https://www.facebook.com/samah.idriss.1/posts/1940024066084455 (accessed 26 April 2019).

7 The political parties involved in student elections are not apolitical; on the contrary, they are deeply embedded in the overall Lebanese political structure, but that is beyond the scope of this chapter.

8 It would be dishonest to say that they are entirely unconcerned, however, as these groups are also affiliated with political groups beyond campus. Further, they sometimes coordinate and organize vigils or protests in response to some atrocity in the region, such as the wars in Yemen, Palestine, or Syria, or Donald Trump's recognition of Jerusalem as the capital of Israel, for example.

References

Abunimah, A. (2014), *The Battle for Justice in Palestine*, Chicago, IL: Haymarket Books.

AUB Faculty United (2018), Facebook post (via Samah Idriss), https://www.facebook.com/samah.idriss.1/posts/1940024066084455 (accessed 1 December 2019).

AUB Office of Communications (2018), 'Statement by the Office of Communications at AUB', https://www.aub.edu.lb/communications/media/Documents/oct-18/Official-Statement-%20Oct-24-2018-EN.pdf (accessed 1 December 2019).

AUB President's Office (2017), 'Policy on Compliance with Economic Sanctions', https://aub.policytech.eu/dotNet/documents/?docid=1293&public=true (accessed 1 December 2019).

'AUB Students Against Normalization with the Zionist Entity' (2018), https://tinyurl.com/uhvkaoz (accessed 1 December 2019).

AUST (n.d.), 'Policy on Rights and Responsibilities', https://www.aust.edu.lb/Content/uploads/Policies/1.pdf (accessed 27 April 2019).

Boycott Campaign in Lebanon (2018), 'On AUB and Normalization', http://www.boycottcampaign.com/index.php/ar/test/letters/1850-from-the-boycott-campaign-in-lebanon-on-aub-and-normalization (accessed 16 November 2018).

Cuomo, A. (2016), 'If You Boycott Israel, New York State Will Boycott You', *The Washington Post*, 10 June, https://www.washingtonpost.com/opinions/gov-andrew-cuomo-if-you-boycott-israel-new-york-state-will-boycott-you/2016/06/10/1d6d3acc-2e62-11e6-9b37-42985f6a265c_story.html?utm_term=.9447e95af1fa (accessed 26 April 2019).

Dobuzinskis, A. (2017), 'American University of Beirut Settles Lawsuit for $700,000', *Reuters*, 24 March, https://www.reuters.com/article/us-usa-security-university-idUSKBN16V1X4 (accessed 16 November 2018).

Harvey, D. (2005), *A Brief History of Neoliberalism*, Oxford: Oxford University Press.

Hermez, S. and M. Sukarieh (2015), 'Boycotts against Israel and the Question of Academic Freedom in American Universities in the Arab World' in A. Dawson and B. Mullen (eds), *Against Apartheid: The Case for Boycotting Israeli Universities*, Chicago, IL: Haymarket Books, pp. 73–80.

LAU (2018), 'Discrimination, Harassment, and Sexual Misconduct Policy', https://www.lau.edu.lb/about/policies/harassment_policy.pdf (accessed 1 December 2019).

McMahan, J. (2008), 'Transcript of Episode 7, Jeff McMahan on Proportionality', *Public Ethics Radio*, Canberra: Centre for Applied Philosophy and Public Ethics, https://publicethicsradio.files.wordpress.com/2009/01/per_episode_7_transcript.pdf (accessed 16 November 2018).

McMahan, J. (2019), 'I Was No-platformed: Here's Why It's Counter-productive', *The New Statesman*, 14 January, https://www.newstatesman.com/2019/01/i-was-no-platformed-here-s-why-it-s-counterproductive (accessed 27 April 2019).

QAYON (2018), Twitter Post, 4 March, 2:02 pm, https://tinyurl.com/w5djmrw.

Redden, E. (2017), 'New York Senate Passes Anti-BDS Bills', *Inside HigherEd*, 9 March, https://www.insidehighered.com/quicktakes/2017/03/09/new-york-senate-passes-anti-bds-bills (accessed 16 November 2018).

Salaita, S. (2015), 'How to Practice BDS in Academe' in A. Dawson and B. Mullen (eds), *Against Apartheid: The Case for Boycotting Israeli Universities*, Chicago, IL: Haymarket Books, pp. 135–140.

Sealey-Huggins, L. and A. Pusey (2013), 'Neoliberalism and Depoliticisation in the Academy: Understanding the New Student Rebellions', *Graduate Journal of Social Science*, http://gjss.org/sites/default/files/issues/chapters/papers/Journal-10-03--04-SealeyHuggins-Pusey.pdf (accessed 27 April 2019).

Taraki, L. (2015), 'The Complicity of the Israeli Academy in the Structures of Domination and State Violence' in A. Dawson and B. Mullen (eds.) *Against Apartheid: The Case for Boycotting Israeli Universities*, Chicago, IL: Haymarket Books, pp. 21–30.

Wolfe, P. (2006), 'Settler Colonialism and the Elimination of the Native', *Journal of Genocide Research* 8 (4): 387–409.

FIVE | Precarious work in higher education, academic freedom, and the academic boycott of Israel in Ireland

Sinead Pembroke

Introduction

For many workers around the world, employment is insecure, with temporary and casual work on the increase. According to Guitierrez-Barbarrusa (2016, 477), 'in all developed economies standard employment is declining in favour of flexible employment (i.e. part-time, casual and own account workers, or those with contracts for specific tasks or services, etc.)'. Traditionally, higher education has been associated with well-paid and secure contracts, but since 2008 and the onset of the global financial crisis, precarious work has increased exponentially in this sector in Ireland and internationally. In Ireland, it is estimated that there are as many people on precarious contracts as there are permanent, tenure-track higher education workers. Precarious work has far-reaching and negative consequences both inside and outside the workplace (Pembroke 2018). Furthermore, precarious work also has implications for academic freedom.

Academic freedom is taken to mean the freedom a higher education worker has to express opinions, beliefs, and ideas without risk of official interference or professional disadvantage from the university. Academic freedom means:

> Both faculty members and students can engage in intellectual debate without fear of censorship or retaliation. Academic freedom establishes a faculty member's right to remain true to his or her pedagogical philosophy and intellectual commitments.

It preserves the intellectual integrity of our educational system
and thus serves the public good ... Academic freedom gives
both students and faculty the right to express their views – in
speech, writing, and through electronic communication, both on
and off campus – without fear of sanction. (Nelson 2010a)

The high dependence on precarious contracts has been identified
as a threat to academic freedom because they 'undermine shared
governance, compromise teaching effectiveness' (Orr 2018, 11).
Consequently, with the rise of precarious work in institutions
of higher education, it has led Clausen and Swidler to pose the
question, 'is it meaningful any longer to talk of academic freedom
as a ruling principle in higher education? Or is it incumbent on
us to consider that the conditions and constraints which are the
constant context of this great majority of academics are the new
reality of higher education?' (2013, 3). This chapter explores how
precarious work in higher education limits the space for critical
thinking and engaging in civil society activism, which has serious
consequences for taking part in the academic boycott of Israel.

The chapter is based on empirical evidence from primary
sources (accounts of precarious academics who engaged in
Boycott, Divestment, and Sanctions (BDS) activism in campuses
in Ireland and further afield), and secondary sources that look
at precarious work and the experience of it in higher education
(Courtois and O'Keefe 2015; AAUP 2018; Bobek, Pembroke and
Wickham 2018; Pembroke 2018). This chapter examines three
main features of precarious work that curtail academic freedom:
contractual and financial insecurity, relationships of dependency,
and the transient nature of precarious work.

What is precarious work?
Precarious work is complex; it does not just include low-waged
work, but has other characteristics such as unpredictable

working hours, the uncertainty of tenure, and the frequency of pay. There is no agreed official definition of precariousness, nor what constitutes precarious employment (International Labour Organization 2012, 29). However, Vosko (2010, 2) identified the main features as constituting, 'work for remuneration characterized by uncertainty, low income, and limited social benefits and statutory elements'.

Similarly, when it comes to identifying the various forms of precarious work, there are inconsistencies. Non-standard forms of employment[1] are often associated with precarious work. However, the European Parliament's report on precarious work observed, 'all employment relationships are at some risk of precariousness' (Broughton et al. 2016, 11). The report identified open-ended full and part-time contracts as low risk, while the employment contracts with the highest risk of precariousness are marginal and involuntary part-time work, temporary fixed-term, temporary agency work, self-employment, bogus self-employment and zero hours contracts (Broughton et al. 2016, 16–18).

In Europe, the highest proportion of non-standard employment occurred in the late 1970s and continued until the global financial crash in 2008 (Eurofound 2017). Non-standard, flexible, and precarious work developed as a policy response by European member states and further afield, 'to become more competitive in response to globalization and "financialization" of the economy, by means of an adaptable, mobile workforce' (Guitierrez-Barbarrusa 2016, 478). During this time, reforms to national employment protection legislation facilitated a departure from the standard employment contract, reducing protections against dismissals. The thinking behind this was that regulations inhibit a flexible labour market, though more recently this stance has been heavily criticized (Rubery, Keizer and Grimshaw 2016).

Precarious work affects people of all ages and occupations, and has resulted in a 'precarity trap' (Gash 2008), whereby people remain in precarious employment. Precarious work is also appearing in traditionally secure sectors such as the education sector. The struggles precarious workers face in the workplace continue into their life outside of work. Frase (2013, 14) observed, 'as work becomes more transient, struggles outside of the workplace such as with landlords, can become more significant than with employers'. Essentially, 'precarious work leads to precarious lives' (Pembroke 2018, 97).

Higher education and precarity in Ireland

There has always been a precariat employed in the higher education sector as lecturers, tutors, and researchers, but the numbers have increased exponentially in Ireland. The Cush Report (2016) revealed that 45 per cent of the total Irish university lecturing staff are employed on three types of atypical[2] contracts: permanent and part-time, fixed-term part-time, and fixed-term full-time. In Institutes of Technology, 25 per cent of core staff and 97 per cent of non-core staff are employed on an atypical basis. A combination of factors led to increased numbers of precarious academics: the economic recession in Ireland from 2008 onwards, and the employment control framework that the government imposed on the public sector in Ireland during this time. The latter involved a recruitment ban of public sector workers, and lecturers at public-funded institutions came under this remit.

However, it is important to note that this is not restricted solely to Ireland. Internationally, precarious work has similarly increased in higher education institutions. For instance, in the USA, approximately 70 per cent of faculty across all American higher education institutions are on precarious contracts (AAUP 2018). In the UK in 2016:

> Academics teaching or doing research in British universities
> will typically have spent years earning doctorates or other
> qualifications, yet more than half of them – 53% – manage on
> some form of insecure, non-permanent contract. They range
> from short-term contracts that typically elapse within nine
> months, to those paid by the hour to give classes or mark essays
> and exams. 53% of academics are on precarious contracts, and
> this figure is higher for junior academics, currently at 75%.
> (Chakrabortty and Weale 2016)

Traditionally academics employed by higher education institutions were largely permanent members of staff, who performed
both teaching and research duties. However, with the advent
of precarious contracts, there are now more people employed
on specific purpose contracts. These can be 'teaching-only'
or 'research-only' contracts, the latter specifying an end date.
Many teaching staff are also employed casually; they do not
have a written contract and are paid for the hours they teach and
nothing more. The rate of pay differs from one higher education institution to another, and is supposed to include preparation time. However, the reality is that many more hours go
into lecture or tutorial preparation than what the hourly pay
rate reflects. Casually paid lecturing staff are being paid neither
for follow-up nor for administrative responsibilities, which are
usually performed outside the hours they teach. The most security a casually paid lecturer/teaching assistant has is knowing
the number of hours allocated in an academic teaching term.
However, there is uncertainty over whether teaching hours will
be allocated once that teaching term is over. The hours are so
low that many casual staff must be supplemented by social wel-
fare (if they can get their hours to fit the part-time work supplement criteria[3]). It is also common to hold part-time teaching
jobs in more than one university.

Academic researchers are mostly employed on fixed-term contracts, and postdoctoral researchers in higher education institutions are designated as trainees. Fixed-term contracts can be rolled over for no more than two years, after which a Contract of Indefinite Duration (CID) must be awarded, or an objective reason for not awarding one must be given. Research and teaching staff hired on this basis receive the same entitlements as people on a permanent contract for the specified period of their employment. However, postdoctoral researchers are generally employed on fixed-purpose contracts, which specifies the end of their contract, thus not qualifying them for a CID.

Consequently, the fact that there is no career progression has a significant impact on salaries; although academics on precarious contracts may gain experience, the salary is not commensurate with that (Courtois and O'Keefe 2015, 56). Career progression in universities only comes about after employment as a full-time permanent lecturer, engaged in research for a number of years, and fixed-term or other temporary workers are not eligible for this. Consequently, although the figure is not available, turnover is a significant issue in departments where there is a high number of teaching fellows and research fellows. This means that academics who desire security of employment are forced to leave higher education altogether, or emigrate.

The implication of this is first, that insecurity can lead to self-censorship by precarious workers because they are less likely to challenge major assumptions or do anything that could be interpreted as controversial. Second, the anxiety of reaching the end of their contract and the financial hardship this entails leads their energies to be focused on finding further employment. This leads to problems with casual workers' health, housing, and ability to plan for the future. Third, precarity in higher education leads to marginalization and isolation both in terms of collegiality and of union representation.

Higher education institutions, permanent/tenured-track academics, and the BDS movement

Pledges in support of the academic boycott of Israel have been signed by academics working in higher education institutions around the world. However, academics have not just been signing the boycott pledge, but have also been instrumental in voicing criticism of Israel's human rights abuses in the occupied Palestinian territory and of its violations of international law against the Palestinian people. In some instances, this has led to them being reprimanded by their university or to losing their job.

For example, in October 2018, it emerged that two university teachers in the University of Michigan refused to write letters of recommendation for two students applying to study abroad in Israel. One of them, associate professor of American culture, John Cheney-Lippold, cited the BDS movement for the refusal, explaining, 'his protest didn't interfere with his teaching duties and was protected by his academic freedom'. He added, 'I can't prevent a student from going to Israel ... But everybody has the right to withhold something, and I chose to exercise that right based on what the movement needs from me as a solidarity activist' (Stanley-Becker 2018). Consequently, the dean of Michigan's College of Literature, Science, and the Arts told Cheney-Lippold

> that he would not qualify for a salary increase for the 2018–19 academic year ... and that his eligibility for sabbatical leave would be frozen for two years. Further conduct of this nature, the dean wrote, would be subject to additional discipline, 'up to and including initiation of dismissal proceedings'. (Stanley-Becker 2018)

Stephen Salaita, formerly a professor of English at Virginia Tech, accepted a new post at the University of Illinois Urbana-Champaign in the autumn of 2014, only to have his offer rescinded by the university trustees, following a number of tweets he posted about the

Israeli attack against Gaza in 2014. This led to student walkouts, to more than 5,000 academics pledging to boycott the university, and to condemnations from prominent academic organizations such as the AAUP. Subsequently, Salaita challenged his dismissal in court and was successful, and awarded a settlement. It also resulted in the resignation of the university's chancellor, Phyllis Wise, and the provost, Ilesanmi Adesida. However, while this is a victory for the BDS movement, unfortunately for Salaita, he has since had to leave academia for good. A search committee had selected Salaita for a directorship in the American University of Beirut (AUB). However, pressure put on the university by donors and US senators resulted in the cancellation of his appointment (Salaita 2019).

As Omar Shakir, one of the attorneys who represented Steven Salaita, wrote:

> Salaita has a stellar record as a scholar, having obtained tenure in 2009 at the age of 33 and published six books before the age of 40. If a university could get away with firing someone like him on the basis of tweets criticizing the policies of a foreign government, what does it means for the junior scholar weighing whether to sign a divestment petition? Or the student thinking of organizing a demonstration? (Shakir 2015)

If permanent, tenured academics face reprimand, then what are the prospects for precarious academics who lack the security of a permanent contract, are frequently forced to look for work, and are dependent on relationships with institutions and other academics to get this work?

Precarious work, contractual and financial insecurity, and self-censorship in academia

Contractual insecurity and the lack of employment protections under the law put precarious workers at a higher risk of dismissal and being out of employment. Nelson points out that precarious work is a threat to academic freedom because precarious academic workers 'work in fear of losing their jobs' and have 'no protection from students, parents, administrators, politicians or community members who may be offended by what they say in the classroom' (2010b, 54).

Searching for work forms a major part of the life of a precarious worker. The public nature of taking part in an academic boycott can have a negative impact on finding a new job. The boycott pledge list is usually published online. While there is merit in doing this, especially to demonstrate the effectiveness of the boycott, the personal impact of making your name public has to be acknowledged. Many employers are now using the internet and social media to screen applicants.[4] The public nature of signing up to the boycott pledge can also result in being scrutinized by the media. For example, the reprimands by the University of Michigan of associate professor of American culture John Cheney-Lippold and teaching assistant Lucy Peterson were publicized in the media. This kind of attention can have further implications for a precarious worker in finding new employment.

As we have seen in the case of Salaita's dismissal, permanent academics also face this threat. However, precarious academics have even less protections or no protections at all under the law. It is easier to dismiss a casual academic who does not have a contract, because of the casual nature of his or her work. Temporary academics can simply be told that their contract will not be renewed, and university authorities do not have to cite the real reason; there is a host of other reasons that fall within the law that the university hierarchy can use. In addition, for those on a fixed-term contract, it can simply mean the end of their contract with no possibility of renewal, which again is within the law.

Kristofer Petersen-Overton was employed by the City University of New York (CUNY) as an adjunct lecturer, teaching a graduate-level introductory course on the politics of the Middle East. A very public campaign to have him removed from his position ensued, first by a student, (who complained about the content of the syllabus and his connection to the 'Palestinian activist community'), followed by a New York State assemblyman who launched a public campaign against him. Just after the assemblyman's press statement was released, the college administration decided to intervene and cancelled his appointment. The college administration cited that he 'lacked the credentials necessary to teach a graduate-level course in political science' (Petersen-Overton 2011, 259).

Another example was where a senior colleague informed Mary (pseudonym), a precarious academic in an Irish university, that their contract would not be extended if they continued to co-organize with the Ireland Palestine Solidarity Campaign (IPSC) for visiting academics from Palestine and Israel to give talks and seminars in their university department. Another example is Arthur (pseudonym), who worked on a temporary basis in an Irish university. He was very active on the campus with other academics in raising awareness and campaigning for Palestine and the BDS movement. Arthur had participated in many peaceful demonstrations organized by academics and some students within the university, and his PI (principal investigator) became aware of this. It was at this point that the relationship started to become soured, although Arthur explained that it was discreet at this stage. Soon after, he was dismissed. His activism was not cited as the reason for his dismissal, but Arthur felt it was a catalyst that led to it. Consequently, this reveals how precarious academics are in a more vulnerable position; institutions of higher education can easily dismiss precarious academics without having to allude to the real reason for their dismissal/not renewing their contract. Arthur challenged his dismissal legally, and was awarded redundancy. However, he disclosed, 'this devastated my employability to the extreme'. He has been unable to find work in academia.

Thus, the temporary nature of their employment can lead to self-censorship. Consequently, it is unsurprising that precarious academics fear 'rocking the boat' (Courtois and O'Keefe 2015, 60). However, it is important to point out that many precarious academics do still take part in the BDS movement and the academic boycott of Israel. A case in point is Lucy Peterson, a University of Michigan teaching assistant who declined to recommend a student for a study abroad programme in Israel, citing BDS as her reason for her refusal. Peterson, questioned by the university's administration, was to be sanctioned by the university, although it has not been made public knowledge what this entailed. The contractual insecurity, however, is a feature that can make it easier for universities to sanction precarious academics.

Precarious work and relationships of dependency

Relationships both in work and outside work play an important role in the lives of precarious workers. Precarious workers often develop a social support network of people and organizations in order to cope financially with the insecurity and unpredictability of their working lives. According to the FEPS-TASC report on precarious work, this leads to dependency both in workers' working lives and in their private lives (Bobek, Pembroke and Wickham 2018, 86). Precarious work forces relationships of dependency with people outside the workplace, relying on family and partners to afford a place to live, or to help with food and bills. For precarious workers who have children this adds a further layer of dependency, because their children depend economically on their parents' ability to secure work.

For precarious academics, the relationships with managers, PIs, and supervisors are important networks that can contribute some security to their working lives, because these relationships ensure that more academic work can be obtained. This could work in a number of ways, including an extension to their contract, allocating more working hours, awarding another fixed-purpose contract for another project/teaching fellowship/lectureship, or being made permanent. Even if this network of senior academics cannot offer any of the above, it can open up networks and links for the precariat by writing letters of recommendation and making informal inquiries on behalf of the precarious workers.

For example, Julia (pseudonym) was advised by her permanent lecturing colleagues in the university to keep a low profile and not to take part in any activism related to the BDS movement and Palestine until after being made permanent. So much so that when an international conference was organized at the university on the topic of Israel, for which she was part of the organizing committee, her colleagues did not put her name down as an organizing member. This was done in order to protect Julia's employment prospects in the university.

Other senior permanent academics may also be key to ensuring that the doors are open for more work. We see this most prominently in the area of academic research funding. Only permanent members of staff can apply for most major research-funding calls, and in most instances, precarious academics are only in a position to apply for postdoctoral positions that arise from successful funding applications. Therefore, precarious academics can feel a pressure to maintain good relationships with other academics in their department.

For example, Arthur disclosed that he knew a colleague with whom he had a relatively good relationship in the university. He had asked him whether he was still looking for a job and Arthur had said he was. He said that he would help Arthur by speaking to another colleague in relation to a possible job opening. However, in the meantime, Arthur and this colleague discussed Palestine. The colleague kept silent in relation to his view on the topic. However, after this discussion, he never heard from this colleague again, even after he attempted to contact him to inquire about the prospective job opening.

Of course, if senior academics in a department are sympathetic, this ameliorates the situation. However, if this is not the case, precarious academics' dependency on permanent members of staff for further employment ultimately curtails their academic freedom.

The transient nature of precarious work and collegiality

Precarious work leads to a transient workforce employed for a fixed purpose or on a fixed-term research or teaching contract. The transient nature of precarious work in higher education institutions has a number of negative impacts. First, the precarious academic is constantly moving from one higher education institution to another. Second, the temporary nature of the precarious worker's contract means that she largely feels invisible in the department she works in. Courtois and O'Keefe (2015, 58) observed, 'precarity also isolates temporary workers, as they are often defined as outside department staff complement'. Consequently, for precarious workers this has a detrimental impact on collegiality (Slaughter and Leslie 1997). Precarious academics often complain of feeling invisible and transient and not being able to form relationships with fellow work colleagues. Oftentimes, a precarious academic is not in the department or institution for very long, so that by the time they might start feeling comfortable enough to speak up about an issue, their contract or hourly paid work may be finishing up.

The transience and invisibility associated with precarious work in higher-level institutions also poses a major impediment for academic freedom; if collegiality is low among precarious academics and between them and permanent academics, then it is very difficult to provide collegial support for precarious academics who take part in the academic boycott, or indeed in any form of activism. Therefore, this has a major impact for a precarious worker's academic freedom, because that layer of collegial support, which is so important for putting pressure on a university or head of department who threatens to impose disciplinary procedures or to dismiss a member of staff for the action they are taking, is missing.

Julia's example, where her permanent lecturer colleagues advised and protected her role in organizing a conference, is a case in point that demonstrates the importance of collegiality for precarious workers. Another example of collegial support was experienced by Kristofer Petersen-Overton. Students, activist groups, and prominent academics and advocacy groups pressured the college administration to reverse their decision, which they did. Julia and Kristofer were lucky to have that support; however, many precarious academics are not in the same boat.

Concluding comments

The purpose of this chapter is to highlight the ways in which precarious work in higher education curtails academic freedom, concurring with Clausen and Swidler that precarious academics do not have that right or freedom given that 'most of them risk forfeiting renewal of their teaching contracts ...' (2013, 4). This has a major impact on precarious academics who are taking part in the academic boycott of Israel. In conclusion, precarious work in higher education limits academic freedom in a number of ways.

First, the lack of protection and security of tenure is a major and obvious impediment to exercising academic freedom. Precarious workers' lack of contractual and financial security puts them at a greater risk of becoming unemployed for taking part in activism that the higher education institution, its donors, or permanent members oppose. Precarious working conditions give universities greater power over academics, because they have very few legal protections, thus making it very easy to dismiss a precarious worker on a legal basis. Ultimately, the threat of not finding further employment or not having their contract renewed can potentially have a negative impact on precarious academics who wish to exercise their academic freedom and take part in the academic boycott of Israel. The consequence of this is that precarity affects research and teaching but also the politics of academic activism.

Second, precarious work makes academics more dependent on a network of permanent academics in order to renew their contract, increase their hours, find more work, or be awarded a permanent contract. This support network is central to remaining in employment and out of poverty. Dependency is a subtler way of impeding academic freedom but it is an important one, as academic networks are a renowned source for finding more employment. Taking part in activism has the potential of alienating potential employers, particularly if it involves the workplace. Therefore, this factor alone can create a situation where self-censorship occurs.

Finally, the transient nature of precarious work means that it is quite usual to frequently move from one workplace to another, or even to be attached to more than one workplace, rather than a long period of employment. This has a negative impact on collegiality, where precarious workers feel invisible in the departments they work in. Collegiality is an important aspect of taking part in an academic boycott, because a level of support and pressure is available to challenge college authorities who attempt to threaten or stop an academic exercising her academic freedom. Salaita's dismissal has shown that collegiality was an important element of support. Yet, for precarious academics, collegiality is often missing because of the transient nature of their position, and this can limit academic freedom and participation in campaigns such as the academic boycott of Israel.

Ultimately, precarious work does not just create precarious lives, but also makes academic freedom practically non-existent. For as long as precarious work continues to increase, it will have a negative impact on the freedom not only to take part in academic activism, but also in research and teaching; by denying higher education workers permanent or tenure-tracked positions, the university influences what is taught and researched. In addition, as the number of precarious contracts continue to rise in higher-level institutions all over the world, we 'need to take the adjunct reality of unfreedom as the baseline reality of academia' (Clausen and Swidler 2013, 4).

As argued above, BDS activists are operating in a hostile climate, and this hostility is particularly poignant in higher education institutions. The lack of collegiality combined with limited legal employment protections for precarious workers curtails academic freedom, leading to self-censorship. These factors can potentially impact precarious workers taking part in the academic boycott of Israel.

Notes

1 Non-standard employment is defined as work that deviates from the Standard Employment Relationship (SER), including temporary contracts, fixed-term contracts, part-time work and self-employment (https://www.ilo.org/global/topics/non-standard-employment/lang--en/index.htm accessed 24 June 2019).

2 Atypical contracts are another term used for non-standard employment, and are generally defined as employment contracts that do not conform to a standard, open-ended, and full-time contract.

3 A person can work up to three days per week and receive Job Seekers' Benefit/Allowance. However, for each day that one works and receives Job Seekers' Allowance or Benefit, they lose the daily rate of payment.

4 For more information, see https://www.careerbuilder.com/advice/ social-media-survey-2017 (accessed 24 June 2019).

References

American Association of University Professors (AAUP) (2018), 'Background Facts on Contingent Faculty Positions', American Association of University Professors, http://www.aup.org/issues/contingency/background-facts.

Bobek, A., S. Pembroke and J. Wickham (2018), *Living with Uncertainty: The Social Implications of Precarious Work*, Dublin: FEPS-TASC, https://www.tasc.ie/publications/living-with-uncertainty-the-social-implications-o/ (accessed 24 June 2019).

Broughton, A., M. Green, C. Rickard, S. Swift, W. Eichhorst, V. Tobsch, I. Magda, P. Lewandowski, R. Keister, D. Jonaviciene, N. E. Ramos Martin, D. Valsamis and F. H. Tros (2016), *Precarious Employment in Europe, Part 1: Patterns, Trends and Policy Strategy* (Employment and Social Affairs), Brussels: European Parliament, Directorate-General for Internal Policies, Policy Department A: Economic and Scientific Policy.

Chakrabortty, A. and S. Weale (2016), 'Universities Accused of "Importing Sports Direct Model" for Lecturers' Pay', *The Guardian*, 16 November, https://www.theguardian.com/uk-news/2016/nov/16/universities-accused-of-importing-sports-direct-model-for-lecturers-pay (accessed 2 November 2019).

Clausen, J. and E.-M. Swidler (2013) 'Academic Freedom from Below: Toward an Adjunct-Centred Struggle', *Journal of Academic Freedom* 4: 1–26.

Courtois, A. and T. O'Keefe (2015), 'Precarity in the Ivory Cage: Neoliberalism and Casualisation of Work in the Irish Higher Education Sector', *Journal for Critical Education Policy Studies* 13 (1): 43–66.

Cush, M. (2016), *Report to the Minister for Education and Skills of the Chairperson of the Expert Group on Fixed Term and Part-time Employment in Lecturing in Third Level Education in Ireland*, Dublin: Department of Education and Skills.

Eurofound (2017), *Aspects of Non-standard Employment in Europe*, https://www.eurofound.europa.eu/publications/customised-report/2017/aspects-of-non-standard-employment-in-europe (accessed 24 June 2019).

Frase, P. (2013), 'The Precariat: A Class or a Condition?', *New Labor Forum* 22 (2):

Gash, V. (2008), 'Bridge or Trap? Temporary Workers' Transitions to Unemployment and to the Standard Employment Contract', *European Sociological Review* 24 (5): 651–688.

Guitierrez-Barbarrusa, T. (2016), 'The Growth of Precarious Employment in Europe: Concepts, Indicators and the Effects of the Global Economic Crisis', *International Labour Review* 155 (4): 477–508.

International Labour Organization (2012), *From Precarious Work to Decent Work*, https://www.ilo.org/wcmsp5/groups/public/---ed_dialogue/---actrav/documents/meetingdocument/wcms_179787.pdf (accessed 24 June 2019).

Nelson, C. (2010a), 'Defining Academic Freedom', *Inside Higher Ed*, 21 December, https://www.insidehighered.com/views/2010/12/21/defining-academic-freedom (accessed 24 June 2019).

Nelson, C. (2010b), *No University Is an Island: Saving Academic Freedom*, New York: New York University Press.

Orr, A. M. (2018), 'Teaching Sociology: The Precariousness of Academic Freedom', *Sociological Perspectives* 62 (1): 5–22.

Pembroke, S. (2018), *Precarious Work Precarious Lives: How Policy Can Create More Security*, Dublin: FEPS-TASC, https://www.tasc.ie/download/pdf/precarious_workersweb_version.pdf (accessed 24 June 2019).

Petersen-Overton, K. J. (2011) 'Academic Freedom and Palestine: A Personal Account', *Arab Studies Quarterly* 33 (3/4): 256–267.

Rubery, J., A. Keizer and D. Grimshaw (2016), 'Flexibility Bites Back: The Multiple and Hidden Costs of Flexible Employment Policies', *Human Resource Management Journal* 26 (3): 235–251.

Salaita, S. (2019), 'An Honest Living', 19 February, https://stevesalaita.com/an-honest-living/ (accessed 10 March 2019).

Shakir, O. (2015), 'Why Salaita Settlement Is a Victory for Palestine Solidarity Movement', *The Electronic Intifada*, 24 November, https://electronicintifada.net/content/why-salaita-settlement-victory-palestine-solidarity-movement/15028 (accessed 11 November 2018).

Slaughter, S. and L. Leslie (1997), *Academic Capitalism*, Baltimore, MD: Johns Hopkins Press.

Stanley-Becker, I. (2018), 'University of Michigan Promises to Discipline Faculty in Israel Boycott Controversy', *The Washington Post*, 11 October, https://www.washingtonpost.com/news/morning-mix/wp/2018/10/11/university-of-michigan-promises-to-discipline-faculty-in-israel-boycott-controversy/?noredirect=on&utm_term=.884f4d28fadc (accessed 15 March 2018).

Vosko, L. F. (2010), *Managing the Margins: Gender, Citizenship and the International Regulation of Precarious Employment*, Oxford: Oxford University Press.

PART II | Colonial erasure in higher education

SIX | Colonial apologism and the politics of academic freedom

John Reynolds†

> The intellectual always has a choice either to side with the
> weaker, the less well represented, the forgotten or ignored, or to
> side with the more powerful.
>
> Edward Said (1996, 32–33)

Introduction

In 1969, the board of regents of the University of California,
Los Angeles ordered the firing of Angela Davis on the basis
of her membership of the Communist Party USA. When a
California Superior Court overturned this decision, Governor
Ronald Reagan continued his crusade to have her fired. The
board of regents successfully fired Davis the following year,
based this time on what they adjudged as her unprofessional
conduct and uncivil rhetoric in critiquing institutionalized racism and sexism. Academic freedom did not apply to protect
Angela Davis. Her position and her freedom to speak on and
off campus was rendered contingent on conforming to certain
brands of professionalism and civility, a requirement which
she was adjudged to have failed. During the post-McCarthy
period of the 1960s, the persecution of socialist academics in
the United States had evolved:

> More sophisticated university administrations and boards of
> trustees began to speak of the sanctity of the marketplace-of-
> ideas and the violation of institutional neutrality by radical
> faculty. The overt anti-communist evaluative criteria of the

1950s, and the earlier treatment of faculty as at-will employees, were replaced by more nuanced, yet just as ideologically-biased standards. (Aby 2007, 289-290)

Anti-capitalist, anti-racist, anti-war, and anti-imperial intellectuals were the primary targets; their academic freedom liable to be stripped back. Scholars who by contrast defended the status quo, including its structures of racial and imperial dominance, were not affected in the same way.

Fifty years on, and while we are at a very different political juncture in many ways, contestations over race and colonialism persist in academic discourse and institutions in the Western Anglosphere. The stories of racialized scholars like Steven Salaita, Johnny Eric Williams, and Tommy Curry show that when it comes to the expression of anti-colonial and anti-racist positions, academic freedom remains vulnerable and conditional. At the same time, we have seen in recent years a resurgence of academic freedom arguments being deployed in the service of colonialism. Such arguments are of course not new, but have metastasized in a wider context involving the proliferation of a certain type of free speech advocacy that exudes quite particular right-wing forms and agendas. In this chapter I reflect on how academic freedom has operated in specific instances to defend work that distorts the legacy of historical colonialism and to insulate the status quo in spaces of ongoing colonization.

I begin by sketching out the contemporary context in which scholarly justifications of colonialism and even nostalgia for the privileges of empire have proliferated. The implications of academic journals publishing and defending 'provocative' articles – explicitly exalting the legacies of colonialism – under the banner of academic freedom are significant. A recent journal essay putting forward 'The Case for Colonialism' (Gilley 2017a) is symptomatic of this. This is not a case of arguments about history being advanced in a vacuum; they map closely onto the very real political struggles of the present. I then look at another recent example of this in the framing of a piece of scholarship which presents colonizers as victims rather than aggressors (Bennett 2017). This taps into a certain sense of racial-imperial victimhood in the prevailing political conjuncture.

The central argument of my chapter is that 'academic freedom' claims often operate as a medium through which traditional power dynamics are reproduced. Certain imperial narratives are amplified, while anti-imperial stances and voices are side-lined, and actual experiences of colonialism are rendered debatable. Whereas we might think that anti-colonial challenges to racial and imperial discourses offer a more meaningful illumination of the substance and necessity of academic freedom as an ideal, they must be conscious of the structural context in which they are engaged.

Colonial apologism

In March 2003 *The Spectator* published a think-piece by Daniel Kruger titled 'The Case for Colonialism'. The 'case' in this instance was that 'the [British] empire was essentially a humanitarian undertaking' and that 'Africa's problem today is not the after-effects of colonialism but ... socialism, and its related grievance culture' (Kruger 2003). Countries in the global South are poor, according to Kruger, because they do not have strong property rights or banking systems and have not sufficiently committed themselves to free trade. Centuries of slavery and resource extraction do not factor in this analysis. Indeed, the core 'humanitarian' credential of empire was that it brought about the end of the transatlantic slave trade. The origins of that very trade are left hanging: unacknowledged and esoteric.

Lest we assume that such specious imperial nostalgia would by definition be confined to the pages of a right-wing British magazine boasting Boris Johnson as its editor at the time, this line of argument has repeatedly surfaced in scholarly publications. In 2017, *Third World Quarterly* published an essay by Bruce Gilley, likewise titled 'The Case for Colonialism'. Gilley asserted that European colonialism was 'both objectively beneficial and subjectively legitimate in most of the places where it was found'. He lamented the harm caused by anti-colonial thinking and called for new incarnations of Western colonialism today: 'Colonialism can be recovered by weak and fragile states today in three ways: by reclaiming colonial modes of governance; by recolonizing some areas; and by creating new Western colonies from scratch' (Gilley 2017a, 1). Here we must note that the recurring motifs of reconquest and recolonization which inhabit this brand of colonial apologist scholarship are not without impact. They periodically surface in mainstream Western political discourse. In late 2018, for example, a senior German government official floated a genuine proposal that the European Union or the World Bank be empowered to acquire land in Africa with a mandate to build and run 'charter' cities there to boost development and curb migration to Europe (Zhangaza 2018).

Gilley's essay is perhaps an anomaly in terms of *where* it was published – an academic journal which had been founded in the 1970s as 'an intellectual venue for anti-colonial thought' (Dawes et al. 2017) and widely respected by postcolonial scholars. It is less of an anomaly, however, in terms of *what* it says as a piece of academic work. Gilley is situated within a prevailing neoconservative scholarly milieu. His piece echoes and escalates the revisionist views of empire produced by right-wing historians such as Andrew Roberts and Niall Ferguson from around the time of the Western-led invasions of Afghanistan and Iraq (Ferguson 2003a).

Roberts's work, for example, attempted to justify one of the more infamous British colonial atrocities – the Amritsar massacre, in which British troops emptied round after round of ammunition into a large civilian crowd attending a Sikh new year festival event in Punjab in 1919, killing several hundreds and wounding many more. He likewise defended the concentration camps established in South Africa during the Anglo–Boer War, on the basis that 'they were run as efficiently and humanely as possible' (Roberts 2006, 31). The company that Roberts keeps is also revealing: in 2001 he gave a lecture at a celebratory event of the Springbok Club – a group that considers itself the shadow white government of South Africa in exile and calls for 'the reestablishment of civilised European rule throughout the African continent' (Hari 2009).

A month into the war in Iraq ('a screwed-up, sun-scorched sandpit'), Ferguson, for his part, proudly described himself as 'a fully paid-up member of the neo-imperialist gang'. He advised the US administration that if it was serious about its civilizing mission in Iraq it really should have been stacking its diplomatic corps with genuine Orientalists and planning for a 40-year occupation rather than a fleeting 'crypto-imperial' in-and-out job (Ferguson 2003b).

The work of these academics has had traction in conservative political circles. Roberts's fallacious claim about the humane nature of the British concentration camps in South Africa was recently stretched to the point of absurdity by Tory member of parliament Jacob Rees-Mogg (Saunders 2019). Roberts has also painstakingly and self-importantly documented his cosy relations with the likes of Henry Kissinger, John Bolton, Karl Rove, Dick Cheney, and Nicolas Sarkozy. Most notable here is his mutual admiration society with George W. Bush (Roberts 2007). Roberts advised Bush that mass internment – on the basis of what he saw as its success in Ireland – 'is the way the administration of Iraq should go' (Hari 2009).

Ferguson's intellectual work with Kissinger and role as an advisor to John McCain is well-known. He was also recruited by Tory education minister Michael Gove in 2011 to contribute to an overhaul of the British history curriculum. The curriculum ultimately produced by this process was praised by Ferguson – in the face of widespread criticism from fellow historians that it was 'a Little England version of our national past ... a mindless regression to the patriotic myths of the Edwardian era' (Ferguson 2013). It was also said that Ferguson's 'imprint in British political thinking is clearest, perhaps, in Gove's writing on foreign affairs' (Vasagar 2012). Gove himself has indeed praised Ferguson for analysing 'the legacy of the British empire with a balanced mind ... ready to acknowledge its progressive side' (Gove 2006).

Such a 'both sides' approach to the study of colonialism is replicated in the five-year interdisciplinary 'Ethics and Empire' project, launched in 2017 by Oxford theology professor Nigel Biggar. Its core aim is to conduct a cost–benefit analysis of imperial history to test the critiques of empire, offset its negatives with positives, and to 'develop a nuanced and historically intelligent Christian ethic of empire' (McDonald Centre 2017). In publicizing this project, Biggar wrote in support of Gilley's case for colonialism describing it as a 'courageous call for a balanced reappraisal of the colonial past' which can help 'us British to moderate our post-imperial guilt', so that 'pride can temper shame' (Biggar 2017). While couched as a rational scientific analysis of empire, in opposition to emotive and untested negative characterizations, the starting premise underlying this work is clear – an intuition (and a resulting political sensibility) of colonialism as a benevolent and democratizing force for good. The politics at play are also clear from the further stated intentions of 'Ethics and Empire' ('to enable a morally sophisticated negotiation of contemporary issues such as military intervention for humanitarian purposes in culturally foreign states') and from Biggar's own summation of the lessons of Iraq and Afghanistan: 'that successful intervention requires more, earlier' (Biggar 2017).

This is situated in a particular lineage of pro-colonial scholarship which seeks to sanitize the historical realities of European empire and to justify a continuing imperial dynamic of interference and extraction in the global South. Weighing the pros and cons of five centuries of European conquest, slave-trading, resource plunder, and anti-democratic governance, 'the "costs" of genocide and dispossession of lands are absurdly placed on a plane of equivalence with the supposed "benefits" of colonial rule' (Rose-Redwood et al. 2017). The long tradition of anti-colonial writing by people subjected to empire and the praxis of liberation movements are also nowhere to be found in these balance sheets of colonial nostalgia. As a result, the conclusion often arrived at by those adopting this approach is that on aggregate, colonialism is economically and/or socially beneficial for the colonized (a caricature justification as old as colonialism itself). Such a conclusion has been consistently and persuasively debunked by scholars of empire – both long before (Rodney 1972; Young 1994; Nunn 2008; Dell 2010; Heldring and Robinson 2012; Michalopoulos and Papaioannou 2016; Acemoğlu and Robinson 2017) and in direct response to Gilley's and Biggar's commentaries (Robinson 2017; Khan 2017; Malik 2018).

Apart from the fallacy of the claim to colonialism's net benefit, there are fundamental problems with an approach premised on 'a sinister accounting exercise featuring smallpox vaccination campaigns in one column, forced labour and torture in the other' (Dupraz and Rueda 2017). Such an approach allows the violent, racist, and anti-democratic essence of colonialism to be subtracted (from artificial comparative measurements of socio-economic development) in its final tally. A similarly absurd rationale has been deployed most recently in the reasoning that 'even though Winston Churchill was a lifelong white supremacist his strengths far outweigh his weaknesses' (Finklestein 2019).

From the outset of postcolonial scholarship in the 1950s, Aimé Césaire's *Discourse on Colonialism* powerfully disposed of French geographer Pierre Gourou's 'bourgeois attempt' to draw up 'the balance sheet on colonization' (Césaire 1955, 57, 62). In *How Europe Underdeveloped Africa*, Walter Rodney likewise confronted the 'bourgeois writers' who suggested it necessary and appropriate to perform a balancing act in the appraisal of colonialism: 'On that balance sheet, they place both the "credits" and the "debits", and quite often conclude that the good outweighed the bad'. Drawing on extensive empirical data and multiple examples from across the African continent, Rodney methodically dismantles such conclusions as 'completely false'. At the same time, he questions the underlying premise of the balance sheet methodology. He emphasizes that 'attention should also be drawn to the fact that the process of reasoning is itself misleading'; the sentiment that 'after all there must be two sides to a thing' is deceptive (Rodney 1972, 205). The idea that these two sides exist in some comparable form and warrant symmetrical consideration effectively entails wilful blindness to glaring asymmetry.

These are among the foundational texts in the vast body of postcolonial critique which Gilley does not acknowledge or engage. His case for colonialism is built on an entirely disingenuous premise in blanking out the inherent violence and racism of colonialism. For those reasons, presumably, the recommendation of three out of four peer reviewers in two separate review processes undertaken by *Third World Quarterly* was that Gilley's article be rejected.

In the process that follows we can unpack the work done by academic freedom. Rather than declining the submission after the first two reviewers rejected it for a special issue, an editorial decision was taken to review it again and repackage and publish it as a 'viewpoint' essay (as distinct from a research article). The essay was widely criticized for its historical inaccuracies and lack of scholarly rigour. The journal was criticized for failing in its responsibility to uphold academic standards and the ethical duty to reject work 'promoting the subjugation of peoples and abuses of fundamental freedoms' (Rose-Redwood et al. 2017). The fall-out prompted 15 of the 34 members of *Third World Quarterly*'s editorial board to call for the article to be retracted – on grounds that 'it fails to provide reliable findings, as demonstrated by its failure in the double-blind peer review process' – and then to resign following an editorial decision not to do so (Kapoor et al. 2017). The majority position of the journal's editorial team and board was apparently to stand behind the publication of the article. A statement issued by the editor-in-chief sought to explain the issue away as one of normal and valid academic debate:

> by publishing this article we are not endorsing its pro-colonial views … we are however presenting it to be debated within the field and academy … We will now continue this debate by publishing contradicting anti-colonial viewpoints, to firmly challenge this opinion in the very best academic tradition.

Thus the journal defended its publication of a piece of academic 'clickbait' (Roelofs and Gallien 2017) and then invoked academic freedom in order to legitimate a debate on the merits of colonialism.

The essay was subsequently 'withdrawn' with Gilley's consent, reportedly due to death threats received by the editor-in-chief from Indian nationalists. It was, importantly, not retracted by the journal, whose publisher maintained that 'the essay had undergone double-blind peer review, in line with the journal's editorial policy' (Taylor and Francis 2017). The *Third World Quarterly* version of the article remains freely available on Gilley's university website page, listed as a 'peer-reviewed research article'. It was republished in 2018 by *Academic Questions*, the journal of the conservative US-based National Association of Scholars, 'in support of academic freedom' (Gilley 2018; National Association of Scholars 2018).

While there have been forceful criticisms of Gilley's essay and questions of 'factual inaccuracies, wanting scholarly depth, and sheer disdain for formerly colonised peoples' (Oxford University Africa Society 2017), any suggestions of disciplinary measures or other repercussions were swiftly knocked on the head by the invocation of academic freedom. Gilley's defenders have sought to characterize the situation otherwise, arguing that the principles of academic freedom have been betrayed (Alderman 2017). A letter to *The Times* signed by 82 academics including eight *Third World Quarterly* editorial board members portrayed the voluntary withdrawal of the article as 'a dangerous precedent for academic freedom' (Cunliffe et al. 2017). Gilley's academic freedom – to conduct his research, publishing, and teaching without institutional sanction or censorship – has not been abdicated in any way, however. Another *Third World Quarterly* board member with substantive sway, Noam Chomsky, entered the fray to stress the importance of Gilley's academic freedom (Ngo 2017).

Gilley has described those who criticized his article as a 'hate mob', and analogized them to a Nazi occupation force: 'Taking my family out of Portland and over the Cascade Mountains for a holiday in central Oregon, I felt like Captain von Trapp leading his family out of fascist Austria into Switzerland' (Gilley 2017b). He claims that 'when academic freedom was threatened', his university 'crouched in the dark' (Van Schoonhoven 2018). Gilley has not been disciplined, censored, or persecuted; he has not been stripped of any academic freedom by state or university. There was no question of his position being in jeopardy. In multiple public statements, the university and its senior management were clear in their deference to academic freedom:

> While Portland State University does not endorse the viewpoints of Professor Gilley's article, we are committed to academic freedom. As such, we acknowledge the right of all our faculty to explore scholarship and to speak, write and publish a variety of viewpoints and conclusions. Ever since Professor Gilley's article was published last year, Portland State has consistently stated its commitment to academic freedom. (Portland State University 2018)

Through 2018, Gilley continued to propound his case for colonialism. In May 2018, Oxford University's McDonald Centre for Theology, Ethics and Public Life hosted a full-day colloquium for Gilley to discuss his article with 30 senior academics in the fields of history, economics, ethics, and international relations, as well as former (colonial) civil servants. In November 2018, he was invited to deliver a lecture at the Institute for the Study of Western Civilization at Texas Tech University. A group of faculty members formally objected to this event taking place. The university's president and provost issued a memorandum to staff saying, 'we emphatically believe that there is no case for colonialism. A system built on the subjugation of one people by another cannot be defended'. However, they said, academic freedom and free speech – even to say and publish that which 'we consider objectionable and potentially harmful' – takes priority: 'we encourage those who have concerns to attend and engage in a healthy debate with Dr Gilley' (Schovanec and Galyean 2018).

Despite claims to the contrary, Gilley has continued to enjoy full academic freedom. My point here is not to argue the merits of this, but to emphasize that Western university defences of academic freedom have been unflinching in instances of pro-colonial scholarship. The colonial (senti)mentality that pervades the work being defended here 'provides fertile ground where misconstruals of the past can grow and contribute to mis-education and misguided decisions in the present' (Oxford University Africa Society 2017). European colonialism was a project of capitalist expansionism which necessitated racial ordering. It thus generated, and was structured upon ideologies and legal regimes of racial superiority. Any defence of the specific project of European colonialism incorporates by implication a defence of white supremacy (Saha 2018). Where academic freedom is invoked as a shield in this context, it crystallizes as the freedom to produce scholarship which reproduces a form of race-thinking.

Colonial victimhood

Following the debacle around his article, Gilley did admit to disregarding colonial atrocities and 'overstating' his claim that colonial regimes were viewed as legitimate by Indigenous populations ('we simply don't have sufficient data') (Gilley 2017b). He nonetheless doubled down on his position that 'colonialism's benefits usually exceeded its harms' as somehow a matter of empirical fact (Gilley 2017b). While he criticizes anti-colonial thought for oversimplification – and presents his own work in contrast as being about honestly and intricately tracing the many varied hues, complexities, and layers to the question of colonial rule – Gilley's own stated viewpoint is not complex: 'To say, as I did, that colonialism was mostly good, in the economic and social sense of the word, is merely to state the obvious' (Gilley 2017b). In a subsequent interview he reiterates the point: 'Colonialism did more right than wrong. Period' (Van Schoonhoven 2018).

Gilley refuses to acknowledge the idea that colonialism is comparable (or connected, or formative) to genocide. When it is put to him 'that journals have an ethical responsibility to reject an article defending colonialism just as they do one defending genocide', Gilley dismisses this out of hand, despite the historical facts of the very foundations of European colonialism being rooted in genocide of Indigenous populations: 'It's an absurd analogy. Genocide, I think everyone would agree, is a moral wrong. There's absolutely no plausible philosophical argument that one group of people establishing authority over another is an inherent moral wrong' (quoted in Patel 2018). This claim that there is not even an argument to be made for self-determination (or democracy) on moral terms is staggering. As is Gilley's flippant attitude to colonial genocide:

Interviewer: What of the Tasmanian genocide, in which the aboriginal population was wiped out by colonists with British government connivance?

Gilley: I don't know anything about Tasmania but every time I look at one of these allegedly uncontestable evils of colonialism, I find a more complex story (Macintyre 2018).

It is indeed notable that the only mention of genocide in Gilley's essay is reference to a speculative suggestion that had it not been for British state rule and its necessary 'brutalities' through the 1950s in Kenya, the anti-colonial Mau-Mau movement might have been inclined itself to perpetrate genocide (Gilley 2017a, 3). This is a common trope of pro-colonial scholarship: that colonialism is defensible on the basis that anti-imperial violence and resistance existed, or might have existed were it not for the gift of colonial law and order. In this outlook, given the choice between the supposedly civilized violence of the European state and the supposedly savage violence of the native rabble, the former is preferable.

Elements of the academic literature in this milieu have not only occluded actual historical colonial genocide, but in some instances have also gone as far as characterizing anti-colonial violence against colonial invaders as itself genocidal. I turn now to an example of this from my own field of international law. Historically, international law (in terms of both practice and the academy) has been quite deeply implicated in the justification and facilitation of European colonialism, all the way back to the Spanish conquests of the Americas. Recent Third World scholarship on international law has done significant work in exposing that legacy and sparking a vibrant critical scholarship on the history of international law, with a transformative view to constructing a more egalitarian global order today.

The *Journal of the History of International Law* has been an important forum for this scholarship, and one that explicitly pitches itself as such. The lead article in the 2017 volume was therefore jarring: a piece arguing that Native Americans were responsible for committing genocide against English colonizers in Virginia (Bennett 2017). When it appeared, the article was received by many international lawyers as hugely problematic, as wholly lacking in rigour (O'Donoghue and Jones 2017), and as anachronistic and troubling in its confusion of killing with genocide (Berkowitz 2017). The article was also seen as reflective of a very dubious political agenda. The author, John Bennett, is a practising lawyer who was previously a US military officer in Iraq and Afghanistan. Before publishing this journal article, he was writing semi-regular blog posts on a right-wing website (*American Thinker*) in which he maligned migrants and minorities in the United States, denounced diversity and affirmative action programmes, and critiqued civil rights agendas as incapable of ameliorating 'cultural pathology' (Bennett 2013).

Leaving aside Bennett's own credentials and predilections, the major concern raised by many readers and former authors of the journal was the decision of its editors to publish the article. The primary goal of the response of critical international lawyers was to delegitimize the article and the journal's publication process, rather than to engage with the article substantively. The process here was indicative of what happens when scholarly editors function as professional intellectuals (Said 1996) while lacking a political compass to guide their decisions. The absence of a political ethic had allowed the article to slip through the editor's radar as just another article about just another conflict where there was violence on both sides and one side committed genocide. The significance of publishing an article asserting there was a Native American genocide *against* the colonizers failed to register. That this episode came on the back of a relative renaissance of critical Third Worldist work in international law, and amidst methodological debates over the 'proper' uses of history suggests that it also presented itself as a useful offset for editors concerned with maintaining 'balance'.

After receiving strong criticisms from international legal scholars (O'Donoghue and Jones 2017; Tzouvala et al. 2017 – myself included), the editor-in-chief admitted that the article had not been through a full peer review process. A message was posted on 24 August 2017 on the *Critical Legal Thinking* blog in which the editors collectively 'acknowledge that the paper should not have been published in the JHIL'. This was subsequently replaced by a new statement posted by the editor-in-chief two weeks later which retained the acknowledgement that there were flaws in the review process, but removed the admission that the article should not have been published. It seems clear that some of the other editors were not on board with this admission. Following this, the journal decided not to retract or withdraw the article, nor to attach a disclaimer statement to the published version. The reasoning for this was grounded in the belief that academic freedom protects the author and that this should take precedence. In spite of the fundamental problems highlighted, and the fundamental editorial failings admitted, the editors doubled down and insisted the author's academic freedom should not be abrogated. Again we see the logic of professionalism trumping that of principle, with academic freedom serving as the normative conduit.

The appearance of this alternative historical version of a dubious 'white genocide' narrative in a reputable academic journal at this particular juncture cannot be viewed entirely in isolation from the primary meaning and associations that 'white genocide' has assumed in public discourse in North America and Europe. It was an unhappy but telling coincidence that the controversy over this particular article – alleging anti-white genocide, written by an alt-right pundit – emerged in August 2017 just days after the now-infamous white nationalist march on Charlottesville, Virginia where participants chanted 'you will not replace us', 'Jews will not replace us', 'blacks will not replace us', 'blood and soil', and 'white lives matter' (*Politico* 2018).

The white genocide narrative has become a watchword among white nationalists for phenomena they see as threatening white majority status in the West – immigration, inter-racial relationships, multiculturalism, and ethnic diversity as a form of genocide by integration. It is a figment of the racist imagination which taps into anxieties around the idea of post-racial society and the erasure of white nationhood. It is a myth that allows right-wing commentators like Ann Coulter to garner conservative currency and generate libertarian free speech bandwagons when they embrace the mantra that 'diversity is a code word for white genocide', and argue that if the demographic changes brought about by migration 'were legally imposed on any group other than white Americans, it would be called genocide' (Coulter 2007). It also lingers, unsaid but unavoidable, beneath the framing of scholarly 'debates' that ask: 'Is Rising Ethnic Diversity a Threat to the West?' (Alakbarov et al. 2018). Such debates, like the premise underpinning Bennett's article, are the academic rendering of the 'politics of aggrieved whiteness' produced by increasing sentiments among white majority populations that they have become an oppressed racial group (King 2017). This aggrieved whiteness and the discursive strategies of 'victim–perpetrator reversal' (Wodak 2015) which it engineers have proved very productive for the colonial apologist. While such a notion of majority victimhood is an obvious fabrication, it has found a certain traction for its claims that deference to multiculturalism and political correctness is the hegemonic consensus in academia, that this consensus is disinterested in complexity and intolerant of alternative viewpoints, and thus that conservatives who merely want to 'debate ideas' are the victims being silenced. Their ideas just so happen to fixate on questions of demography, migration, and colonialism in a way that conjures clear racial narratives. They are, however, proffered in a purportedly post-racial paradigm which strips away the material realities of race and imperialism to render it a 'detached' discussion of governance methods. Academic freedom is then commandeered to jettison the argument that this is in fact an expression of racial supremacy.

Academic freedom's contingency

When a term like 'white genocide' starts to gain traction in the Western world, it means that when anti-racist scholars write about structural racism or engage in philosophical debates over the use of violence in self-defence, they are subject to orchestrated right-wing campaigns. The response of their universities, rather than standing with them and defending academic freedom, has in some cases been to publicly rebuke or discipline them. After political scientist George Ciccariello-Maher made mocking reference to the white genocide myth in late 2016, he was met with an organized backlash of far-right, white supremacist harassment. His employer, Drexel University, put out a statement almost immediately condemning his satirical commentary as 'inflammatory' and 'utterly reprehensible'. The chair of the American Association of University Professors Committee on Academic Freedom argued that in doing so Drexel had infringed upon Ciccariello-Maher's academic freedom and should apologize to him (Reichman 2016). Instead, the university placed him under investigation for this and other public statements that had revved up the right-wing outrage machine, including a sociologically grounded interrogation of the question as to why mass shootings in the United States are almost always perpetrated by white males (Ciccariello-Maher, 2017). Following this, Ciccariello-Maher was put on forced administrative leave. This only served to fan the flames of his ongoing harassment, culminating in his decision at the end of 2017 to resign from Drexel.

Johnny Eric Williams, an African-American sociology professor, was likewise put on forced leave by his institution (Trinity College, Connecticut) over his public engagement on questions of race. Williams called for an 'end to the vectors of the destructive mythology of whiteness and the white supremacy system'. When he was criticized by conservative outlets for advocating violence (and in some interpretations genocide) against white people, he made clear that this was absolutely not the case; that what he was advocating was for people to oppose systemic racism and the construct of race itself. The president of his university nonetheless issued a fairly scathing criticism of Williams and made the somewhat vacuous assertion that his situation evoked 'principles that concern how we think about academic freedom and freedom of speech, as well as the responsibilities that come with those fundamental values' (Flaherty 2017). The university then made quite clear how it thought about academic freedom by putting Williams on punitive leave after he had declined a request to go on voluntary leave. The American Association of University Professors characterized this as an adverse disciplinary action which amounted to a 'clear violation of the professor's academic freedom'. Republican state legislators and alumni donors continued to call for him to be fired. A subsequent review cleared Williams of any wrongdoing and the university partially rolled back on its earlier position, though without acknowledging the harm done to Williams by the disciplinary measures and public reprimands to which he was subjected.

The story of Palestinian-American scholar of Native American studies, Steven Salaita is another well-known case (Salaita 2015; Reynolds 2016). The University of Illinois at Urbana-Champaign revoked his appointment to a tenured professorship over his critiques of Israeli colonial violence. The extent to which academic freedom was rendered meaningless in that instance is starkly highlighted by Corey Robin's summation of the university's position: 'at the University of Illinois at Urbana-Champaign, academic freedom is the freedom to pursue the widest possible range of viewpoints and positions, except for those that are not consistent with our values, which must reflect the values of the state' (Robin 2015). Salaita has been purged not just from that particular tenured position, but from the Western academy in general. He took a temporary position at the American University in Beirut, where he was unable to secure another full-time appointment. He now works, 'content with a new sense of purpose', as a school bus driver (Salaita 2019).

Thus we see that there are particular challenges for academics who critique racism and colonialism as part of their work, or who partake in anti-colonial boycotts that are increasingly threatened by legal sanction. The application of academic freedom principles in these contexts has been mixed at best. When we contrast the measures taken against these scholars on the one hand with the protections guaranteed to pro-colonial academics and positions discussed earlier on the other, we see the ways in which the indeterminacy of academic freedom often still results in practice in its alignment with establishment conservatism. Academic freedom has been strongly defended in relation to academics who publish problematic pro-colonial work or who host academic events (as the European Society of International Law did in 2018) in Israeli universities involved in the colonization of Palestinian territory (Abi-Saab at el. 2017). Academic freedom does not cut so clearly the other way to protect anti-colonial speech, scholarship, and association. This illustrates how the politics of academic freedom in the West are to a large extent ensnared by the tentacles of managerialism and the professional orthodoxies which underpin power dynamics in the modern university.

The critical point, then, is that when we talk about academic freedom, we have to be cognizant that critical or dissenting speech is subject to background limitations that precede the explicit limitations on speech defined by courts and institutions. Like freedom of expression more broadly, academic freedom is a form of 'non-partisan tolerance' (Marcuse 1969) insofar as it is formally granted in equal measures to all protagonists – but in doing so it practically functions to lock in any already established disparities, so that the premise of a level playing field is often illusory. As a result, some people effectively have more academic freedom than others.

Writing after the experience of his own academic freedom being curtailed by disciplinary measures, Johnny Eric Williams found that the academic freedom to speak out and pursue political or provocative research is most often 'not afforded faculty who are of the wrong political persuasion, "race", or religion. Suppression of academic freedom is especially pronounced for socially defined black faculty who critically examine white supremacy'. The ways in which academic freedoms are contingent and loaded in this sense have a depoliticizing effect which serves 'to ensure that most faculty will not use their teaching and scholarship to foment the social seeds necessary to mobilize revolt against systemic oppressions' (Williams 2018).

Judith Butler explains that the conservative seizure of academic freedom in the USA has emphasized an orthodoxy of 'balance' – with the consequence that state legislatures are empowered to enforce this balance, necessitating surveillance and interference. Academic freedom as such is 'restrictively liberal':

> [I]f the conservative seizure of academic freedom is to fail, there must be more robust and substantive ways to relate academic freedom to ideals of democracy that include not only right of free expression but opposition to forms of surveillance that target political viewpoints. (Butler 2006, 16–17)

In a similar vein, Herbert Marcuse called for pursuit of 'a partisan goal, a subversive liberating notice and practice' as a counterpoint to the pre-existing imbalances of power and the entrenched aversion to partisanship in liberal intellectual work. Thinking about this in relation to the academic space specifically, Walter Rodney conjures the metaphor of the guerrilla intellectual, whose mission is to subvert the pre-existing power disparities. For Rodney, the struggle to overcome the established imbalance of power in academic institutions must be based first on an honest awareness and acknowledgement of the initial disparity, and second on the need to think tactically and strategically about how to use the limited tools available to expose and challenge existing inequalities. The task of the guerrilla is to wage a struggle on her own terms, not by confronting the dominant power directly but by occupying the terrain, entering the institutions, and setting free the entire structure (Rodney 1990, 112).

For academic freedom to be meaningful, it has to be rooted to an emancipatory political ethic and an underlying claim to justice. The academic freedoms afforded to pro-colonial scholarship or to association with a colonizing university remind us that academic freedom in itself is not an inherently progressive force. Progressive scholars should invoke and accentuate it where it makes tactical sense to do so, while understanding that there may be limits to how far it can take you and remaining conscious of its pitfalls. Sophie Smith makes a similar point in response to a controversy over the writings on homosexuality of the conservative Oxford legal philosopher John Finnis: 'Academic freedom is a principle worth defending, but it is foolish to ignore its costs, and who (disproportionately, quietly) bears them' (Smith 2019). In the academic discourses on race and colonialism, those who remain most at risk of bearing those costs are typically radical and racialized scholars. In the ongoing struggles over legitimacy in institutional spaces and the emancipation of knowledge production, their voices should be amplified so that the case for colonialism can no longer be heard.

Note

† I would like to thank Usha Natarajan, Gavan Titley, and Ntina Tzouvala for their important thoughts and insights on a draft of this essay, as well as Ronit Lentin, David Landy, and Conor McCarthy for their editorial improvements and for putting this important collection together.

References

Abi-Saab, G. et al. (2017), 'Statement by Legal Scholars and International Lawyers against Holding ESIL Forum at the Hebrew University in East Jerusalem', *Critical Legal Thinking*, 23 November, http://criticallegalthinking.com/2017/11/23/statement-against-holding-esil-at-the-hebrew-university (accessed 7 May 2019).

Aby, S. (2007), 'Angela Davis and the Changing Paradigm of Academic Freedom in the 1960s', *American Educational History Journal* 34 (2): 289–301.

Acemoğlu, D. and J. Robinson (2017), 'The Economic Impact of Colonialism' in S. Michalopoulos and E. Papaioannou (eds), *The Long Economic and Political Shadow of History*, Vol. 1, London: Vox.

Alakbarov, F. et al. (2018), 'Framing Ethnic Diversity as a "Threat" Will Normalise Far-Right Hate, Say Academics', *Open Democracy*, 23 October, https://www.opendemocracy.net/en/opendemocracyuk/framing-ethnic-diversity-debate-as-about-threat-legitimises-hat-0/ (accessed 7 May 2019).

Alderman, G. (2017), 'Academic Freedom Is Now Being Betrayed by Academics', *The Spectator*, 17 October, https://blogs.spectator.co.uk/2017/10/academic-freedom-is-now-being-betrayed-by-academics (accessed 7 May 2019).

Bennett, J. (2013), 'Civil Rights and the Collapse of Birmingham, Ala.', *American Thinker*, 25 February, https://www.americanthinker.com/articles/2013/02/civil_rights_and_the_collapse_of_birmingham_ala.html (accessed 7 May 2019).

Bennett, J. (2017), 'The Forgotten Genocide in Colonial America: Reexamining the 1622 Jamestown Massacre within the Framework of the UN Genocide Convention', *Journal of the History of International Law*, 19 (1): 1–49.

Berkowitz, R. (2017), 'The Jamestown Genocide?' *Hannah Arendt Center Amor Mundi Newsletter*, 27 August (copy on file with the author).

Biggar, N. (2017), 'Don't Feel Guilty about Our Colonial History', *The Times*, 30 November, https://www.thetimes.co.uk/article/don-t-feel-guilty-about-our-colonial-history-ghvstdhmj (accessed 7 May 2019).

Butler, J. (2006), 'Israel/Palestine and the Paradoxes of Academic Freedom', *Radical Philosophy*, 135: 8–17.

Césaire, A. (1972 [1955]), *Discourse on Colonialism* (Joan Pinkham trans.), New York: Monthly Review Press.

Ciccariello-Maher, G. (2017), 'Conservatives Are the Real Campus Thought Police Squashing Academic Freedom', *The Washington Post*, 10 October, https://www.washingtonpost.com/news/posteverything/wp/2017/10/10/conservatives-are-the-real-campus-thought-police-squashing-academic-freedom (accessed 7 May 2019).

Coulter, A. (2007), 'Bush's America: Roach Motel', 6 June, http://www.anncoulter.com/columns/2007-06-06.html (accessed 7 May 2019).

Cunliffe, P. et al. (2017), 'Our Colonial History and Guilt over Empire', *The Times*, 2 December, https://www.thetimes.co.uk/article/our-colonial-history-and-guilt-over-empire-kct89g775 (accessed 7 May 2019).

Dawes, S. et al. (2017), 'Open Letter to *Third World Quarterly* on the Publication of "The Case for Colonialism"', *OpenDemocracy*, 20 September, https://www.opendemocracy.net/en/open-letter-to-third-world-quarterly-on-publication-of-case-for-coloniali/ (accessed 7 May 2019).

Dell, M. (2010), 'The Persistent Effects of Peru's Mining *Mita*', *Econometrica*, 78 (6): 1863–1903.

Dupraz, Y. and V. Rueda (2017), 'There Is No "Case for Colonialism": Insights from the Colonial Economic History', *London School of Economics Blog*, 17 October, https://blogs.lse.ac.uk/africaatlse/2017/10/17/there-is-no-case-for-colonialism-insights-from-the-colonial-economic-history/ (accessed 7 May 2019).

Ferguson, N. (2003a), *Empire: How Britain Made the Modern World*, London: Allen Lane.

Ferguson, N. (2003b), 'The Empire Slinks Back', *New York Times Magazine*, 27 April, https://www.nytimes.com/2003/04/27/magazine/the-empire-slinks-back.html (accessed 7 May 2019).

Ferguson, N. (2013), 'On the Teaching of History, Michael Gove Is Right', *The Guardian*, 15 February, https://www.theguardian.com/commentisfree/2013/feb/15/history-teaching-curriculum-gove-right (accessed 7 May 2019).

Finklestein, D. (2019), 'Winston Churchill Was a Racist but Still a Great Man', *The Times*, 12 February, https://www.thetimes.co.uk/article/churchill-was-a-racist-but-still-a-great-man-vnhkhfnpm (accessed 7 May 2019).

Flaherty, C. (2017), 'Trinity Suspends Targeted Professor', *Inside Higher Ed*, 27 June, https://www.insidehighered.com/news/2017/06/27/trinity-college-connecticut-puts-johnny-eric-williams-leave-over-controversial (accessed 7 May 2019).

Gilley, B. (2017a), 'The Case for Colonialism', *Third World Quarterly* (withdrawal notice September 2017).

Gilley, B. (2017b), 'How the Hate Mob Tried to Silence Me', *Standpoint*, December 2017 – January 2018, https://standpointmag.co.uk/issues/december-2017-january-2018/features-december-17-bruce-gilley-how-the-hate-mob-tried-to-silence-me/ (accessed 7 May 2019).

Gilley, B. (2018), 'The Case for Colonialism', *Academic Questions*, 31 (2): 167–185.

Gove, M. (2006), 'There's Only One Fergie in the History Game', *The Times*, 14 June, https://www.thetimes.co.uk/article/theres-only-one-fergie-in-the-history-game-76brwc2gqvv (accessed 7 May 2019).

Hari, J. (2009), 'The Dark Side of Andrew Roberts', *The Independent*, 31 July, https://www.independent.co.uk/voices/commentators/johann-hari/johann-hari-the-dark-side-of-andrew-roberts-1765229.html (accessed 7 May 2019).

Heldring, L. and J. Robinson (2012), 'Colonialism and Economic Development in Africa', National Bureau of Economic Research, Working Paper 18566.

Kapoor, I. et al. (2017), 'Letter of Resignation from Members of the Editorial Board of *Third World Quarterly*', 19 September, https://urpe.wordpress.com/2017/09/19/letter-of-resignation-from-members-of-the-editorial-board-of-third-world-quarterly/ (accessed 7 May 2019).

Khan, S. (2017), 'The Case against "The Case for Colonialism"', *Duck of Minerva*, 19 September, http://duckofminerva.com/2017/09/the-case-against-the-case-for-colonialism.html (accessed 7 May 2019).

King, M. (2017), 'Aggrieved Whiteness: White Identity Politics and Modern American Racial Formation', *Abolition Journal*, 1.

Kruger, D. (2003), 'The Case for Colonialism', *The Spectator*, 15 March, https://www.spectator.co.uk/2003/03/the-case-for-colonialism/ (accessed 7 May 2019).

Macintyre, B. (2018), 'Why a Provocative Academic Is Challenging Orthodoxies about the Evils of Empire', *The Times*, 12 May, https://www.thetimes.co.uk/edition/news/i-ve-chosen-to-offend-away-and-keep-writing-about-colonialism-7cwl5nxbp?CMP=Sprkr (accessed 7 May 2019).

Malik, K. (2018), 'The Great British Empire Debate', *New York Review of Books*, 26 January, https://www.nybooks.com/daily/2018/01/26/the-great-british-empire-debate (accessed 7 May 2019).

Marcuse, H. (1969), 'Repressive Tolerance' in H. Marcuse, B. Moore Jr. and R. P. Wolff (eds), *A Critique of Pure Reason*, Boston, MA: Beacon Press, pp. 95–137.

McDonald Centre (2017), 'Ethics and Empire: Project Description', https://www.mcdonaldcentre.org.uk/ethics-and-empire (accessed 7 May 2019).

Michalopoulos, S. and E. Papaioannou (2016), 'The Long-Run Effects of the Scramble for Africa', *American Economic Review* 106 (7): 1802–1848.

National Association of Scholars (2018), 'NAS Re-publishes "The Case for Colonialism"', 13 June, https://www.nas.org/articles/nas_re_publishes_the_case_for_colonialism (accessed 7 May 2019).

Ngo, A. (2017), 'Noam Chomsky Defends Academic Freedom of Pro-colonialism Professor under Fire', *The College Fix*, 21 September, https://www.thecollegefix.com/noam-chomsky-defends-academic-freedom-pro-colonialism-professor-fire (accessed 7 May 2019).

Nunn, N. (2008), 'The Long-Term Effects of Africa's Slave Trades', *Quarterly Journal of Economics* 123 (1): 139–176.

O'Donoghue, A. and H. Jones (2017), 'The Jamestown Massacre: Rigour and International Legal History', *Critical Legal Thinking*, 24 August, http://criticallegalthinking.com/2017/08/24/jamestown-massacre-rigour-international-legal-history/ (accessed 7 May 2019).

Oxford University Africa Society (2017), 'Statement in Rejection of Attempts to Sanitise Empire and Justify "Recolonialisation" Led by Oxford University's Nigel Biggar', 19 December, http://www.oxforduniversityafricasociety.com/statement-19-12-17/ (accessed 7 May 2019).

Patel, V. (2018), 'Last Fall This Scholar Defended Colonialism: Now He's Defending Himself', *The Chronicle of Higher Education*, 21 March, https://www.chronicle.com/article/Last-Fall-This-Scholar/242880 (accessed 7 May 2019).

Politico (2018), 'What Charlottesville Changed', *Politico Magazine*, 12 August, https://www.politico.com/magazine/story/2018/08/12/charlottesville-anniversary-supremacists-protests-dc-virginia-219353 (accessed 7 May 2019).

Portland State University (2018), 'Statement on Bruce Gilley's Article', 28 March.

Reichman, H. (2016), 'Drexel Must Defend Academic Freedom', *Academe Blog*, 26 December, https://academeblog.org/2016/12/26/drexel-must-defend-academic-freedom (accessed 7 May 2019).

Reynolds, J. (2016), 'Disrupting Civility: Amateur Intellectuals, International Lawyers and TWAIL as Praxis', *Third World Quarterly* 37 (11): 2098–2118.

Roberts, A. (2006), *A History of the English Speaking Peoples since 1900*, New York: HarperCollins.

Roberts, A. (2007), 'Diary', *The Spectator*, 21 March, https://www.spectator.co.uk/2007/03/diary-270 (accessed 7 May 2019).

Robin, C. (2015), 'Academic Freedom at UIUC: Freedom to Pursue Viewpoints and Positions that Reflect the Values of the State', *Crooked Timber*, 10 August, http://crookedtimber.org/2015/08/10/academic-freedom-at-uiuc-freedom-to-pursue-viewpoints-and-positions-that-reflect-the-values-of-the-state/ (accessed 7 May 2019).

Robinson, N. (2017), 'A Quick Reminder of Why Colonialism Was Bad', *Current Affairs*, 14 September, https://www.currentaffairs.org/2017/09/a-quick-reminder-of-why-colonialism-was-bad (accessed 7 May 2019).

Rodney, W. (1972), *How Europe Underdeveloped Africa*, Dar es Salaam: Tanzanian Publishing House.

Rodney, W. (1990), *Walter Rodney Speaks: The Making of an African Intellectual*, Trenton, NJ: Africa World Press.

Roelofs, P. and M. Gallien (2017), 'Clickbait and Impact: How Academia Has Been Hacked', *London School of Economics Impact Blog*, 19 September, https://blogs.lse.ac.uk/impactofsocialsciences/2017/09/19/clickbait-and-impact-how-academia-has-been-hacked/ (accessed 7 May 2019).

Rose-Redwood, R. et al. (2017), 'Scholars and the Debate about Colonial Rule', *The Times*, 8 December, https://www.thetimes.co.uk/article/scholars-and-the-debate-about-colonial-rule-6ksjjhfr6 (accessed 7 May 2019).

Saha, J. (2018), 'Safe Spaces for Colonial Apologists', *Critical Legal Thinking*, 8 January, http://criticallegalthinking.com/2018/01/08/safe-spaces-colonial-apologists/ (accessed 7 May 2019).

Said, E. (1996), *Representations of the Intellectual: The 1993 Reith Lectures*, New York: Vintage.

Salaita, S. (2015), *Uncivil Rites: Palestine and the Limits of Academic Freedom*, Chicago, IL: Haymarket.

Salaita, S. (2019), 'An Honest Living', 17 February, https://stevesalaita.com/an-honest-living/ (accessed 7 May 2019).

Saunders, R. (2019), 'British Concentration Camps: A Response to Jacob Rees-Mogg', *The Gladstone Diaries*, 16 February, http://gladstonediaries.blogspot.com/2019/02/british-concentration-camps-response-to.html (accessed 7 May 2019).

Schovanec, L. and M. Galyean (2018), 'Memorandum to Concerned Faculty Members', Office of the President, Texas Tech University, 27 November (copy on file with the author).

Smith, S. (2019), 'Academic Freedom', *London Review of Books Blog*, 14 January, https://www.lrb.co.uk/blog/2019/january/academic-freedom (accessed 7 May 2019).

Taylor and Francis (2017), 'Withdrawal Notice: The Case for Colonialism', https://www.tandfonline.com/doi/abs/10.1080/01436597.2017.1369037 (accessed 7 May 2019).

Tzouvala, N. et al. (2017), 'Letter to the Editors of the Journal of the History of International Law', *Critical Legal Thinking*, 6 September, http://criticallegalthinking.com/2017/09/06/letter-editors-journal-history-international-law (accessed 7 May 2019).

Van Schoonhoven, G. (2018), 'The Good Side of Colonialism: An Interview with Bruce Gilley', *Elsevier Weekblad*, 3 March, https://www.elsevierweekblad.nl/nederland/achtergrond/2018/02/the-good-side-of-colonialism-interview-bruce-gilley-597263 (accessed 7 May 2019).

Vasagar, J. (2012), 'Niall Ferguson: Admirable Historian, or Imperial Mischief Maker?', *The Guardian*, 18 June, https://www.theguardian.com/books/2012/jun/18/niall-ferguson-bbc-reith-lecturer-radio4 (accessed 7 May 2019).

Williams, J. E. (2018), 'The Academic Freedom Double Standard: "Freedom" for Courtiers, Suppression for Critical Scholars', *American Association of University Professors Journal of Academic Freedom*, 9, https://www.aaup.org/sites/default/files/Williams.pdf (accessed 24 June 2019).

Wodak, R. (2015), *The Politics of Fear: What Right-Wing Populist Discourses Mean*, London: Sage.

Young, C. (1994), *The African Colonial State in Comparative Perspective*, New Haven, CT: Yale University Press.

Zhangaza, T. (2018), 'German Minister for Africa's Selective and Neo-Colonial Amnesia', *Africa Blogging*, 26 November, https://www.africablogging.org/german-minister-for-africas-selective-and-neo-colonial-amnesia (accessed 7 May 2019).

SEVEN

The academic boycott and beyond: towards an epistemological strategy of liberation and decolonization

Yara Hawari

Introduction

In 2005 hundreds of Palestinian civil society organizations came together and put out a call for boycotts, divestment, and sanctions against the State of Israel. The call noted that all attempts at international intervention and negotiations had failed to force Israel to comply with international law and to recognize the Palestinian right to self-determination. The call took inspiration from the boycott movement against South African apartheid and recognized the historical precedence of international solidarity against such regimes. The movement became known as the Boycott, Divestment and Sanctions Movement (BDS) and centred on three demands. First, the ending of the occupation and colonization of the lands occupied in 1967, the West Bank, the Gaza Strip, and the Golan Heights (the Sinai Peninsula, also occupied in 1967, was returned to Egyptian rule in 1977); second, the recognition of the fundamental rights of the Palestinian citizens of Israel to full equality; and third, the right of return of Palestinian refugees as stipulated by UN Resolution 194.[1] In these three demands, the BDS movement managed to unite the majority of Palestinians without following a particular party platform. Indeed, its foundation in civil society has helped the movement remain both grassroots and non-partisan.

While the BDS movement also emphasizes the need for sanctions and divestment, the boycott aspect has received a lot of attention because this is the tactic most successfully implemented. Boycott, as an age-old tactic of civil disobedience, is 'deeply embedded in the long history of Palestinian popular resistance' (Maira 2018, 43). In the case of the BDS movement the boycott focuses on three areas: economic, cultural, and academic. This chapter is focused on the latter in both the individual and collective sense.

The academic boycott preceded the 2005 civil society boycott statement but actually followed earlier calls to boycott Israel in a variety of spheres. It was established in 2004 by a group of academics based in Ramallah and was called the Palestinian Campaign for the Academic Boycott of Israel (PACBI). Palestinian academics called for international colleagues to comprehensively boycott Israeli academic institutions until Israel withdraws from the lands occupied in 1967, agrees to the right of return for refugees, and ends its system of apartheid (PACBI, 2008). Later PACBI came under the umbrella of the BDS National Committee (BNC). The essence of this boycott is the recognition that 'Israeli universities are major, willing and persistent accomplices in Israel's regime of occupation, settler-colonialism and apartheid'. Further details of complicity include:

> developing weapon systems and military doctrines deployed in Israel's recent war crimes in Lebanon and Gaza, justifying the ongoing colonization of Palestinian land, rationalizing gradual ethnic cleansing of indigenous Palestinians, providing moral justification for extra-judicial killings, systematically discriminating against 'non-Jewish' students, and other implicit and explicit violations of human rights and international law.[2]

The boycott also extends to individuals if they represent the State of Israel. Importantly, mere affiliation to an Israeli institution is not grounds for boycott on its own, rather a clause called 'common sense boycott' applies to all individuals (Israeli and non-Israeli) who advocate or are complicit in the violations of international law. In other words, BDS does not target identity unlike the boycott movement against South African apartheid, which called for a blanket boycott. BDS rather targets complicity with the Israeli state through discourse and/or action. The boycott also calls attention to funding and demands that academic projects, events, and programmes sponsored by Israel or Israeli institutions be boycotted. This call for boycott thus challenges the normalization of Israeli state oppression and violations of international law by highlighting the complicit nature of Israeli academic institutions as well as holding individuals directly responsible for affiliations and complicity.

The academic boycott has faced many criticisms from adversaries who support Israel and who minimize the violations against the Palestinian people. For example, in *The Case against BDS: Why Singling Out Israel for Boycott Is Anti-Semitic and Anti-Peace*, Alan Dershowitz argues that the BDS movement has its roots in the Nazi boycott of Jewish establishments in the 1930s and thus is founded on antisemitism (Dershowitz 2018, 5). The academic boycott has also faced controversy and accusations from more liberal academics who argue that it is a barrier in the way of free speech. Thus, for example, 'Anthropologists Against the Boycott of Israeli Institutions' argue that the act of boycotting 'forecloses listening to others' and 'undermines academic freedom'.[3]

The concept of academic freedom is worth unpacking. In essence, it aims to protect knowledge producers and knowledge production itself. More simply put, academic freedom means the right to research, publish, and teach without hindrance (Abowd et al. 2006, 5), yet crucially this does not come at any cost. Indeed, the co-founder of the BDS campaign, Omar Barghouti, has responded to accusations that the boycott stifles academic freedoms by explaining that it comes with obligations to uphold the liberty of others through the recognition of violations against such freedoms and through the avoidance of complicity with such violations (Barghouti 2013). Likewise, Judith Butler (2006) explains that 'privileging of academic freedom as a value above all other freedoms is antithetical to the very foundation of human rights'. Importantly, it has been asserted many times that boycott is a legal form of political expression that does not constitute a hindrance to free speech. This was affirmed in 2016 by a group of 200 European legal scholars who stated:

> States that outlaw BDS are undermining this basic human right and threatening the credibility of human rights by exempting a particular state from the advocacy of peaceful measures designed to achieve its compliance with international law. (*Middle East Monitor* 2016)

BDS came about as a tactic after decades of failure of so-called 'peace negotiations' and attempts at international pressure on Israel to comply with international law.[4] The negotiations demonstrated that Israel would not be willing to end its aggression towards the Palestinians let alone compromise on a solution. Moreover, the negotiations demonstrated clearly that the so-called international community would neither challenge Israel in demanding that the Palestinians make even greater concessions nor implement international law. The unequal level in which both parties were situated meant that Palestinians have always been under-prepared, under-resourced, and without political leverage compared to the Israeli negotiators. This was acutely demonstrated with the signing of the Oslo Accords in 1993 that Edward Said described as an 'instrument of Palestinian surrender, a Palestinian Versailles' (Said 1993, 3). These failings at the higher echelons of politics were recognized by many in Palestinian civil society. They thus sought to develop a grassroots tactic of non-violent measures of pressuring and isolating Israel. BDS therefore emerged out of both a change in tactics and of an exhaustion from political negotiations.

Since the BDS movement was established there have been many victories, particularly in the academic sphere. For example, in 2013 the American Studies Association Council voted unanimously (while the majority of the ASA itself voted) to endorse the academic boycott of Israel,[5] while the Native American and Indigenous Studies Association issued a declaration on the academic boycott though the members did not vote on the matter. Other professional associations, including the African Literature Association and the Critical Ethnic Studies Association followed suit.[6] Similarly, in 2015, a group of over 300 British academics from dozens of British universities signed a declaration to boycott Israeli academic institutions as well as academic events funded by them. It was published as a full-page advertisement in *The Guardian* under the title 'A Commitment by UK Scholars to the Rights of Palestinians' (Walker and Black 2015). In June 2019 the British Society for Middle East Studies (BRISMES) voted at its annual conference to support the Palestinian call for a boycott of complicit Israeli academic institutions.[7] Additionally, support has also come from students, and dozens of student unions around the world have passed motions endorsing BDS on their campuses.

While the support for the boycott in the academy is a critical tool that has the ability to increase pressure on Israel to comply with international law, it is important to analyse it and its supporters critically within the wider struggle for Palestinian liberation. While knowledge production and reproduction has always played a key role in Western expansion and domination (Mignolo

2002, 62) it should also play an important and central place in the quest for liberation and decolonization from such domination. Indeed, knowledge production sites can be where oppressed and colonized peoples can reclaim histories and 'take back control of our destinies' (Tuhiwai Smith 2016, 142). It is thus imperative that the boycott is not isolated as the only practical step for those in solidarity with Palestine. Other efforts within the academy must be taken in order to contribute towards Palestinian liberation, including a critical pedagogy centred on the oppressed and the colonized. Paulo Freire writes that critical pedagogy

> must be forged with, not for, the oppressed … this pedagogy makes oppression and its causes objects of reflection by the oppressed and from that reflection will come their necessary engagement in the struggle for their liberation. (Freire 2005, 48)

Making oppression an 'object of reflection by the oppressed', as Freire writes, means the reframing of narratives so that they focus on the experiences of the oppressed. While Freire remains ambiguous when he talks about the oppressed, we can identify them as those who are dominated by the prevailing structures of power such as patriarchy, colonialism, and white supremacy. In the case of Palestine, this requires a recalibration of knowledge production where Palestinians are not seen merely as subjects of Israeli oppression. This also means returning to a lexicon that uses words such as liberty, justice, and decolonization rather than one that talks of conflict resolution and state building. This is highlighted by Salamanca et al. in a special issue on settler colonialism in Palestine, where they question the discourse used by contemporary literature which creates an 'ontological category distinct from the larger structures of Israeli settler colonialism' (Salamanca et al. 2013, 3). In particular, they note that the notion of the 'Green line' (the colonial border between historic Palestine, reconfigured as the State of Israel, and the West Bank) simultaneously contributes to the fragmentation of the Palestinian people and ignores the macro structure (Salamanca et al. 2013, 3).

This chapter therefore highlights the prevailing structures in the academy that help to maintain dominating forces while also proposing to re-frame the boycott as a tactic in a much larger strategy of liberation and decolonization. Beginning by addressing the origins of the Western academy as deeply connected to empire, the chapter looks at how hierarchies in the academy continue to enforce not only colonial ideas in the epistemic realm but also ongoing colonial projects in the material realm. I then address the notion of a politicized scholarship, making the argument that the neoliberalization of the academy has had a significant impact on separating scholarship from a political agenda. In light of this, my argument is that the academic boycott must be accompanied by a wider commitment to challenging academic hegemonies which continue to erase native and indigenous experiences.

Hierarchies in the academy

The Western academy was built on the understanding that knowledge can dominate and conquer peoples and that it was implicit in the material manifestations of colonialism. In *Decolonising the University*, Bhambra et al. explain:

> It was in the (Western) university that colonial intellectuals developed theories of racism, popularised discourses that bolstered support for colonial endeavours and provided ethical and intellectual grounds for the dispossession, oppression and domination of colonised subjects. In the colonial metropolis, universities provided would-be colonial administrators with knowledge of the peoples they would rule over, as well as lessons in techniques of domination and exploitation. (Bhambra, Gebrial and Nişancioğlu 2018, 5)

Likewise, Anaheed Al Hardan writes that knowledge production has been an 'accomplice to Empire, and is ongoing through the American Empire's colonial and neocolonial ventures' (Al Hardan 2014, 61). Anthropological and historical research was particularly complicit in domination as it sought to shed light on the 'other' through a particular lens. Said (1978) illuminated this in the context of European colonialism through the concept of orientalism that explained an authoritative and dominating knowledge practice of the Arab East. This practice maintained and continues to maintain material and epistemic hierarchies to the present day. Said's work on orientalism inspired much of the postcolonial scholarship that followed; among many other things this scholarship was committed to bringing to light in the Western academy the human cost of colonialism. Gayatri Chakravorty Spivak's seminal essay 'Can the Subaltern Speak' (1988) continued this critique of Western scholarship, but also included an important critique of postcolonial studies for mirroring the power structures of colonialism and its complicity in maintaining white heteropatriarchy.

Today the academy remains complicit in the misuse of power through the development of weapons, dehumanizing narratives, centring the victors' histories and erasing existences. In Israel for example, the Technion (Israel Institute of Technology) conducts weapons research and develops arms for the Israeli Defense Forces (IDF). This has included a remote-controlled bulldozer used to destroy Palestinian homes (White 2012). In April 2019 the Hebrew University of Jerusalem announced that it would be hosting a programme for the IDF Intelligence Corps where officers will receive intelligence training as well as concentrating on Islamic and Middle Eastern studies (Kubovich 2019).

Even in spaces considered 'progressive' and 'liberal' scholarship can reproduce dangerous structures of power by giving space to dehumanizing rhetoric that justifies mass violence.

Such was the case at the 2017 International Studies Association Conference, San Francisco, which included a panel titled 'Arab–Israeli Conflict: Israel's Approach' that discussed whether it was more strategic for Israel to 'mow the lawn' or 'destroy the garden' in Gaza.[8] 'Mowing the Lawn' in Israeli parlance refers to the routine but endless military operational practice of bombarding its enemies in order to debilitate them. In Gaza this is manifested through the countless bombardments and assaults by Israel. 'Destroying the Garden' in this panel referred to an even more violent strategy of neutralizing the enemy entirely, which would result in an even deadlier outcome for the besieged Gaza Strip. This form of epistemic violence translates into very real material consequences, particularly as the siege of Gaza is ongoing.

Epistemic violence can also be replicated through the silencing or marginalizing of certain voices. In a lecture-performance entitled 'Decolonizing Knowledge', Portuguese artist and writer Grada Kilomba delivered the following powerful words:

> They place the discourses of Black/People of Colour scholars back at the margins, as deviating knowledge, while white discourses remain at the centre, as the norm. When they speak, it is scientific. When we speak, it is unscientific. When they speak, it is universal. When we speak, it is specific. When they speak, it is objective. When we speak, it is subjective. When they speak, it is neutral. When we speak, it is personal. When they speak, it is rational. When we speak, it is emotional. When they speak, it is impartial. When we speak, it is partial. When they speak, it is they have facts. When we speak, it is we have opinions. When they speak, it is they have knowledge. When we speak, it is we have experiences. These are not simple semantic categorizations; they possess a dimension of power that maintains hierarchical positions. We are not dealing here with simple semantics, but rather with a violent hierarchy, which defines who can speak. (Kilomba 2015)

Kilomba highlights the prevailing structures of power in knowledge production arenas, particularly in the West, that ascribe binaries to white scholars and 'other' scholars. These binaries hold very serious implications for what narratives and ideas are held valid or become known 'truths'. This has certainly been the case for Palestinians who for many decades had their narrative obscured and their voices ignored. The emergence of the Nakba in mainstream Western academia was initiated largely by the Israeli 'New Historians' in the late 1980s. These historians wrote a 'revised' history of the establishment of Israel in 1948 based on sources obtained from the Israeli military archives which had been closed for decades. The claim was that the opening of these military archives allowed these scholars to offer a source-based challenge to the official Zionist narrative. Yet, Palestinian and Arab scholars had been writing about the Nakba for decades and Palestinian people had been sharing testimonies and stories of the Nakba since 1948.

The first written work on 1948 was published in Arabic by the Syrian intellectual Constantine Zurayk, one of the first to term what happened in 1948 as the Nakba in his book *The Meaning of the Catastrophe* (Zurayk 1948). In 1965 the Palestinian Research Centre was established in Beirut and set about conducting academic research and collecting books and documents on Palestine. The centre was targeted by Israel on several occasions, most notably during the 1982 invasion of West Beirut by the Israeli army which ransacked the building and looted some of the collections (Qallab 1985, 186). The *Journal of Palestine Studies* in Beirut and the *Arab Studies Quarterly* were among the non-governmental organizations that published pioneering articles on interviews and memories from the Nakba including from the Palestinians in the 1948 Territory (Masalha 2012, 215). In 1984, Edward Said published his pivotal article 'Permission to Narrate'. Written in reaction to Israel's 1982 invasion of Lebanon, Said calls for a critical re-examination of the Zionist narrative and historical record. Even after the horrific scenes of indiscriminate bombing by Israel, much of the so-called international community still maintained that Israel was a civilized and democratic state. Said argued that this was made possible through institutionalized mechanisms, particularly in the media, that stopped any adverse narratives about Israel being published. Said elaborated, writing that 'facts do not at all speak for themselves, but require a socially acceptable narrative to absorb, sustain and circulate them' (Said 1984, 34). Said's Gramscian analysis of the hegemonic narrative demonstrates that the representation of Israel since its establishment has enabled the total marginalization of any Palestinian voices in the mainstream West. Moreover, 'the Palestinian narrative has never been officially admitted to Israeli history, except as that of non-Jews' (Said 1984, 33).

Some of the Israeli 'New Historians' offered some important insights into the Zionist strategy, notably Ilan Pappe who analysed the blueprint to ethnically cleanse Palestine known as Plan D (Pappe 2006). However, much of it reiterated the Palestinian version of events, backing it with 'official' Zionist sources and making it more palatable to Western audiences. Meanwhile Zionist military archival sources were given more credibility than Palestinian sources and many of these 'new historians' failed to recognize the nexus between power and knowledge production. Writing on this scholarship, Nur Masalha provides a strong critique:

> Almost inevitably since the late 1980s the Israeli 'new historians'
> in general and Benny Morris in particular have come to be
> seen in the West as the 'ultimate authority' on 1948, the birth
> of the Palestinian refugee problem and the Nakba. The 'new
> historians' fitted the bill. They were all Western-educated
> (with connections to Oxford and Cambridge), male, white,

young, Ashkenazi descendants of the ancient Hebrews, highly
professional and scientifically-minded and authoritative, their
work was grounded in official documents and state archives and
so they could now universally represent everyone, especially
those indigenous Palestinians located at the bottom of the pile.
(Masalha 2011, 23-24)

This critique explains how the structural hierarchy of knowledge
was maintained by a hegemony that favoured the voice of the
powerful, in this case Ashkenazi (white) male scholars.

Similarly, writing on indigenous studies, Jodi Byrd explains
that one of the challenges facing the field is how to 'resist the con-
tinual prioritizing of an effect for a cause, of requiring the settler
and the frontier rather than the indigenous as the structuring ana-
lytic through which to assess the consequences of colonialism'
(Byrd 2014, 153). In other words, how is it possible for scholars
to avoid falling into the trap of centring the narrative on the experience of the settler and replicating the silencing of indigenous
voices? While postcolonial, subaltern, and indigenous studies
scholars have long sought to deconstruct these power structures
and to limit their devastating material consequences, Western
institutions and many Western academics are still very much
wedded to making 'theoretical nods' and 'paying homage to what
is usually dead European men' (Al Hardan 2014, 64). bell hooks
writes about her experience with this in a meeting to discuss transformative pedagogy while teaching at university. hooks explained
how during the meeting 'it was necessary to remind everyone that
no education is politically neutral'. She also had to explain that 'a
white male professor ... who teaches only work by "great white
men" is making a political decision' (hooks 1994, 37).

As hooks implies, choosing who narrates, who is read, and who
is given a platform to share knowledge are all inherently political
and deliberate acts. While Palestine Studies as a discipline has

been institutionalized in Western universities (for example in the UK at the University of Exeter and SOAS, and in the US at Brown University) and critical scholarship on Palestine and Israel can be found in abundance, the replication of authoritative hierarchies continues. For example, in 2017 the University of Sussex held a conference to reflect on 50 years of the 1967 Israeli occupation and its implications for both Palestinians and Israelis. The conference had promised to host both academic and non-academic speakers including activists. Yet not only did the conference have some incredibly problematic presentations using racist and negating language, it also hosted twice as many Israeli as Palestinian presenters. Indeed 'the structural issues in the wider academy were manifested in the composition and content of the conference' (Hawari and Sleiman 2017).

This context of structural hierarchies of knowledge production manifesting themselves even in critical spaces requires a serious strategy of epistemic liberation and decolonization. In her book *Decolonizing Methodologies* (1999), Linda Tuhiwai Smith not only highlights that knowledge is produced and understood within a context of ongoing colonialism, she also talks about very real and practical efforts to decolonize the academy. This has included acknowledging that because indigenous knowledge has long been dismissed as ignorant or not scientific, incorporating more indigenous/native voices from within and outside the academy is key. Different methodologies and research practices that deviate from hegemonic and dominating theoretical norms must also be engaged with. This expansion of epistemologies and methodologies will encourage researchers to think more critically about who the research is for and who it will benefit. This critical analysis of power structures and re-thinking of research moves the academy towards a practice that is politically committed and accountable to the communities being researched and spoken about.

Scholarship with a political agenda

In many historically revolutionary contexts the boundaries between scholars and revolutionaries were often blurred. An obvious example is Frantz Fanon, who is so often referenced in scholarship on colonialism and settler colonialism for his analysis of the colonial condition. Yet Fanon was also an active member the Algerian National Liberation Front and much of his writing intersected thought and practice, offering a revolutionary praxis (Fanon 1964). For Fanon, the intellectual and the revolutionary were not mutually exclusive terms, but rather played complementary roles. Similarly, in the 1960s there was a cohort of Palestinian scholars who were producing scholarship from the PLO Research Centre including Sabri Jiriyis (1976) and Fayez Sayegh (1965). For these scholars and many others, liberation, revolution, and knowledge production was understood to be intimately connected.

The African American feminist scholar-activist Audre Lorde also recognized the need to be a politically engaged scholar, particularly in the context of an academy that was and still is colonial and heteropatriarchal. In 1979 at a conference commemorating the thirtieth anniversary of the publication of *The Second Sex* (1949) by Simone de Beauvoir, Lorde delivered what would become her best known speech. In it, she challenged the legitimacy of a conference in which women of colour and queer women were seriously underrepresented:

> It is a particular academic arrogance to assume any discussion of feminist theory without examining our many differences, and without a significant input from poor women, Black and Third World women, and lesbians. (Lorde 1984, 110)

Using her own experience as a black and queer woman, Lorde highlighted the need for politically engaged scholarship in order to challenge the overarching structures of dominance within spaces of knowledge production. Importantly she also challenged the notion of reform and put forward a radical feminist approach by stating that 'the master's tools will never dismantle the master's house' (Lorde 1984, 111). Lorde and others emphasize that being a politically engaged scholar never was and continues not to be a choice for many marginalized and oppressed people. Rather it is born out of existential necessity to challenge hegemonic discourses that seek to erase and marginalize the experiences of the oppressed. Gerald Taiaiake Alfred expresses this well:

> It has been said that being born Indian is being born into politics. I believe this to be true; because being born a Mohawk Kahnawake I do not remember a time free from the impact of political conflict. (Alfred 1995, 1)

Yet since the onset of neoliberalism, many academic spaces have significantly been depoliticized and have seen the entrenchment of hierarchical knowledge structures (Harvey 2005). In terms of the academy, neoliberalism means that 'universal education' was replaced with profit-based practices. In other words, education has become a commodity where students are seen as consumers and teachers are seen as delivering a product not as conduits of knowledge. Moreover, students and teachers are encouraged to spy on each other and to note signs of ideological radicalization. In the UK this was put forward in 2015 through the 'Prevent' programme which placed an obligation on British universities to carry out assessments and trainings to identify 'extremist' ideas.[9]

While the neoliberalization of the academy has led to the depoliticization of the institutional academy, on an individual level there has been a re-emergence of the term 'scholar-activist' to refer to scholars who are also involved in or whose scholarly work is heavily intertwined with political activism. For them, understanding knowledge production in the Foucauldian sense is crucial: knowledge is power and control over the hegemonic narrative has very real implications on the ground. Moving towards a more politically engaged scholarship requires academics to consider in depth the lived realities of the communities they study. It also means making sure that scholarly work has a positive and potentially transformative impact. Indeed, Fanon argued that 'it's no longer a question of knowing the world, but of transforming it' (Fanon 1967, 1). This move from knowing to transforming is an essential part of the decolonization process.

Tuck and Yang importantly write that 'decolonization is not a metaphor', noting the ease with which this word has been used in social science discussions and scholarship, while simultaneously the 'contributions of indigenous intellectuals and activists' to these decolonizing frameworks remain limited (Tuck and Yang 2012, 3). Decolonization, they stress, requires very real, material, and transformative changes that will be inherently disruptive and unsettling, 'a program of complete disorder' (Fanon 1963, 36). In terms of the academy this means a disruption of 'accepted' methodologies and theoretical nods and elevating indigenous ways of knowing and producing knowledge.

Writing about decolonizing as both theory and praxis, Bhambra et al. explain what it means for them:

> Firstly, it is a way of thinking about the world which takes colonialism, empire and racism as its empirical and discursive objects of study; it re-situates these phenomena as key shaping forces of the contemporary world, in a context where their role has been systematically effaced from view. Second, it purports to offer alternative ways of thinking about the world and alternative forms of political praxis. (Bhambra, Gebrial and Nişancioğlu 2018, 2)

Importantly, Bhambra et al. recognize the contestations over the definition of decolonization while highlighting that difference and reflexivity remain key in decolonial work.

Part of the process of decolonization is also the imagining and conceptualizing of the future. Tuhiwai Smith explains that much of the impetus behind recent indigenous research and knowledge production has been 'the survival of peoples, cultures and languages: the struggle to become self-determining and the need to take back control of our destinies' (Tuhiwai Smith 2016, 142). This taking back control of 'destinies' is a highly political endeavour in a world where colonized and indigenous peoples are so often denied a future. Discussing the case of French colonialism in Algeria, Fanon wrote that it 'always developed on the assumption that it would last forever'. He went on to explain that 'the structures built, the port facilities, the airdromes, the prohibition of the Arab language' all gave the impression of a rupture in the colonial time impossible (Fanon 1965, 179–180). Similarly, writing in the context of settler colonialism in the US and Canada (Turtle Island), Waziyatawin explains how life beyond colonialism is especially difficult to perceive in the context of the 'world's greatest and last superpower' (Waziyatawin 2012, 76). In the case of Palestine, it is particularly difficult to conceive of a realistic future in which the Palestinian refugees are allowed to return home and Palestinians are given full rights in their historic homeland. Waziyatawin's call to indigenous people to think beyond the spatial and temporal confines speaks to this difficulty:

> As Indigenous Peoples, it is essential that we understand the direness of the global situation, recognize the fallacy of industrial civilization's invulnerability, and begin to imagine a future beyond empire and beyond the colonial nation-states that have kept us subjugated. (Waziyatawin 2012, 77)

Thinking 'beyond empire' for Palestinians and their allies means thinking beyond the hegemonic concept and definition of what and where Palestine is and who is Palestinian. Hegemonic understanding limits Palestine and Palestinians to the West Bank and Gaza and those who reside within those areas. Indeed, spaces in which Palestine's futures are discussed have for so long not only excluded Palestinians but have also been bound in particular frameworks. Outside the academy these spaces include political negotiations and diplomatic discussions, where for the most part the interest of Israel and its allies are prioritized and Palestinians are underrepresented. These spaces have unfortunately also set the frameworks for discussions within the academy as noted by Salamanca et al. who ask:

> since when did the ongoing struggle for land and for return become a 'post-conflict situation' … and when did the establishment of the Palestinian Authority and the consequent fortification of Palestinian reserves become 'state-building'? (Salamanca et al. 2013, 3)

An example in which Palestinians were underrepresented in discussions of the future was the Brown University 2018 conference 'Future Scenarios in Israel-Palestine', which hosted 27 panellists to talk about imagination and future possibilities. Of those panellists, 16 were Israeli and only six were Palestinian. Even more worrisome was that of the six Palestinians there was not a single woman. This highly problematic yet predictable imbalance of panellists has serious implications for what the organizers of the conference hoped to achieve. The conference's stated aim was to 'explore the manner in which several generations of Jews and Palestinians have imagined the future since the beginning of Zionist settlement in the land in 1882' (Watson Institute, Brown University 2018). Simply through the make-up of the panellists, the conference could not have even scratched the surface of Palestinian imagined futures. However, while the academy's expectations to properly represent Palestinian voices are not that high, the more troublesome issue was the presence of academic allies. The voices of academic allies cannot and should not replace Palestinian voices. Furthermore, their ally-ship necessitates them to recognize and call out these problematic academic spaces without being prompted to do so by Palestinians.

Conclusion

This chapter began by noting that the BDS movement has had significant victories in the academy ranging from a large number of institutional and individual endorsements. Yet BDS, in the academy and beyond, has also mistakenly been regarded as a strategy rather than a tactic. Indeed, Palestinians charge BDS with the onus of filling the void created by the lack of a coherent national liberation strategy, as Hazem Jamjoum writes:

> It is well beyond the mandate of BDS campaigns to address
> the socio-politics of Palestinian communities, let alone
> decide on the politics of liberation strategies and 'solutions'.
> BDS organizations do not, and indeed cannot, claim to be
> representative organizations or parliaments, and since they
> overwhelmingly take aim at third parties – corporations,
> investment funds, cultural institutions, inter-state arrangements –
> that are neither the Israeli state nor its Palestinian quisling
> regime, they cannot be held responsible for the failures of the
> liberation movement at large. (Jamjoum 2018)

As Jamjoum notes, it is beyond the mandate of the BDS campaign to tackle the issue of a wider strategy for liberation. The disintegration of the Palestinian national movement has left the

Palestinian people without a unifying strategy of liberation and perhaps herein lies the reason for the popularity of the BDS campaign among Palestinians. Its political mandate manages to unite most Palestinians through its call for the right of return of Palestinian refugees, for the end to the occupation of the 1967 territories, and for equal rights for the Palestinian citizens of Israel. This mandate accounts for all the fragments of the Palestinian people and has been adopted by many Palestinian groups and activists.

Within this understanding, every aspect of the BDS movement, including the academic boycott, must be reaffirmed as a tactic in a wider strategy. This chapter argues that those committed to the academic boycott of Israel's settler colonial regime must also be committed to the wider practice of decolonizing and re-politicizing the academy. The practice of boycotting Israeli academic institutions, projects, and events as well as individuals who are directly complicit in Israel's oppression of the Palestinian people, while inherently important, is not enough. The structural hierarchies within the academy and the material consequences these have for Palestinians and Palestine necessitate much more.

The political agenda in the academy may currently be set to follow a neoliberal trajectory, yet there are opportunities for scholars and allies to create critical spaces that are geared to a more liberatory and decolonial approach. In particular, these individuals and spaces must fight against epistemic violence and its very real consequences while also challenging epistemic norms that contribute to the erasure of indigenous voices and knowledge production. Importantly, space has to be created in which Palestinians are able to speak about and conceptualize their futures free from imposing frameworks and theoretical norms. In this way, we may reach a more radical scholarly practice that is committed to liberation and decolonization.

Notes

1 https://bdsmovement.net (accessed 16 April 2019).
2 https://bdsmovement.net/academic-boycott (accessed 17 April 2019).
3 https://anthroantiboycott.wordpress.com/ (accessed 16 April 2019).
4 The failure of the peace process is argued by various scholars including Khalidi (2014), Pappe (2013), and Roy (2002).
5 https://bdsmovement.net/tags/american-studies-association (accessed 17 April 2019).
6 https://usacbi.org/academic-associations-endorsing-boycott/ (accessed 17 April 2019).
7 https://bdsmovement.net/news/british-society-middle-eastern-studies-endorses-palestinian-call-boycott-complicit-israeli (accessed 26 June 2019).
8 http://web.isanet.org/Web/Conferences/San%20Francisco%202018-s/San%20Francisco%202018%20-%20Full%20Program.pdf (accessed 17 April 2019).
9 https://www.gov.uk/government/publications/prevent-duty-guidance (accessed 17 April 2019).

References

Abowd, T. et al. (2006), 'Academic Freedom and Professional Responsibility after 9/11: A Handbook for Scholars and Teachers', Taskforce on Middle East Anthropology, https://s3.amazonaws.com/academia.edu.documents/31198763/Handbook-1.pdf?AWSAccessKeyId=AKIAIWOWYYGZ2Y53UL3A&Expires=1554112319&Signature=XUzoTqucKhnIRwojw%2BO%2BKkfzwnQ%3D&response-content-disposition=inline%3B%20filename%3DAcademic_freedom_and_professional_respon.pdf (accessed 17 April 2019).

Al-Hardan, A. (2014), 'Decolonizing Research on Palestinians: Towards Critical Epistemologies and Research Practices', *Qualitative Inquiry* 20 (1): 61–71.

Alfred, G. T. (1995), *Heeding the Voices of Our Ancestors: Kahnawake Mohawk Politics and the Rise of Native Nationalism*, Oxford: Oxford University Press.

Barghouti, O. (2013), 'On Academic Freedom and the BDS Movement', *The Nation*, 14 December, https://www.thenation.com/article/academic-freedom-and-bds-movement/ (accessed 27 April 2019).

Bhambra, G. K., D. Gebrial and K. Nişancioğlu (eds) (2018), *Decolonising the University*, London: Pluto Press.

Butler, J. (2006), 'Israel/Palestine and the Paradoxes of Academic Freedom', *Radical Philosophy* 135, https://www.radicalphilosophy.com/article/

israelpalestine-and-the-paradoxes-of-academic-freedom (accessed 17 April 2019).

Byrd, J. A. (2014), 'Follow the Typical Signs: Settler Sovereignty and Its Discontents', *Settler Colonial Studies* 4 (2): 151–154.

De Beauvoir, S. (1949), *The Second Sex*, Paris: Gallimard.

Dershowitz, A. (2018), *The Case against BDS: Why Singling Out Israel for Boycott Is Anti-Semitic and Anti-Peace*, New York: Post Hill Press.

Fanon, F. (1963), *The Wretched of the Earth*, New York: Grove Press.

Fanon, F. (1964), *Toward the African Revolution*, New York: Grove Press.

Fanon, F (1965), *A Dying Colonialism*, New York: Grove Press.

Fanon, F. (1967/2008), *Black Skin White Masks*, London: Pluto Press.

Freire, P. (2005), *Pedagogy of the Oppressed*, New York: Continuum.

Harvey, D. (2005), *A Brief History of Neo-liberalism*, Oxford: Oxford University Press.

Hawari, Y. and H. Sleiman (2017), 'Challenging Knowledge Production in the British Academy: Who Can Speak on Palestine?', *Jadaliyya*, 29 May, http://www.jadaliyya.com/Details/34308/Challenging-Knowledge-Production-in-the-British-Academy-Who-Can-Speak-on-Palestine (accessed 26 April 2019).

hooks, b. (1994), *Teaching to Transgress*, New York: Routledge.

Jamjoum, H. (2018), 'Reclaiming the Political Dimension of the Palestinian Narrative', *Al Shabaka*, 12 September, https://al-shabaka.org/circles/reclaiming-the-political-narrative-in-palestinian-politics/ (accessed 26 April 2019).

Jiriyis, S., (1976), *The Arabs in Israel*, New York: Monthly Review Press.

Khalidi, R. (2014), *Brokers of Deceit: How the US Undermined Peace in the Middle East*, Boston, MA: Beacon Press.

Kilomba, G. (2015), 'Decolonizing Knowledge', Lecture-Performance, https://voicerepublic.com/talks/grada-kilomba-decolonizing-knowledge-016ae920-48de-445f-845d-dcfe6926c4b4 (accessed 17 April 2019).

Kubovich, Y. (2019), 'Hebrew University to Host Army Base on Campus', *Haaretz*, 14 April, https://www.haaretz.com/israel-news/.premium-hebrew-university-to-host-israeli-army-base-on-campus-1.7113981 (accessed 27 April 2019).

Lorde, A. (1984), 'The Master's Tools Will Never Dismantle the Master's House' in *Sister Outsider*, Freedom, CA: Crossing Press, pp. 110–113.

Maira, S. (2018), *Boycott! The Academy and Justice for Palestine*, Berkeley, CA: University of California Press.

Masalha, N. (2011), 'New History, Post-Zionism and Neo-Colonialism: A Critique of the Israeli "New Historians"', *The Journal of Holy Land and Palestine Studies* 10 (1): 1–53.

Masalha, N. (2012), *The Palestine Nakba*, London: Zed Books.

Middle East Monitor (2016), 'European Legal Scholars Uphold Right to BDS in Struggle for Palestinian Rights', 8 December, https://www.middleeastmonitor.com/20161208-european-legal-scholars-uphold-right-to-bds-in-struggle-for-palestinian-rights/ (accessed 16 April 2019).

Mignolo, W. (2002), 'The Geopolitics of Knowledge and the Colonial Difference', *South Atlantic Quarterly* 10 (1): 57–96.

PACBI (2008), 'History', http://pacbi.org/pacbi140812/?page_id=2551 (accessed 27 April 2019).

Pappe, I. (2006), *The Ethnic Cleansing of Palestine*, London: One World Publications.

Pappe, I. (2013), 'Revisiting 1967: The False Paradigm of Peace, Partition and Parity', *Settler Colonial Studies* 3 (3–4): 341–351.

Qallab, S. (1985), 'An Interview with Sabri Jiriyis', *Journal of Palestine Studies* 14 (4): 185–187.

Roy, S. (2002), 'Why Peace Failed: An Oslo Autopsy' in *Failing Peace: Gaza and the Israeli-Palestinian Conflict*, London: Pluto, pp. 233–249.

Said, E. (1978 [1995]), *Orientalism: Western Conceptions of the Orient*, London: Penguin Books.

Said, E. (1984), 'Permission to Narrate', *Journal of Palestine Studies* 3 (13): 27–48.

Said, E. (1993), 'The Morning After', *London Review of Books* 15 (20): 3–5.

Salamanca, O. J., M. Qato, K. Rabie and S. Samour (2013), 'Past Is Present: Settler Colonialism in Palestine', *Journal for Settler Colonial Studies* 2 (1): 1–8.

Sayegh, F. (1965), *Zionist Colonialism in Palestine*, Beirut: PLO Research Center.

Spivak, G. (1988), 'Can the Subaltern Speak' in C. Nelson and L. Grossberg (eds), *Marxism and the Interpretation of Culture*, London: Macmillan, pp. 271–314.

Tuck, E. and K. W. Yang (2012), 'Decolonization Is Not a Metaphor', *Decolonization: Indigeneity, Education and Society* 1 (1): 1–40.

Tuhiwai Smith, L. (2016 [1999]), *Decolonizing Methodologies: Research and Indigenous Peoples*, London: Zed Books.

Walker, P. and I. Black (2015), 'UK Academics Boycott Universities in Israel to Fight for Palestinian's Rights', *The Guardian*, 27 October, https://www.theguardian.com/world/2015/oct/27/uk-academics-boycott-universities-in-israel-to-fight-for-palestinians-rights (accessed 17 April 2019).

Watson Institute, Brown University (2018), 'Conference: Future Scenarios in Israel-Palestine', https://watson.brown.edu/events/2018/conference-future-scenarios-israel-palestine (accessed 16 April 2019).

Waziyatawin (2012), 'The Paradox of Indigenous Resurgence at the End of Empire', *Decolonization: Indigeneity, Education and Society* 1 (1): 68–85.

White, B. (2012), 'Why a Boycott of Israeli Academics Is Fully Justified', *The Guardian*, 12 September, https://www.theguardian.com/science/blog/2012/sep/12/boycott-israeli-academics-justified (accessed 16 April 2019).

Zurayk, C. (1948 [2001]), *The Meaning of the Catastrophe*, Beirut: Markaz Dirasat al-Wihda al-Arabiyya.

EIGHT | Colonial academic control in Palestine and Israel: blueprint for repression?

Ronit Lentin

Introduction

In January 2018 the Israeli Knesset approved a bill bringing academic institutes in the occupied West Bank under the jurisdiction of Israel's Higher Education Authority. According to *Haaretz*, the legislation is 'one of a series of laws designed to enact creeping annexation of the West Bank and apply Israeli law to the settlements' (Zur 2018). The bill was enacted despite opposition by leading Israeli academics who warned that it would damage the agreement reached between Israel and the European Union to maintain the separation between institutions within the State of Israel and in the Palestinian territory occupied in 1967, and that it would lead to demands that Israel be removed from scientific cooperation programmes such as the prestigious EU Horizon 2020 programme (Zur 2018).

The key academic institution benefiting from this law is Ariel University. Founded in 1982, the Ariel University Centre of Samaria[1] became an independent college in 2004 and was granted accreditation as a university by the Council for Higher Education in Judea and Samaria in 2012. Ariel University is built on occupied Palestinian land, in the illegal colony-settlement Ariel, established in 1978 on Palestinian land declared 'state land', although under the Fourth Geneva Convention, building Israeli settlements on occupied Palestinian or Syrian territory constitutes a war crime.[2] Israel's commitment to double the size of Ariel University within

five years is part of its plan to control the Israeli higher education sector both in the Palestinian territory occupied in 1967 and
within the State of Israel.

Bringing Israeli higher education institutions in the occupied
West Bank under the jurisdiction of Israel's Council for Higher
Education was announced by former right-wing Education
Minister Naftali Bennett on their Facebook page in October 2018.
Absurdly, Bennet said this was essential to ensure academic freedom and break 'the universities' cartel that had been in existence
since the establishment of the state'.[3] The project of increasing
state control over the higher education sector includes establishing the Herzliya Interdisciplinary Centre as Israel's first private
university, and approving the Ariel University medical school
(Jaffe-Hoffman 2019).

This chapter begins by arguing that Israel's attempts to control the academic sector are not new and that Israeli academia has
always been complicit in upholding the colonization of Palestine
in a variety of ways. It then argues that controlling academic
expression inevitably breeds resistance, internationally through
the Palestinian Academic and Cultural Boycott of Israel (PACBI)
campaign, and nationally through 'Academia for Equality', established by Israeli academics concerned about the oppression of
Palestinian academic institutions in the occupied territory and the
state's campaign against academic freedom in the Israeli higher
education sector. The chapter concludes by arguing that, having
successfully recruited Israeli academics as active collaborators
in the colonization of Palestine, Israel's campaign of curtailing
academic freedom in Palestine and in Israel is a resource, or a
blueprint, for stymieing academic freedom and free debate on the
Israeli colonization of Palestine elsewhere in the world.

Israeli state control of academics and academic institutions
in the State of Israel has several aspects. In order to consolidate

state control over research and teaching, Israel does all it can to monitor dissent and free expression in Israeli academic institutions by, *inter alia*, closing down 'left-wing' departments and courses in Israeli universities. More seriously, Israel exercises surveillance and control over educational institutions in occupied Palestine by regularly raiding and closing down Palestinian universities and schools, disrupting the free movement of students and faculty, preventing the holding of international conferences, and not renewing the visas of Palestinian faculty with foreign passports, as discussed later. Israeli control of dissent within the state and the Occupied Palestinian Territory (OPT) is then exported through its well-funded campaign of controlling critical discourse and spaces for debating its colonization of Palestine on campuses throughout the world. Monitoring dissent, I propose, imposes a colonial agenda on Israel's higher education, making a mockery of the very principle of academic freedom.

Before I begin, it is worth noting that Western universities are key sites through which colonialism and colonial knowledge have been produced, institutionalized, and naturalized, and that universities in the global North were founded and financed through the spoils of colonial plunder, enslavement, and dispossession. As Bhambra et al. (2018, 5) remind us:

> It was in the university that colonial intellectuals developed theories of racism, popularised discourses that bolstered support for colonial endeavours and provided ethical and intellectual grounds for the dispossession, oppression and domination of colonised subjects. In the colonial metropolis, universities provided would-be colonial administrators with knowledge of the peoples they would rule over, as well as lessons in techniques of domination and exploitation. The foundation of European higher education institutions in

colonised territories itself became an infrastructure of empire, an institution and actor through which the totalising logic of domination could be extended; European forms of knowledge were spread, local indigenous knowledge suppressed, and native informants trained.

Bhambra et al.'s argument is relevant to my discussion of the colonial aspect of the Israeli academy. As a colonial European project, Zionism relied on academic knowledge to deepen its hold on Palestine and the Palestinians. Since the early days of the Zionist movement, universities were key to enabling the colonization of Palestine and the racialization of the Palestinians. As this chapter argues, Israeli universities and third-level institutes of science and technology are central to the development of Israel's weapons and security industries, the training of military and security personnel, and the provision of theoretical backing for the Israeli occupation, as argued by Israeli scholars Shir Hever (2009, 2018), Idan Landau (2017), and Eyal Weizman (2017). At the same time, the State of Israel exercises control and surveillance over academic institutions in occupied Palestine, curtailing academic freedom but also students' and academics' freedom of movement and the actual freedom to educate the younger generations of Palestinians at all levels.

Academic complicity in the colonization of Palestine

This section discusses four aspects of the complicity of the Israeli academy in the colonization of Palestine: the implications of a controversial ethics code imposed on Israeli higher education institutions; the ways in which the Israeli higher education sector upholds and supports the Israeli colonization of Palestine (Hever 2009); the control Israel exercises over Palestinian higher education; and the surveillance of dissent within the Israeli state itself.

Ethics as a means of surveillance

In December 2016 Israel's then Education Minister Naftali Bennett announced a new ethics code for Israeli universities. The move followed the minister prohibiting school visits by the Israeli soldier whistle-blower group 'Breaking the Silence – Israeli Soldiers Talk about the Occupied Territories'[4] (Adamkar 2017); reprimanding teachers who criticize the Israeli Defense Forces (IDF) in class; and removing a novel depicting a love affair between a Jewish woman and a Palestinian man from the secondary school literature syllabus (*The Guardian* 2016). Bennett's ethics code was particularly sinister because the academic charged with writing it, philosophy professor Asa Kasher, was the controversial author of the IDF's 1994 ethics guidelines, *The Spirit of the IDF: Values and Basic Norms* (Roth 2016). In 2014, Kasher expressed satisfaction with the IDF's conduct during Israel's 'Protective Edge' assault on Gaza in which 2,251 Gazans were killed, claiming that the IDF acted in accordance with their own belief in the supremacy of the lives of Israeli soldiers over the lives of 'their' civilians (Matar 2016). The ethics code bans discriminating against lecturers or students based on their political views, prohibits participating in, or calling for, academic boycotts of Israeli institutions, bans 'party propaganda' and the expression of a personal political view as that of the institution (Bachner 2018).

Palestinian-Canadian sociologist Elia Zureik (2016, 108–109) writes that surveillance is central to colonial rule and argues that as a settler colonial occupying power, Israel is more interested in surveillance, control, and exclusion ultimately aimed at appropriating the territory in which the colonized population resides than in population management. The effects of the ethics code remain to be seen, but the code's guidelines would most probably necessitate drastically increased levels of surveillance.

Following the initiation of the academic ethics code, right-wing
Knesset member Oded Forer proposed a bill that would allow
cutting state funding to Israeli universities that employ lecturers backing the academic boycott of Israel. The proposed bill,
Forer told *Haaretz*, aims 'to prevent a situation in which the state
pays the wage of a professor who calls for a boycott of it. The bill
doesn't ban universities from employing such lecturers, but if they
continue employing them they would fund them through private
donations, not state funds' (Lis 2017). At the time of writing the
bill had not yet been enacted, but in March 2018 the Council for
Higher Education decided to voluntarily adopt the ethics code,
instructing Israeli universities and colleges to incorporate it into
their disciplinary codes. Paradoxically, Minister Bennet disingen-
uously insisted that the ethics code promotes academic freedom
rather than curtails it:

> We must keep the world of academia free of politics and foreign
> interests. Complete academic freedom – yes. Promoting political
> agendas and calling for a boycott – no. We are in fact limiting
> the freedom of condemnation and increasing the freedom of
> expression, so the academic discourse in Israel remains free
> of politics and discrimination. At the gates of academia, leave
> politics outside. (Yanko 2018)

In fact, the voluntary adoption of the controversial ethics code is
in line with the long history of collusion by Israeli universities in
the colonization of Palestine. According to Israeli sociologist Uri
Ram (1993, 10), the Israeli academy has always been central to
Zionism's statist approach advocated by its first Prime Minister
David Ben Gurion, who regarded the state as the source of institutional authority and moral inspiration. Academics were mobilized as agents of statism and were instrumental in constructing
policy, and in turn the state funded the universities and accorded

them prestige. Academics in the pre-state *Yishuv* and later in the State of Israel have always been centrally involved in maintaining white European Jewish supremacy, and in policies of colonization, Jewish immigration, forging Jewish identity, and denigrating 'Israeli Arab' identity, the 1948–1966 military government regime, and Zionist land ownership. Since the 1967 occupation, academics have become ever more central to policies of occupation, segregation, domination, and military prowess.

The ongoing collusion of Israeli academia in the Zionist project

According to the Israeli economist Shir Hever (2009), Israeli academia colludes in the colonization of Palestine in several ways. To start with, Israeli academic research and development has been servicing the Israeli armed forces and security industries by developing weapons and security systems, by training military personnel, and by contributing to Israel's lucrative weapons and security exports (see also Katz 2007; Landau 2017).

What comes to mind here is the concept of the 'military-industrial complex', first coined by US president Dwight Eisenhower in their 1961 farewell address to the nation, in which they warned, 'We must never let the weight of this combination endanger our liberties or democratic processes'.[5] Interestingly, Henry Giroux (2007) claims that the speech originally used the term 'military-industrial-academic complex'. Though arguing that Eisenhower saw the academy as part of the complex, and that the warning was prescient for twenty -first-century America, Giroux defends the university as one of the few public spaces capable of raising important questions and educating students to be critical and engaged agents.

Israeli anthropologist Jeff Halper (2013, 3–4) argues that Israel transforms 'its military and securocratic prowess into political clout in pursuing … "security politics'". The Occupied Palestinian Territory, Halper writes, serves as a resource for Israel as a testing ground for the development of weapons, tactics, security systems, and models of population control without which Israel would be unable to compete in international arms and security markets.

However, Israel's weapons and security industries would not be as successful without the active collaboration of academics and universities, on which these industries depend. According to Hever (2018), the recent crisis in Israeli arms exports due to the collapse of the concept of the Occupied Palestinian Territory as the 'laboratory' for Israel's military technology, and the parallel crisis in the Israeli academy, due to the impact of the Boycott, Divestment and Sanctions (BDS) movement, have led to both the academic and the security elites seeking to join forces and apply jointly for government funding. Hever cites Major General Professor Isaac Ben Israel, a member of both elite groups, who says that the security system funnels large amounts of money for the development of information technologies to the universities. Academia is also the main provider of training for the arms industry, training thousands of engineering and science students in the security system's R&D centres; these students later return to the civilian market, thus consolidating the relationship between the security industries and the universities.

Academics also provide theoretical grounding for new IDF warfare modes. Israeli forensic architect Eyal Weizman (2017, 187–192) cites the example of Tel Aviv University philosophy professor (and retired IDF brigadier-general) Shimon Naveh, who was instrumental in designing the IDF's 'swarming' mode of urban warfare, a non-linear polycentric strategy first developed by the US Army, and a central component of the IDF's attacks on refugee camps and densely populated urban centres in the OPT. In Yotam Feldman's documentary *The Lab* Naveh is filmed boasting of having designed a phantom city in the southern Negev region, where the IDF practises urban warfare.[6]

Hever also outlines the public support by Israeli universities for student soldiers (including those serving in Israel's 2008–2009, 2012, and 2014 attacks on the Gaza Strip), who receive grants, extra exam dates, and extra credits for their army reserve duty (Gravé-Lazi 2018). This discriminates against Palestinian students, most of whom, with the exception of some male Druze and Bedouin Palestinians, are not conscripted to the IDF and are thus not eligible for university grants and deferred exam dates available to serving Israeli student soldiers.[7]

Furthermore, all Israeli higher education institutions provide training programmes for military and security personnel. On the lowest level, the Israeli College for Security and Investigation prepares graduates to work in Israel's multi-faceted, privately run security industry.[8] More prestigious institutions – such as the army's flagship Command and Staff College (PUM), which provides both military and academic training programmes in several Israeli universities and colleges – enjoy closer relationships with the security and secret service agencies.

An example of the universities' deep involvement in military training is the tender won in April 2019 by the Hebrew University of Jerusalem (HUJI) to host the IDF's *Havatzalot* training programme for military intelligence officers. According to Academia for Equality, this means that the IDF would establish a highly secured military installation on campus with an armed force deploying surveillance technologies that may affect everyone on campus; that the personal details of all university employees related to the programme would be available to the IDF; that hundreds of uniformed and armed soldiers in departments of Islamic and Middle Eastern studies, political science, and philosophy would receive preferential treatment including a commitment that only high-ranking tenured lecturers would be allocated to the programme, effectively discriminating against civilian students; that programme commanders would be allowed to intervene in the soldiers' academic performance; and finally, that high-ranking army officers would attend classes and affect their contents.[9]

Hever also argues that several Israeli universities are already directly involved with the occupation. Ariel University has been party to Israel's highly lucrative arms and security industries through partnering with weapons manufacturer Israel Aerospace Industries (IAI) in joint research employing nanotechnology to develop miniature satellites.[10] Another example is HUJI's Mount Scopus Campus, which is partly built on Palestinian land in occupied East Jerusalem. Its buildings and facilities were expanded after Israel's 1968 illegal confiscation of Palestinian lands, used to build car parks and student dormitories, and the university's presence stimulates settler activities in occupied East Jerusalem. HUJI benefits from settlement infrastructure, transport lines, and access roads in the occupied territory, some of them on privately owned Palestinian land.[11]

Besides benefiting from the occupation, Israeli universities play an active role in forming occupation policies. A notorious example is the Haifa University Professor of Demography and Geo-strategy Arnon Sofer, who has authored policies relating to the West Bank Separation Wall, the Palestinian Right of Return, and what he terms Israel's 'demographic problem' – the high birth rate among Palestinians. Sofer's comments on Gaza are typical of his demographic outlook:

> We will tell the Palestinians that if a single missile is fired over the fence, we will fire ten in response. And women and children will be killed and houses will be destroyed ... it's going to be a human catastrophe. Those people will be even bigger animals

than they are today, with the aid of an insane fundamentalist Islam ... So, if we want to remain alive, we will have to kill and kill and kill. All day, every day. (Abunimah 2006, 85–86)

Another example of the collusion by the Israeli academy in the colonization of Palestine outlined by Hever is the practice of parachuting high-ranking IDF officers into academic posts.[12] Hever concludes by arguing that Israel curtails academic freedom by regularly raiding and closing down Palestinian universities and colleges in the West Bank and bombing educational institutions in Gaza, and by setting limits on the academic freedom of individual academics within the State of Israel itself as argued later.

Controlling Palestinian academics and students

Unsurprisingly, the highest level of control and surveillance in Israeli universities has been and continues to be exercised against Palestinian academics and students. According to a 2013 report, 'Pluralism and Equality of Opportunity in Higher Education: Extending Access to the Academy for Arab, Druze and Circassians in Israel',[13] Palestinian students in Israel face many barriers to accessing university education. These include low proficiency in Hebrew and English, insufficient preparation for university entry exams, accessibility (many Palestinians live far from Israeli universities and colleges), economic difficulties, and Palestinian students' relatively young age compared with Israeli Jewish students who begin university after their military service. Due to occupational barriers, Palestinian students tend to favour medicine and nursing, pharmacy, natural sciences, and engineering. Barred from many government posts and prevented from taking degree courses such as geography for spurious 'security reasons', many Palestinian students take less challenging and more politically safe courses, ending up in professions that do not require military service or security clearance (Abdo 2002, 135–139).

Politically active Palestinian students in Israeli universities are often harassed. One example was the September 2014 notice served by the Hebrew University to 12 Palestinian students who participated in an 'unauthorized demonstration' that the students insisted was a 'spontaneous gathering' in response to the hunger strike by Palestinian prisoners in Israeli jails. Though not the first time HUJI was accused of limiting Palestinian students' freedom of expression, this time the university targeted individual students rather than political groups. According to 24-year-old law student Riham Nassra, this 'can end in suspension, probation or even expulsion ... They probably think that personal targeting will serve as more effective deterrence' (Younis 2014).

In the OPT Israel routinely raids and closes Palestinian higher education institutions. On 14 July 2018 the Israeli police closed down the Hind Al-Husseini College and Al-Quds University's College of Art in occupied East Jerusalem, and banned the holding of a two-day conference organized by the Jerusalem Islamic Waqf and the Heritage Society on the status of Muslim endowment and property, detaining 15 conference participants. The move was condemned by the Arab American University president, Ali Abu Zuhri, who said that the Israeli occupation aims to obstruct the educational system and prevent the teaching of Palestinian curricula, imposing the Israeli curriculum in an attempt to change Jerusalem's cultural and historical identity.[14] In 2019 the UN refugee agency for Palestinians said Israel was planning to replace UNRWA-run schools in occupied Jerusalem with schools run by the Jerusalem municipality, teaching the Israeli curriculum which is alien to Palestinian Jerusalemites, and further extending Israeli colonial control (*Al Jazeera* 2019).

Equally damaging is the Israeli policy of imposing entry and residency restrictions on international academics with US or European passports working in Palestinian universities. In June 2018 Israel refused to grant visa extensions to seven international Bir Zeit University academics, and several others had already been forced to leave the country. International academics seeking to work in the OPT have long faced obstacles, and the situation has dramatically worsened since 2017.[15] A Palestinian Ministry of Education survey of Palestinian universities found that over half of all foreign staff in eight universities have been negatively affected in 2017 and 2018, causing serious disruptions to academic programmes and university administrations, and undermining Palestinian universities in attracting external expertise. According to Israeli Law Professor Daphna Golan (2018):

> Without international researchers, universities experience a 'ghettoization of knowledge'. Many deported foreign academics are Palestinians who studied in the US or Europe ... Israel ... makes the entry of Palestinian academics who study abroad near impossible, permitting them to teach in Palestine for only five years. Deporting Palestinian lecturers will inevitably cause the slow destruction of Palestinian universities.

Controlling dissent in Israeli universities

State control extends beyond occupied Palestine to the Israeli higher education sector itself, where dissenting academics face a high level of surveillance and are often penalized by their universities. Probably the best known example is the 'new historian' Ilan Pappe, whose work on the 1948 Nakba brought him into conflict with his employer, the University of Haifa. Pappe (2010) writes about a Master's thesis by Theodore Katz who documented the 1948 massacre of the inhabitants of the Palestinian village Tantura. The thesis was challenged by IDF veterans interviewed as the perpetrators of the massacre and was eventually rejected by the university. Pappe's support for Katz and the hostile reactions to their solidarity with the 13 Palestinians shot to death by the Israeli police in October 2000 eventually made them realize that working in the University of Haifa was no longer tenable. In 2002, Pappe was summoned to appear before a university disciplinary committee, and was accused, like other Israel-critical academics, including Steven Salaita (discussed by several contributors in this volume), of non-collegial, *uncivil* behaviour. Pappe insisted that the charges were not about 'incivility' but rather about denial of academic freedom. Although the disciplinary committee ultimately dropped the complaint, Pappe's family members were harassed for a long period following the hearing. When death threats and abusive phone calls and letters became a regular occurrence, and after Pappe's endorsement of the academic boycott of Israel led to the university president calling for their resignation, Pappe did in fact resign. Unlike the Palestinian-American Salaita,[16] who was unable to secure an academic position, Pappe, a privileged white Ashkenazi Jew, was at least able to find a professorial job in Britain.

Two more recent examples: first, when Israeli Ben Gurion University Professor Neve Gordon called to boycott Israel in a *Los Angeles Times* article in 2011, they were heavily criticized by the university administration; they now work in London (Breiner 2011). Second, in February 2019 Palestinian Hebrew University Professor Nadera Shalhoub-Kevorkian lectured at Columbia University on Israel using Palestinian prisoners and Palestinian children in drug experiments. Shalhoub-Kevorkian said that 'Palestinian spaces are laboratories for the Israeli security industry, [they] are using them as showcases', and argued that the Israeli occupation authorities issue permits to large pharmaceutical firms to carry out tests on Palestinian prisoners, and that Israeli military firms are testing weapons on Palestinian children and carry out these tests in Palestinian areas in occupied Jerusalem. In response, former Education Minister Bennett called for Shalhoub-Kevorkian's dismissal, saying, 'It's a shame that an Israeli lecturer in Israeli academia is slandering IDF soldiers around the world'. In its own statement, HUJI distanced itself from Shalhoub-Kevorkian and said their opinions 'do not represent or express those of Hebrew University or its administration in any way' (Moshe 2019).

Resisting academic control: PACBI and Academia for Equality

One response to Israeli universities being willing accomplices in Israel's colonial regime and the suppression of Palestinian academics, students, and universities was the launch in April 2004 of the international Palestinian Academic and Cultural Boycott of Israel (PACBI) by a group of Palestinian academics and intellectuals in Ramallah, occupied West Bank, discussed in the introduction.

Within Israel, the clampdown on academic freedom and the suppression of Palestinian universities, academics, and students prompted a group of Israeli academics to resist academic surveillance and control by forming Academia for Equality. The group, which numbers some 400 Israeli academics, argues that Israeli universities collude with state policies, particularly the occupation. As a first step, it published 'Complicit Academy',[17] a database of Israeli and international newspaper articles, documents, NGO reports, and official university publications, with the aim of 'shedding light on Israeli universities' repression of dissent, institutionalized discrimination against Palestinian-Israeli students and faculty, collusion with the settlement enterprise, military R&D, and *hasbara*' (Konrad 2018). The database shows how, contrary to its 'liberal' image, Israeli academia works in the service of the racial state's permanent war against the Palestinians (see Lentin 2018). It demonstrates the growing number of university programmes designed to battle the 'delegitimization' of the State of Israel, state racism against Palestinian students and faculty, and Israeli universities' role in researching, manufacturing, and marketing Israel's hugely lucrative arms and security industries.

Though Academia for Equality does not support the academic boycott of Israel as policy, the group regularly protests against the State of Israel and against universities abroad silencing academics who criticize Zionist policies. Thus in October 2018 the group sent a letter to the University of Michigan (UM) protesting against UM penalizing professor John Cheney Lippold, and teaching assistant Lucy Peterson, both of whom refused to write references for a student wishing to study in Israel.[18] In April 2019, Academia for Equality published a public letter protesting the militarization of the Hebrew University following the establishment of the *Havatzalot* project mentioned earlier,[19] and among its other activities, the group protested the jailing of Turkish academics,[20] and the raiding of the West Bank Kadoorie College.[21] However, while Academia for Equality is an important, albeit minority, protesting voice against Israel infringing academic freedom and silencing dissent, it seems that most of its members ultimately aim to reform the Israeli academy, rather than transform it into a site of anti-Zionist action.

Conclusion: blueprint for global control of academic freedom?

This chapter argues that understanding the suppression of academic freedom and dissent by the Israeli government in Israel and in Palestine is central to understanding the silencing of criticism and dissent as debated by contributors to this book, because, as this conclusion shows, suppressing dissent starts with Israel and its Zionist US and European supporters. My argument is that Israel's ongoing campaign of controlling dissent in Palestine's higher educational institutions and in Israeli academia should be understood as a resource, perhaps even a blueprint, for exerting control over the academic freedom to debate and criticize its permanent war against Palestine, and to discuss the validity of BDS and the academic boycott worldwide. The chapter further argues that just as resistance to surveillance and control of academic freedom in Palestine and in Israel is intensifying, so resistance, particularly through PACBI, but also through groups such as Students for Justice in Palestine and a variety of pro-Palestine academic organizations, is increasing, despite Israel's relentless and well-funded campaign to control critical discourse and silence dissent.

While Israeli universities have always been central to upholding the colonization of Palestine, and while Israel's *hasbara* efforts to justify its policies have always existed, in recent years, with the growing success of the BDS movement, the campaign against dissent and criticism has intensified as this conclusion details.

In 2014 the University of Haifa launched the first academic programme aiming to combat the online 'delegitimization of Israel'. Programme students, the university said, were being prepared 'to be unofficial "ambassadors" for Israel on the Internet'. The programme was initiated in the wake of Israel's 2014 Gaza war and the university lists among its 'achievements' an operation room that 'propagated the reality in Israel during the Gaza war', initiating 'propaganda delegations abroad', and creating 'viral memes' (White 2014).

Though typical of Israeli initiatives aimed at combatting dissent and campaigning against BDS, the University of Haifa programme predated the establishment of the official anti-BDS campaign masterminded by the Ministry for Public Security, Information and Strategic Affairs.[22] The Ministry granted this campaign a 72-million dollar budget while also calling on American Jewish communities to set up parallel not-for-profit organizations to oversee the first 'civil society infrastructure servicing the state of Israel and the pro-Israel lobby to fight against the delegitimization of Israel' (*Forward* 2017).

The depth of Israel's commitment to the anti-BDS campaign was revealed in June 2019 by *Haaretz* gaining access to the 2018 diaries of Strategic Affairs Minister Gilad Erdan (Landau 2019), disclosing the minister's collaboration with the Mossad (Israel's national intelligence agency) in the fight against the BDS movement. Erdan's diaries also show meetings with representatives of numerous international Jewish organizations, including the American Jewish Committee, B'nai B'rith, the American Jewish Congress, the umbrella organization of French Jewry, and the US Reform Movement. The meetings focused on establishing a 'public benefit corporation' which received 128 million shekels (about 36 million US dollars) in Israeli government funding and was set to collect a matching amount in private contributions.

As part of its campaign against pro-Palestine activism, the Israeli government supports right-wing groups such as the Jerusalem-based NGO Monitor, which reports on the output of international NGOs from a pro-Israel perspective, and whose tactic of aggressive surveillance has led to these groups being accused by an Israeli report of 'spearheading the shrinking of space for Israeli and Palestinian human rights NGOs' (*Middle East Monitor* 2018). In January 2018 Israel published a list of 20 pro-Palestine organizations, including *Jewish Voice for Peace*, whose members are now prevented from entering the country due to supporting BDS (Eglash 2018).

The involvement of Israeli diplomats in pro-Israel groups in Britain and the US was revealed by *Al Jazeera*'s four-part documentary series *The Lobby*, focusing on Britain.[23] A subsequent US series, produced by an undercover *Al Jazeera* reporter who infiltrated pro-Israel US groups such as The Israel Project and Emergency Committee for Israel, was censored by the Qatari government as part of its attempt to win the support of Jewish American organizations, demonstrating the depth of interference by the State of Israel against any criticism (Tibon 2018).

US groups such as Campus Watch and Canary Mission, the latter dedicated to documenting 'people and groups that promote hatred of the USA, Israel and Jews on North American college campuses',[24] are directly involved in the surveillance of pro-Palestine campus activities. Though Campus Watch is purportedly 'a project of the Middle East Forum, (that) reviews and critiques Middle East Studies in North America, with an aim to improving them',[25] it has long been accused of being a pro-Israel group involved in harassing, blacklisting, and intimidating academics critical of Israel. However, the collusion of the Zionist lobby in silencing dissent in academia is nothing new. In 'The Israel Lobby and US Foreign Policy', Mearsheimer and Walt (2006) wrote that the Campus Watch website was established by neoconservative academics Martin Kramer and Daniel Pipes in order to post dossiers on 'suspect' academics and encourage students to report remarks or behaviour considered hostile to Israel, with the aim of monitoring what professors write and teach. Without the Israel lobby, Mearsheimer and Walt insist, the relationship between Israel and the US would not be as intimate as it is.

In October 2018 the Israeli government proposed legislation that would subject Israeli and foreign activists promoting BDS – including the academic boycott – to prison terms of up to seven years (Lis 2018). Proposing this legislation, which has not yet materialized, proves how seriously Israel takes the threat to its legitimacy posed by the BDS campaign, and how determined it is to silence any criticism.

This chapter argues that Israel's colonial surveillance and control of higher education in occupied Palestine and the silencing of dissent and criticism in Israeli academic institutions should be understood as a blueprint for its relentless campaign of silencing its academic critics and controlling the debate regarding its colonization of Palestine on campuses throughout the world.

Notes

1 Samaria is a biblical name that together with Judea is used by the State of Israel to name the occupied West Bank.

2 https://www.btselem.org/settlements/20100830_facts_on_the_settle ment_of_ariel (accessed 16 September 2018).

3 https://www.facebook.com/search/top/?q=%D7%A0%D7%A4%D7% AA%D7%9C%D7%99%20%D7%91%D7%A0%D7%98%20-%20naf tali%20bennett (accessed 14 October 2018).

4 http://www.breakingthesilence.org.il/ (accessed 25 January 2017).

5 https://en.wikipedia.org/wiki/Eisenhower%27s_farewell_address (accessed 23 September 2019).

6 http://www.gumfilms.com/projects/lab (accessed 12 October 2018).

7 Though Palestinian citizens make up 21 per cent of Israel's population, they constitute 16.1 per cent of undergraduate students, 13 per cent of graduate students, 6.3 per cent of PhD students (Lieber 2018), and just 2–3 per cent of the academic staff in Israeli academic institutions (Hager and Jabareen 2016).

8 https://www.israeldefense.co.il/en/company/isci-israeli-college-secu rity-investigation (accessed 10 February 2019).

9 https://www.facebook.com/academiaforequality/posts/2269 447039977949 (accessed 12 April 2019).

10 http://www.afau.org/blog/2015/05/14/ariel-university-aerospace-and-nano-satellite-research-center/ (accessed 13 March 2019).

11 See 'No Academic Business as Usual with Ariel University', a PACBI Campaign for Non-Recognition of and No-Ties with Ariel University, https://noarielties.org/ (accessed 12 April 2019).

12 An example is ex-Colonel Pnina Sharvit-Baruch whose part in overseeing the legal justification of Israel's bombing of the Gaza Strip in December 2008 – January 2009 did not deter Tel-Aviv University from appointing her as a law lecturer (Hever 2009).

13 Published by the Abraham Fund Initiative: Building a Shared Future for Israel's Arab and Jewish Citizens, https://www.abrahamfund.org (accessed 12 March 2019).
14 https://www.alaraby.co.uk/english/news/2018/7/15/anger-after-israel-shuts-down-palestinian-universities-in-jerusalem (accessed 28 October 2018).
15 https://www.aljazeera.com/news/2018/07/foreign-residents-palestinian-territories-denied-visa-renewals-180713112441505.html (accessed 28 October 2018).
16 https://www.chronicle.com/interactives/08282019-salaita-academic-freedom (accessed 16 September 2019).
17 https://www.zotero.org/groups/1551835/a4e_complicit_acad emy_-___-__ (accessed 10 February 2019).
18 Facebook post, 23 October 2018, https://www.facebook.com/academia forequality/ (accessed 23 October 2018).
19 http://maki.org.il/en/?p=18274 (accessed 16 September 2019).
20 https://afp.hypotheses.org/372 (accessed 17 September 2019).
21 http://maki.org.il/en/?p=9921 (accessed 16 September 2019).
22 http://www.inss.org.il/minister-public-security-minister-strategic-affairs-mr-gilad-erdan/ (accessed 23 October 2018). The Ministry for Strategic Affairs, Information and Public Security replaces the Ministry for Public Security, in existence since 1948 to deal with matters of internal security.
23 https://www.aljazeera.com/investigations/thelobby/ (accessed 24 October 2018).
24 https://canarymission.org/ (accessed 12 April 2019).
25 https://www.meforum.org/campus-watch/about (accessed 24 October 2018).

References

Abdo, N. (2002), 'Dislocating Self, Relocating "Other": A Palestinian Experience' in N. Abdo and R. Lentin (eds), *Women and the Politics of Military Confrontation: Palestinian and Israeli Gendered Narratives of Dislocation*, Oxford and New York: Berghahn Books, pp. 119–154.

Abunimah, A. (2006), *One Country: A Bold Proposal to End the Israeli–Palestinian Impasse*, London: Picador.

Adamkar, Y. (2017), 'The Destruction of Democracy: The "Breaking the Silence" Law Unanimously Approved by the Knesset', *Walla*, 8 January, http://news.walla.co.il/item/3029757?utm_source=facebook&utm_medium=sharebutton&utm_term=social&utm_content=facebook&utm_campaign=socialbutton (accessed 8 January 2017).

Al Jazeera (2019), 'Israel Plans to Close UNRWA Schools in Occupied East Jerusalem', 20 January, https://www.aljazeera.com/news/2019/01/israel-plans-close-unrwa-schools-occupied-east-jerusalem-190120112744547. html (accessed 12 March 2019).

Bachner, M. (2018), 'Universities Urged to Enforce Code Banning Politics in Lectures', *Times of Israel*, 25 March, https://www.timesofisrael.com/israel-approves-code-banning-partisan-politics-from-academic-classrooms/ (accessed 11 March 2019).

Bhambra, G. K., D. Gebrial and K. Nişancioğlu (eds) (2018), *Decolonising the University*, London: Pluto Press.

Breiner, Y. (2011), 'The Senior Lecturer Who Refused to Serve in the Reserve and Was Jailed', *Walla*, 11 May, http://www.gumfilms.com/projects/lab (accessed 12 October 2018).

Eglash, R. (2018), '20 Groups that Boycott Israel Will Now Be Denied Entry', *The Washington Post*, 7 January, https://www.washingtonpost.com/news/worldviews/wp/2018/01/07/18-groups-that-advocate-boycotting-israel-will-now-be-denied-entry/?utm_term=.52b6f634761b (accessed 24 October 2018).

Forward (2017), 'Israeli Government OKs $72 Million Anti-BDS Project', 31 December, https://forward.com/fast-forward/391129/israeli-government-oks-72-million-anti-bds-project/ (accessed 24 October 2018).

Giroux, H. (2007), *The University in Chains: Confronting the Military-Industrial-Academic Complex*, Boulder, CO: Paradigm Publishers.

Golan, D. (2018), 'Destroying Palestinian Universities', *Haaretz*, 26 July, https://www.haaretz.com/opinion/.premium-israel-is-destroying-palestinian-universities-1.6315086 (accessed 14 October 2018).

Gravé-Lazi, L. (2018), 'Universities to Grant Credits for Reserve Duties', *The Jerusalem Post*, 1 May, https://www.jpost.com/Israel-News/Universities-to-grant-credits-for-reserve-duty-553244 (accessed 11 March 2019).

The Guardian (2016), 'Novel about Jewish–Palestinian Love Affair Is Barred from Israeli Curriculum', 1 January, https://www.theguardian.com/world/2016/jan/01/novel-about-jewish-palestinian-love-affair-is-barred-from-israeli-curriculum (accessed 18 October 2018).

Hager, T. and Y. Jabareen (2016), 'From Marginalisation to Integration: Arab-Palestinians in Israeli Academia', *International Journal of Inclusive Education* 20 (5): 455–473, DOI: 10.1080/13603116.2015.1090488 (accessed 13 March 2019).

Halper, J. (2013), *War against the People: Israel, the Palestinians and Global Pacification*, London: Pluto Press.

Hever, S. (2009), 'Academic Boycott of Israel and the Complicity of Israeli Academic Institutions in Occupation of Palestinian Territories', *Economy of the Occupation, Socioeconomic Bulletin*, No. 23, October, Jerusalem: Alternative Information Centre.

Hever, S. (2018), ' Oppression Education: Israeli Academic Institutions Throw Their Lot with the Israeli Security Elite', *AURDIP*, 14 August, http://www.aurdip.org/oppression-education-israeli.html?lang=fr (accessed 11 March 2019).

Jaffe-Hoffman, M. (2019), 'CHE Approves Medical School in Ariel University in the West Bank', *Jerusalem Post*, 11 April, https://www. jpost.com/Israel-News/CHE-approves-Medical-School-at-Ariel-University-586503 (accessed 12 April 2019).

Katz, Y. (2007), '2006: Israel Defense Sales Hit Record', *Jerusalem Post*, 1 January, https://www.jpost.com/Israel/2006-Israel-defense-sales-hit-record (accessed 10 February 2019).

Konrad, I. (2018), 'Is Academia the Last Bastion of Progressive Thought in Israel?', *+972 Magazine*, 23 January, https://972mag.com/is-academia-the-last-bastion-of-progressive-thought-in-israel/132623/ (accessed 15 October 2018).

Landau, I. (2017), 'On the Public Role of Academics in These Times', *Don't Die Stupid*, 17 March, https://idanlandau.com/2017/03/17/on-the-public-role-of-academics/ (accessed 10 October 2018).

Landau, N. (2019), 'Mossad Involved in Anti-Boycott Activity, Israeli Minister's Datebooks Reveal', *Haaretz*, 12 June, https://www.haaretz. com/amp/israel-news/.premium-mossad-involved-in-anti-boycott-activity-israeli-minister-s-diaries-reveal-1.7360253? (accessed 12 June 2019).

Lentin, R. (2018), *Traces of Racial Exception: Racializing Israeli Settler Colonialism*, London: Bloomsbury Academic.

Lieber, D. (2018), 'Number of Arab Students in Israeli Universities Grows 78% in Seven Years', *Times of Israel*, 25 January, https://www. timesofisrael.com/number-of-arab-students-in-israeli-universities-grows-78-in-7-years/ (accessed 11 March 2019).

Lis, J. (2017), 'Israeli Bill Would Cut Funds to Universities with Lecturers Backing Boycott', *Haaretz*, 3 February, http://www.haaretz.com/israel-news/.premium-1.769255 (accessed 28 October 2018).

Lis, J. (2018), 'Israeli Ministers to Discuss Bill Calling to Imprison BDS Activists for up to Seven Years', *Haaretz*, 18 October, https://www. haaretz.com/israel-news/.premium-israeli-ministers-to-talk-bill-calling-to-imprison-bds-activists-for-up-to-7-years-1.6572953?utm_source=dlvr.it&utm_medium=twitter (accessed 18 October 2018).

Matar, A. (2016), 'What Enables Asa Kasher?', www.wisdom.weizmann. ac.il/~oded/PS/anat.doc (accessed 28 October 2018).

Mearsheimer, J. J. and S. M. Walt (2006), 'The Israel Lobby and US Foreign Policy', *Middle East Policy Council* 13 (3): 29–87, http://mearsheimer. uchicago.edu/pdfs/IsraelLobby.pdf (accessed 24 October 2018).

Middle East Monitor (2018), 'New Israel Report Exposes Role of NGO Monitor in Defaming Rights Activists', 1 October, https://www.

middleeastmonitor.com/20181001-new-israel-report-exposes-role-of-ngo-monitor-in-defaming-rights-activists/ (accessed 20 February 2019).

Moshe, S. (2019), 'Hebrew University Distances Itself from Lecturer Who Said Palestinian Kids Face "Death Machine" in Jerusalem', *The Algemeiner*, 18 February, https://www.algemeiner.com/2019/02/18/hebrew-university-distances-itself-from-lecturer-who-said-palestinian-kids-face-death-machine-in-jerusalem/ (accessed 12 March 2019).

Pappe, I. (2010), *Out of the Frame: The Struggle for Academic Freedom in Israel*, London: Pluto Press.

Ram, U. (1993), 'Society and Social Science: Institutional Sociology and Critical Sociology in Israel' in U. Ram (ed.), *Israeli Society: Critical Perspectives*, Tel Aviv: Breirot Publishing, pp. 7–39.

Roth, N. (2016), 'Former IDF Ethicist Tapped to Censor "Political Speech" in Israeli Universities', *+972 Magazine*, 9 December, http://972mag.com/former-idf-ethicist-tapped-to-censor-political-speech-in-israeli-universities/123600/ (accessed 28 October 2018).

Tibon, A. (2018), 'Parts of Censored *Al Jazeera* Documentary on D.C. Israel Lobby Leaked', *Haaretz*, August 18, https://www.haaretz.com/israel-news/.premium-parts-of-censored-al-jazeera-documentary-on-pro-israeli-lobby-leaked-1.6432835 (accessed 24 October 2018).

Weizman, E. (2017), *Hollow Land: Israel's Architecture of Occupation* (new ed.), London: Verso.

White, B. (2014), 'Haifa University Launches Course in Pro-Israel Propaganda', *Middle East Monitor*, 18 April, https://www.middleeastmonitor.com/20140418-haifa-university-launches-course-in-pro-israel-propaganda/ (accessed 21 October 2018).

Yanko, A. (2018), 'Controversial Academic Ethical Code Advances', *YNet*, 25 March, https://www.ynetnews.com/articles/0,7340,L-5194926,00.html (accessed 9 October 2018).

Younis, R. (2014), 'Hebrew U Threatens Palestinian Students over Political Activity', *+972 Magazine*, 24 October, https://972mag.com/hebrew-u-threatens-palestinian-students-with-expulsion-for-political-activities/97987/ (accessed 14 October 2018).

Zur, Y. (2018), 'Israel's Creeping Annexation: Votes to Extend Israeli Law to Academic Institutions in the West Bank', *Haaretz*, 12 February, https://www.haaretz.com/israel-news/israel-votes-to-expand-israeli-law-to-academic-institutions-in-w-bank-1.5810994 (accessed 28 October 2018).

Zureik, E. (2016), *Israel's Colonial Project in Palestine: Brutal Pursuit*, London and New York: Routledge.

PART III | Interrogating academic freedom

NINE | Lawfare against academics and the potential of legal mobilization as counterpower

Jeff Handmaker

BDS as legal mobilization[1]

On 27 April 2016, Omar Barghouti, an internationally known and respected scholar, addressed a conference at Stanford University regarding the Boycott, Divestment and Sanctions (BDS) movement for Palestinian rights. He explained the underpinnings of the BDS Call issued by the movement in 2005 as being framed by three separate demands, each of which flowed from Palestinians' inalienable rights to self-determination, all of which were based on international law and outlined later in this chapter (BNC 2005).

During his contribution to the 2016 Stanford conference, Barghouti was not physically present. He was speaking through a Skype connection since the Israeli government had (again) refused to grant him an exit permit to leave the country. This was neither the first, nor the last attempt by the Israeli government to try to curb Barghouti's academic freedom by way of repressive, law-based measures, or *lawfare*. Barghouti has continually been the target of an Israeli-government-funded *tarnishing unit* that was designed to smear Palestinian, Israeli, and international BDS advocates (Oren 2016). In addition, an Israeli government minister has publicly threatened Barghouti and other BDS advocates with 'targeted civil assassination' (Zonszein 2016). This particular threat was condemned by Amnesty International (2016).

The response of Barghouti and a global network of supporters in the BDS movement has been to consistently follow a strategy of law-based, civic confrontation, serving as an important and legitimate form of *legal mobilization* that has gained inspiration from the global movement to end apartheid in South Africa. As Barghouti remarked in April 2017 on the occasion of his being awarded the 2017 Gandhi Peace Award:

> We had to take the South African path, so to speak, to bring Israel to account by citizens around the world, institutions around the world, civil society, getting together and taking measures that would isolate Israel academically, culturally, economically, and eventually impose sanctions on it, as was done against South Africa. (Goodman 2017)

As I explain in this chapter, it is both analytically and practically useful to regard the legal content of Barghouti's talk, as well as the other case studies of BDS addressed in this chapter as forms of legal mobilization (Handmaker 2019). By analysing (international) law-based advocacy, I am cognisant of the widespread scepticism that many critical and particular decolonial legal scholars have articulated about the role and function of international law. Erakat (2019, 6) has noted this concern with particular regard to the Palestinian struggle.

> There are at least two reasons to be skeptical that international law has the capacity to overcome geopolitical realities and advance the Palestinian struggle for freedom. One is the sordid origin of international law as a derivative of a colonial order … that reifies, rather than unsettles a symmetry of rights and duties among international actors. The other is the fact that the international system lacks a global sovereign, thereby politicizing enforcement by leaving it to the discretion of states to decide when, how and whom, to punish.

With specific reference to the BDS movement, Erakat warns of the risk of invoking international law in the absence of 'a corresponding political programme' and hence the risk of depoliticizing the Palestinian struggle 'by framing it as a movement for equality'. The struggle, she argues, is fundamentally 'against settler-colonial dominance' (Erakat 2019, 231). Hence, campaigns that are based on a rights-based approach are not only incapable of redressing the historical dispossession of Palestinian land and livelihoods, but situate the struggle in terms of 'competing rights' without addressing the massive power differentials between settler-colonial Israelis and Palestinians who are claiming those rights (Erakat 2019, 232). Instead, Erakat argues – like other scholars of Third World Approaches to International Law or TWAIL, such as Samour (2017) and Reynolds (2017) – in favour of an historical understanding of international law and institutions in order to reimagine the potential of international law to support the Palestinian struggle.

Notwithstanding these valid concerns, much of the law-based, civic-led advocacy is highly refined in Israel–Palestine, where there is a significant amount of legal knowledge, and international human rights law has formed a significant role in the normative architecture. Rather than passively insisting on its enforcement, international law has been mobilized by Palestinian civic actors in a political response to what has been described as 'an unmet obligation of the organized international community to resolve a conflict partially generated by its own actions' (UN 2017, iv).

It is well-documented that the government of Israel takes a highly exceptionalist position with regard to international law, particularly with regard to Palestinian self-determination, meaning Israel only follows international law when it suits its interests (Akram et al. 2011). Just as the case during the 1980s in South Africa, which also faced global criticism of its apartheid policies, such blatant disregard for the global applicability of international law explains why appealing to international law to substantiate criticisms of Israel's treatment of Palestinians, particularly manifested through a call for BDS, has such global resonance.

This chapter proceeds as follows. In the following section, I explain Israel's legal regime in which lawfare and legal mobilization are expressed. I then discuss the use of law in relation to academic freedom claims, making a distinction between legal mobilization and lawfare. An analytical framework that can be used to evaluate how law is strategically used by civic actors as either legal mobilization or lawfare is not fully developed in this particular chapter, though I have explained this elsewhere (Handmaker 2019). Instead, I briefly introduce the framework and develop legal mobilization and lawfare as analytical concepts, which are then applied against various examples of law-based advocacy, either from proponents of, or objectors to the global BDS movement for Palestinian rights.

The chapter then goes on to evaluate the transformative potential of drawing on international human rights law, using legal mobilization to support a global movement for BDS aimed at ending Israel's violations of Palestinian rights under international law, and defending academics and other advocates critical of Israel against lawfare. I then analyse examples of lawfare where legal and/or policy measures have been imposed by the Israeli government against academic critics of Israel, and particularly BDS advocates to try to suppress their freedom of speech and freedom of association, which have been wielded by a range of government-linked, but mostly privately funded lawfare organizations. This then allows me to revisit, in the penultimate section, the crucial distinction between lawfare and legal mobilization and finally to draw conclusions in the final section regarding both the potential and challenges of law-based BDS advocacy to pursue a progressive social justice agenda.

But first I briefly outline the context in which both legal mobilization and lawfare take place in relation to Israel–Palestine, explaining the nature of Israel's legal regime.

Israel's legal regime of apartheid

From a normative standpoint, Israel's legal system has entrenched the socially constructed, ethno-nationalist *Jewish* character of the State of Israel, which takes the form of a racialized, settler-colonial regime that is profoundly discriminatory, perhaps most visibly reinforced by the 2018 Nation-State Law (Ben-Youssef and Tamari 2018). Also in its implementation, Israel's legal regime has been profoundly repressive towards Palestinians, as extensively documented, particularly regarding the situation in the Occupied Palestinian Territory, by organizations such as Al-Haq, B'tselem, Addameer, the Palestinian Center for Human Rights, and international organizations such as Human Rights Watch, Amnesty International, and Fédération Internationale des Droits de l'Homme (FIDH). Hence, on a range of legal criteria, the situation in the Occupied Palestinian Territory can be readily described as a regime of apartheid (Dugard and Reynolds 2013; UN 2017).

Moreover, the situation of apartheid extends beyond the Occupied Palestinian Territory to all areas under Israeli control. Discrimination and other human rights violations in Israel have further been extensively documented by the Haifa-based Adalah Human Rights Organization, Ittijah Union of Arab Community-Based Associations, and the Nazareth-based Human Rights Association. Moreover, apartheid incorporates not only legal, but also ideological, architectural, and physical dimensions (Abdelnour 2013).

Added to this is the also well-documented, although officially unacknowledged history that Israel's creation in 1948 was only made possible following the forcible dispossession of several hundred thousand Palestinians from their homes and lands, described by the Israeli historian Ilan Pappe (2006) as a deliberate policy of ethnic cleansing.

Confronted with such an oppressive situation, and triggered by Israel's continued building of a wall, despite the International Court of Justice declaring the wall to be illegal, Palestinians issued the international law-based BDS Call in 2005 (Bot 2019).

Pragmatic mobilization versus hegemonic instrumentalization of law

As Barghouti specifically and the BDS movement in general have demonstrated, law can be mobilized pragmatically by civic actors, including academics in their critiques of Israel's behaviour. The concept of legal mobilization therefore refers generally to the use of law as a *legitimate* form of political counterpower, to underpin political claims, and more specifically as the basis for non-violent, law-based protests against oppressive regimes. As I argue in this section, legal mobilization is to be contrasted with the concept of lawfare, which refers to the hegemonic and *illegitimate* use of law by state and/or corporate bodies to undermine legal mobilization, including to silence dissent and to persecute individual critics of Israel.

Legal values are firmly embedded in the BDS Call (BNC 2005). The first demand of the Call is that Israel '(end) its occupation and colonization of all Arab lands and dismantl(e) the Wall' that Israel constructed in 2002, affirmed a year prior to the Call as illegal by the International Court of Justice (2004). The second demand is that Israel 'recognize the fundamental rights of the Arab-Palestinian citizens of Israel to full equality', a demand for equality incorporated in numerous international legal instruments, notably the Universal Declaration of Human Rights, which was passed in the same year as Israel's creation (UN 1948). The final demand of the BDS Call is that Israel commit to 'respecting, protecting and promoting the rights of Palestinian refugees to return to their homes and properties as stipulated in UN resolution 194', a cornerstone of Palestinian self-determination (UN 1949; Handmaker 2011).

Since the broad BDS Call in 2005, and through national and international legal processes, BDS advocates, including a very large global coalition of academics, have advocated for structural change using international law and especially rights-based arguments (Bisharat et al. 2018, 5). This use of law by civic actors striving for social change, or what can be broadly regarded as legal mobilization, has two characteristics. Legal mobilization is a term to describe the *practice* of legal advocacy; it is also an analytical *concept* and interdisciplinary lens to understand the role of law in civic advocacy, in terms of its normative and its functional dimensions (Handmaker 2019).

An important distinction should be made between *legal mobilization* and other uses of law, including oppressive legal measures by a state and/or corporation, which should be conceptualized as *lawfare*. These two law-based concepts might both be superficially regarded as forms of legal instrumentalism on the assumption that the political character of the claim inevitably undermines the rule of law (Tamanaha 2005). However, I argue that they are fundamentally different. Indeed, understanding these distinctions is key to appreciating the legitimate use of law as a form of counterpower against the powerful, suppressive arm of a state. Beyond *what* legal mobilization and lawfare are as analytical concepts, it can also be analysed *how* they operate.

Clearly, law is used not only by civic actors such as academics critical of Israel and other advocates, but by a range of stakeholders, including lawfare groups such as Shurat HaDin, Legal Insurrection, and the Brandeis Center, as discussed later in this chapter. As a practice, the legal mobilization of human rights adopts positive, legitimating, and empowering forms, reinforcing the underlying social justice claims of BDS in what Hoffman (2003, 121) has referred to as 'an indispensable rhetorical tool against any form of dominance and attempted hegemony'. By contrast, lawfare takes negative, delegitimizing, and oppressive forms, justifying retrogressive policies and even reinforcing the hegemonic actions of states, such as denying access to legal representation and holding accused persons without charge in the operation of Israel's military tribunals or validating the superiority of one group of people over another in the case of Israel's Nation-State Law.

The strategic use of law by civic actors to advance human rights provides legal legitimacy to a political claim (legal mobilization), which Bot has argued is based on political principles of 'emancipation, transformation, and civility' (Bot 2019, 16). This should be seen in contrast to the hegemonic manner in which law is instrumentalized by powerful states as well as individuals, groups, and corporations to serve an oppressive agenda (lawfare). Legal mobilization as an analytical framework recognizes: first, the capacity of civic actors to challenge the state; second, that the values underpinning international human rights law can be translated by civic actors into a locally relevant context, rather than merely reproducing and transplanting these rules in a technocratic manner (Merry 2006); and third, international law's inherent structural bias is crucial in understanding the strategic potential for law-based advocacy, both in terms of the institutions against which legal mobilization is directed as well as the substantive law that forms the basis of any legal claim, including lawfare (Handmaker and Arts 2019, 12). The third of these elements will be applied further in this chapter.

This three-dimensional framework forms an analytical basis for assessing the legitimate potential of legal mobilization, as a lens to assess socially progressive forms of legal mobilization, as well as – and against the contrasting lens of – lawfare as an oppressive instrumentalizing of law (Handmaker 2019). To illustrate the former, I next discuss how academics have used legal mobilization as a legitimate form of counterpower through their support for the Palestinian call for a boycott of Israeli academic and cultural institutions.

Legal mobilization in promoting Palestinian rights and academic freedom

Faced with few credible domestic legal remedies in Israel, Palestinians, together with some Israelis and a global network of supporters, including numerous academics and lawyers, have been compelled to mobilize international law in order to advocate for a socially progressive agenda, including academic freedom for Palestinian students and scholars. Thousands of academics around the world answered the initial call by their Palestinian colleagues through the Palestinian Academic and Cultural Boycott of Israel (PACBI), which was released in 2004, the same year as the ICJ (2004) judgement and immediately preceding the 2005 Call referred to earlier. The BDS Call was signed by a broad-based collective of Palestinian civil society organizations, including political parties, trade unions, and professional associations.

The BDS Call advocates that boycotts, divestment, and sanctions 'should be maintained until Israel meets its obligation to recognize the Palestinian people's inalienable right to self-determination and fully complies with the precepts of international law' (BNC 2005).

This Call has been accompanied by three clear demands, each of which, it already noted, is grounded in international legal norms. Beyond the legal basis of justification, the several hundred signatories of the Call have appealed for different kinds of measures, each of a punitive, though non-violent character, which are equally grounded in international law and comprise: institutional boycotts, including academic boycotts, corporate divestment, and ultimately sanctions against Israel. These forms of BDS can be analytically regarded as forms of legal mobilization.

In analysing the BDS movement, several arguments can put forward, both with regard to the substantive content of the BDS Call and the character of the global movement, within the broader rubric of legal mobilization.

The first argument is that by drawing on international law, the legitimate normative character of the BDS Call is enhanced, on the basis of individual claims enshrined in multiple sources of international law. This is confirmed by Barnette (2010), who observes that the legitimacy of the Palestinian narrative has been enhanced by high-profile UN reports, to which critics of Israel often make reference. One of the most damning of these reports, which has formed the basis for preliminary enquiries by the office of the Prosecutor of the International Criminal Court, is the Goldstone Commission's report confirming the commission of widespread violations of human rights and international humanitarian law in Gaza and the West Bank by Israel's military during 2008/09.

The second argument is that the capacity of Palestinian civic actors to participate in international legal process has been an explicit claim of the BDS movement. This right to participate is embedded in international legal norms, deliberately mentioned in the BDS Call as a core principle of self-determination and supported by a broad social justice movement comprising a global network of advocates, including academics, based in Europe,

North America, South Africa, Australia, India, Brazil, the Arab world, and elsewhere. Through persistent and very vocal campaigns, the BNC leadership have become active participants in international and national law-based processes, from national legislatures to the European Union and various United Nations fora. In the BNC's frequent interactions with the media, advocates routinely reaffirm the relevance of respecting international law. Similarly, the public figures engaged by the movement have also based their arguments on the need to respect international law. One notable example is a statement in solidarity with the BNC by the well-known theologian and South African anti-apartheid advocate Archbishop Desmond Tutu:

> Many black South Africans have travelled to the occupied West Bank and have been appalled by Israeli roads built for Jewish settlers that West Bank Palestinians are denied access to, and by Jewish-only colonies built on Palestinian land in violation of international law. (Tutu 2012)

Another example comes from the American civil rights author and scholar Alice Walker, who served, along with other eminent scholars and jurists, on the jury of the Russell Tribunal on Palestine (2011) that held hearings in different parts of the world concerning alleged violations of international law by Israel, including in Cape Town concerning the crime of apartheid. Numerous prominent scholars critical of Israel, including Sara Roy (2012), John Dugard (2018), John Reynolds (2017), Richard Falk (2017), and Noura Erakat (2019), to name just a few, have documented Israel's extensive violations of international law obligations.

Consistent and accurate reference to international law as a principal basis for their arguments renders these cultural icons and scholars powerful advocates of legal mobilization. Through the sustained efforts of the BDS movement and the prominent public figures who support the BNC, a wide range of activities by the State of Israel, and its numerous cultural, political, academic, and other institutions, have been called into question at a global level.

The third argument is that, by forming a broad-based and grass-roots network of civic actors, the BDS movement has managed to connect with both the global context that has generated basic protective principles of international law as well as the local context in which these international norms find normative expression. In doing so, the BNC has been a powerful translator in reinforcing Palestinians' social justice claims, which are articulated in international human rights law. Accordingly, the BNC has charted a persistent, confrontational, non-violent, and highly strategic course of action that Omar Barghouti (2011) terms a global struggle for Palestinian rights.

A further argument is that in making consistent reference to law-based justifications, the founders of the BDS movement strategically highlight some of the core legal biases present in international legal vocabularies, and particularly human rights enforcement institutions. This is visible in the preamble to the original BDS petition:

> In light of Israel's *persistent violations* of international law; and
> Given that, since 1948, hundreds of UN resolutions have condemned Israel's *colonial and discriminatory policies* as illegal and called for immediate, adequate and effective remedies; and
> Given that *all forms of international intervention and peacemaking have until now failed* to convince or force Israel to comply with humanitarian law, to respect fundamental human rights and to end its occupation and oppression of the people of Palestine. (BNC 2005; emphasis added)

By consistently referencing international law in this historicized form that explicitly acknowledges Israel's 'persistent violations', the drafters of the BDS Call have acknowledged that international law reinforces unequal power relations, notably within the academy. Moreover, human rights law possesses an inherent normative bias that, when wielded in a historically grounded and anti-imperial manner, favours a socially progressive agenda, underpinning the threefold demands embodied in the BDS Call and affirming the need to question institutional practices.

While affirming international human rights values, the drafters of the Call are also sceptical of the transformative effect of human rights on the basis of legalistic explanations alone. This is what led the American Studies Association (ASA), comprising thousands of academics, to call for a boycott of Israeli academic institutions. In its call, the ASA explicitly mentions US complicity in 'enabling' actions by the Israeli government and settlements as being:

> in violation of international law, as well as in supporting the systematic discrimination against Palestinians, which has had documented devastating impact on the overall well-being, the exercise of political and human rights, the freedom of movement, and the educational opportunities of Palestinians. (ASA 2013)

Consequently, the drafters of the BDS Call, as well as academics and other advocates who have responded, have shifted their emphasis away from a reliance on formal legal institutions designed to enforce it, in favour of a broad-based, civic-led platform focused on advocating for the international isolation of Israel at an institutional level, until Israel complies with international law.

Israel's campaign of lawfare and legal mobilization as a defence

Legal mobilization for Palestinian rights, particularly through BDS, has triggered a well-financed counter-campaign of lawfare waged by the State of Israel and its global supporters. Around ten years after the BDS movement was launched, the government of Israel and its supporters began responding to non-violent legal mobilization with a barrage of oppressive legal instruments. Adopting highly-politicized interpretations of criminal law, civil liability, and even municipal regulations in countries abroad, lawfare organizations have sought to harass, intimidate, slander, and otherwise seek to harm individual scholars, activists, student organizations, and companies critical of Israel. Unlike the BDS movement, which is inclusive and aimed at triggering critical political dialogue, these mostly government-sponsored measures to suppress the movement are profoundly discriminatory, aimed at politicizing and subverting the rule of law as a 'political tool' (Bot 2019, 9).

Palestinian scholars such as Barghouti and Haidar Eid have been particularly affected by such lawfare measures, primarily taking the form of movement restrictions. Students have also been seriously affected by Israel's lawfare, with one Palestinian university (Birzeit) having faced repeated closures by the Israeli occupation forces since 1973, including an extended period of 1,571 days between 1988 and 1992. Critical Israeli scholars have also been affected by Israel's lawfare. For example, there have been persistent efforts, including the use of a sham 'international review process', to shut down the Department of Politics at Ben Gurion University, which has been known for the outspoken views of many faculty members (B.N. 2012). Professor Nadera Shalhoub-Kevorkian of Hebrew University of Jerusalem has been subject to years of in-faculty and external abuse, including bogus accusations from the Israeli media and the Israeli Education Minister Naftali Bennett of 'anti-Semitism' (Tucker and Brand 2019).

Israel's campaign of lawfare has built on earlier legal forms of repression since the creation of the State of Israel in 1948, the establishment of which triggered an official State of Emergency that has persisted throughout its existence. Around the sixtieth anniversary of its creation, Israel sought to intensify legal and financial incentives aimed at attracting Israeli and foreign corporations. At the same time, the government has sought to protect corporate profits through a so-called anti-BDS law (Lis 2011). The law attacks freedom of expression by allowing corporations, including those profiting from business activities inside the occupied Palestinian territory (in violation of international law), to make claims for damages against individuals if it can be established that their advocacy (e.g. exposing complicity of these companies in international crimes) harms the corporation's economic interests. The anti-BDS law has been accompanied by a so-called 'Loyalty Oath' law, which seeks to ensure allegiance to the 'Jewish democratic state' and to ban a range of activities deemed to question it (Ananth 2013, 134).

There has been very limited opposition to such repressive measures among liberal Israeli human rights organizations, which generally lack a critical perspective and fail to listen to Palestinian organizations (Handmaker 2018), and none at all from Israel's higher education institutions. Instead, human rights have been invoked to rationalize the inequalities between Jewish settlers and Palestinians and to give the impression that Israel is a liberal, democratic state. Aharon Barak (2006), a former president of the Supreme Court of Israel and law professor at the Hebrew University of Jerusalem has adamantly maintained that there is normative equality in Israel, irrespective of religion or ethnicity. Another prominent human rights scholar, David Kretzmer (1992) has referred to the 1992 Basic Laws on Human Rights in Israel as amounting to a mini-revolution in terms of Israeli constitutional law, without fundamentally questioning its racist ideological basis. However promising these normative claims

may be, functionally speaking such claims are largely meaningless; Israel's legal regime has routinely betrayed these normative
promises, particularly when measured against international law.
By failing to seriously engage with the ideological character of
these laws, and at best superficially engaging with their functional
character (generally limited to criticisms of Israel's practices in
the Occupied Palestinian Territory, if at all), liberal human rights
scholars in Israel have reinforced, and even become complicit in
Israel's policy of exceptionalism and lawfare.

Israel's lawfare has been followed by a string of laws in other
countries, notably the United States and Britain, where publicly financed entities have been informed that they will no longer receive state funding if they take a position in support of the
Palestinian BDS movement (Hager 2016). These laws have been
promoted by well-funded lawfare organizations such as the Reut
Institute, pledging to challenge what they refer to as 'delegitimization' and 'resistance' networks critical of Israel (Ananth 2013,
130–136).

Another well-funded, pro-Israel lawfare organization is Shurat
HaDin, based in Israel and exposed by Wikileaks as tied to Israeli
intelligence agencies (Winstanley 2017), but operating transna-
tionally and especially in the United States. On its website, the
organization sensationally claims to be 'bankrupting terrorism,
one lawsuit at a time', while misleadingly suggesting that it is not
they, but those engaged in legal mobilization that are engaged in
lawfare, although the organization fails to substantiate this claim
(Shurat HaDin 2018). Among other spectacular claims on its
website, the organization declares itself to be:

> dedicated to protecting the State of Israel. By defending against
> lawfare suits, *fighting academic and economic boycotts*, and
> challenging those who seek to delegitimize the Jewish State,

> Shurat HaDin is utilizing court systems around the world to go
> on the legal offensive against Israel's enemies. (Shurat HaDin
> 2018; emphasis added)

Among many other cases brought by Shurat HaDin was a lawsuit against an Australian professor, Jake Lynch, regarding his support for the academic boycott. Raising wildly unsubstantiated allegations of racial discrimination, the organization called for his dismissal from the University of Sydney, although later dropped its claim, which appeared to be solely designed to intimidate and otherwise discourage academics from speaking out on BDS (Safi and Davidson 2014).

Another organization engaged in lawfare is Legal Insurrection (2018), which actively (and successfully) campaigned for the withdrawal of an employment contract that had been offered to US academic and prominent Israel critic Stephen Salaita. Following intervention by Salaita's lawyers at the Center for Constitutional Rights, the university paid extensive compensation, but refused to reinstate its initial offer of employment (LaHood 2016). Legal Insurrection also reported the ASA to the IRS, alleging (unsuccessfully) that the ASA was not fulfilling the requirements of its tax-exempt status due to its endorsement of the academic boycott of Israel. Later, joined by another lawfare organization, the Brandeis Center, claims were filed (albeit later dismissed) against the ASA, erroneously alleging that the association over-reached its contractual obligations to its members (Palestine Legal 2019).

Legal mobilization as a defence against lawfare

The cases of lawfare highlighted in this chapter are just the tip of an iceberg. There are many more examples of threats to individual academic freedom, hundreds of which have been carefully documented by the Chicago-based organization Palestine Legal, a legal services organization providing crucial support to academics, student associations, and other targets of pro-Israel lawfare organizations. Faced with a growing range of lawfare attacks, there has been a need to invoke legal mobilization in defence of academic freedom, particularly in the United States where lawfare has mainly been focused. Various organizations have emerged that have taken the lead in support to academics critical of Israel, notably the Center for Constitutional Rights (CCR) – which has supported Palestine Legal – as well as the National Lawyers Guild (NLG) and American Civil Liberties Union (ACLU), primarily on the basis that BDS and scholarly critiques of Israel ought to be regarded as protected speech (Hauss 2017).

Basing arguments on US constitutional law, particularly concerning free speech and anti-discrimination provisions, and probono support to individuals and organizations who would potentially face extensive legal bills, organizations such as CCR, NLG, and ACLU have brought robust legal argumentation in defence of baseless accusations and spurious legal claims made by lawfare organizations. Drawing on decades of engagement with American legal culture, a highly developed legal consciousness in relation to the use of the US Constitution and international human rights, and the local complexities of the cases they have been handling, as well as a keen awareness of how US citizens have developed a growing criticism of Israel's human rights record, CCR have been able to make quick, creative use of the law (Asmy 2017).

Accordingly, CCR and other organizations have mobilized law as a shield to defend Lynch, Salaita, and others against lawfare efforts to silence them and to a significant extent redress the otherwise massively unequal power relations between a corporate and state-sponsored regime and individual activists and public interest groups. Moreover, CCR has carefully framed their statements to the media, showing they had made a strategic assessment of the positive bias embedded in international human rights law that supported their legal claims, which were able to thwart the efforts of groups who intended to silence critics of Israel as part of a well-financed campaign of lawfare.

False antisemitism allegations

One of the more recent (though somewhat exaggerated) lawfare efforts in Europe has been to define criticism of Israel as antisemitic and to secure official endorsement of this definition in support of bogus allegations of antisemitism. In the United States and Britain, antisemitism claims in response to criticisms of Israel are relatively easy to equate with allegations of antisemitism, in Europe there is much greater scepticism about these claims, particularly within the academy.

The efforts to equate criticisms of Israel with antisemitism have mainly been led by a lobby group known as the International Holocaust Remembrance Alliance (IHRA), which, in its proposed definition of antisemitism, has argued that 'the targeting of the state of Israel, conceived as a Jewish collectivity' amounts to antisemitism (IHRA 2016). This wide formulation makes it practically impossible to challenge the *Jewish character* of the State of Israel, parroting a position that the Supreme Court of Israel has routinely affirmed, and the Nation-State Law of 2018 has entrenched at the legislative and executive levels. More specifically, the IHRA argues that '(d)enying the Jewish people their right to self-determination, e.g. by claiming that the existence of a State of Israel is a racist endeavor' amounts to antisemitism. In other words, the IHRA implies that it is perfectly acceptable for Israel to deny Palestinians, as well as Israelis (including Jews) who identify as Palestinians their right to self-determination, and to exclusively declare Hebrew as Israel's official language (while downgrading Arabic), yet it would be antisemitic to argue that any of this is racist. Indeed, suggesting that there is a situation of apartheid in Israel would also amount to antisemitism according to the IHRA definition.

There has been a lot of discussion regarding the German Bundestag's passing of a non-binding 'motion' in May 2019, which appeared to declare that BDS was antisemitic. This immediately triggered an open protest by Jewish and Israeli scholars condemning the motion (Oltermann 2019). This not-withstanding, efforts to paint critics of Israel as antisemitic are clearly waning. At an event in The Hague that I had organized at my university in October 2018, the respected journalist, scholar, and writer Ali Abunimah outlined the consequences of Israel's claim to have a right to exist as a Jewish state as confirmed by the 2018 Nation-State Law (Abunimah 2018). Drawing on illustrations from his earlier book *The Battle for Justice in Palestine* (2014), Abunimah explained how Israel's right to exist effectively allowed the Israeli government, military, and supporters worldwide to pursue a state-sponsored agenda of lawfare. As a practical consequence of this agenda, Abunimah argued that Israel creates legal backing to discriminate, kill, and persecute Palestinians.

At the start of his presentation, Abunimah noted that the announcement of the October 2018 event had led to a string of online messages and letters by pro-Israel groups, including a letter addressed to my university, invoking the IHRA definition and attempting to smear Abunimah as antisemitic (Abunimah 2018). These lawfare efforts to condemn and seek to censor Abunimah were unsuccessful in the Netherlands, where BDS has been confirmed as protected free speech (Lazaroff 2016; Bot 2019). Accordingly, Dutch lawyers advised Abunimah, at no cost, that he could respond by way of legal mobilization and register both a civil claim and a criminal complaint in response to the accusations against him, which he ultimately chose not to pursue.

The Hague event illustrated vividly why lawfare and legal mobilization are fundamentally different, the former aimed at suppressing criticism, while the latter is aimed at protecting individual rights, including freedom of expression. The final section of this chapter revisits this crucial distinction.

Why should Israel's lawfare be distinguished from legal mobilization?

Evaluating the crude instrumentalization of law by Israel and its supporters, such as Shurat HaDin and Legal Insurrection, confirms the importance of an analytical distinction between lawfare and legal mobilization. They are not the same. In the case of the counter-BDS campaign waged by Israel and its supporters, the legitimacy question has been turned entirely on its head, suggesting that legitimacy is something inherent in the State of Israel itself, and that any actions that challenge this are *de facto* illegitimate.

From a legal capacity point of view, both the tone and the content of measures taken by the Israeli government have explicitly rejected the role of civic actors to participate in the (international) legal process. Through the anti-BDS law and other measures, notably travel bans as experienced by Barghouti and other advocates, the Israeli government seeks to curtail the work of leading figures in the BDS movement. As part of the battle for legitimacy by Israel and its supporters, arguments have been reinforced by misplaced references to the historical persecution of Jews, which political science professors Mearsheimer and Walt have argued are a key part of a well-organized 'Israel lobby' intent on distorting key facts, and obscuring Israel's responsibility for international crimes, including third-state support for Israel's regime (Mearsheimer and Walt 2008).

Curiously, while the use of structural bias has been clearly evident in the use of law by all parties, the results of such efforts have tended to favour the legal mobilizers rather than those engaged in lawfare. Unlike legal mobilization advocates who reinforce the values underpinning international law, organizations engaged in lawfare have been informed by hollow claims that Israel has faced increasing delegitimization and has been treated unfairly by the United Nations and other international law institutions (Bayefsky 1995). Rather than engage with these international law institutions, lawfare organizations have relied on principles of 'necessity', and describe their perceived enemies as operating 'outside and against the law threatening the life of the state of Israel' (Kearney 2010, 126). In this way, Israel's military commanders, government lawyers, and overseas supporters who are engaged in lawfare reflect Israel's exceptionalist treatment of international law, oppressively instrumentalizing national laws against Palestinians and other BDS advocates that bear little to no relation to international law in general, and human rights law in particular.

Such efforts reaffirm that lawfare can readily serve as a basis for systematic discrimination by elites against particular groups, which adapted to the BDS Call has taken the form of an 'entrenched system of racial discrimination against … Arab-Palestinians' (BNC 2005). Hence, the legitimacy of lawfare can be strongly questioned from a legal values standpoint; whereas self-determination, equality and (non-)discrimination are mobilized as fundamental legal values, in contrast to the derisive dismissal of these values by Israel and its supporters.

Conclusions

Applying the legal mobilization concept to case studies of academics and associations speaking critically of Israel and in solidarity with Palestine vividly reveals how Palestinian and global social justice advocates within the BDS movement have mobilized law to pursue a socially progressive agenda. Law has been mobilized as a dynamic means of emancipating people from injustice, as a defence against repressive state measures, to challenge official impunity, and as a means to try to hold individuals, states, and corporations accountable for (complicity in) violations of international law, and especially human rights.

As I have argued, the BDS Call and accompanying global movement is more than merely another form of legal instrumentalism; it is a politically legitimate means of claiming rights and holding violating states and their corporate agents accountable. It is, accordingly, a form of legal mobilization. Furthermore, this form of law-based advocacy should be distinguished from lawfare, which is designed to undermine legal mobilization and indeed undermine the rule of law.

A conclusion that can be drawn here is that the potential of legal mobilization aimed at holding governments accountable to protect human rights has common drivers, both thematically and across different social and political contexts, each of which highlight BDS as a very significant, civic-led form of law-based advocacy. Three of these common drivers deserve specific mention.

First, legal mobilizers have shown how important it is not only to appreciate, but to explain to the rest of the world the social, economic, political, and legal context against which BDS takes place. This context includes the appalling treatment of Palestinian children, particularly by the Israeli military tribunal system (Parker 2016), the confiscation of Palestinian land to benefit the illegal activities of agricultural companies (Tonutti 2013), and severe restrictions on Palestinians' movement (OCHA 2016), which in turn relate to the state and corporate actors as well as to complicit universities and cultural institutions against whom BDS advocates, including academics, have targeted their efforts.

Second, the structural bias that conditions BDS advocates utilizing legal mobilization can be reflexively understood (i.e. built into an organization's programming), and critically assessed when academics and other advocates in solidarity with Palestine are making strategic choices to mobilize the law in a particular way, not only through expensive litigation, but also through broad-based movements of civic-led boycotts and divestment.

Finally, the success of strategic legal mobilization interventions is their capacity to go beyond legal-technocratic jargon and invoke multiple strategies, most notably use of the media, that combine legal and other forms of social mobilization to give a human face to, and facilitate a broader and critical engagement with, the issues at stake.

Note

1 This chapter is based initially on a talk I gave at Trinity College Dublin in September 2017.

References

Abdelnour, S. (2013), 'Beyond South Africa: Understanding Israeli Apartheid', Policy Brief, Washington, DC: Al-Shabaka.

Abunimah, A. (2014), *The Battle for Justice in Palestine*, Chicago, IL: Haymarket.

Abunimah, A. (2018), 'Introductory Statement' at the seminar *Israel's Nation-State Law: A Discussion*, The Hague: International Institute of Social Studies.

Akram, S., M. Dumper, M. Lynk and I. Scobbie (2011), *International Law and the Israeli–Palestinian Conflict*, London: Routledge.

Amnesty International (2016), 'Israeli Government Must Cease Intimidation of Human Rights Defenders, Protect Them from Attacks', London, Index number MDE 15/3824/2016, 12 April 2016, https://www.amnesty.org/en/documents/mde15/3824/2016/en/ (accessed 9 May 2019).

Ananth, S. (2013), 'The Politics of the Palestinian BDS Movement', *Socialism and Democracy* 27 (3): 129–143.

ASA (2013), 'Boycott of Israeli Academic Institutions', Resolution of the American Studies Association, 16 December, https://www.theasa.

net/about/advocacy/resolutions-actions/resolutions/boycott-israeli-academic-institutions (accessed 9 May 2019).

Asmy, B. (2017), 'Legal Mobilization in the United States' in J. Handmaker, *Legal Mobilization in a World Marked by Populism and Crisis: Report of a Colloquium and Public Event*, Princeton University, June 12–13, pp. 16–19.

B.N. (2012), 'How the Israeli Right Conspired to Shut Down "Lefty" Department at BGU', *+972 Magazine*, 24 October, 2012, https://972 mag.com/who-and-what-are-behind-the-attacks-on-ben-gurion-universitys-politics-and-government-department/58296/ (accessed 10 October 2019).

Barak, A. (2006), 'Human Rights in Israel', *Israel Law Review* 39 (2): 12–34.

Barghouti, O. (2011), *Boycott Divestment Sanctions: The Global Struggle for Palestinian Rights*, Chicago, IL: Haymarket.

Barnette, J. (2010), 'The Goldstone Report: Challenging Israeli Impunity in the International Legal System?', *Global Jurist* 10 (3): 1–28.

Bayefsky, A. (1995), 'Israel and the United Nations' Human Rights Agenda: The Inequality of Nations Large and Small', *Israel Law Review* 29 (3): 424–458.

Ben-Youssef, N. and S. Tamari (2018), 'Enshrining Discrimination: Israel's Nation-State Law', *Journal of Palestine Studies* 48 (1): 73–87.

Bisharat, G., J. Handmaker, G. Karmi and A. Tartir (2018), 'Mobilizing International Law in the Palestinian Struggle for Justice', *Global Jurist* 18 (3): 1–6.

BNC (2005), 'Palestinian Civil Society Call for BDS', Boycott National Committee, Ramallah, bdsmovement.net/call (accessed 9 May 2019).

Bot, M. (2019), 'The Right to Boycott: BDS, Law, and Politics in a Global Context', *Transnational Legal Theory*, https://doi.org/10.1080/2041400 5.2019.1672134 (accessed 11 October 2019).

Dugard, J. (2018), *Confronting Apartheid*, Auckland Park, South Africa: Jacana.

Dugard, J. and J. Reynolds (2013), 'Apartheid, International Law, and the Occupied Palestinian Territory', *European Journal of International Law* 24 (3): 867–913.

Erakat, N. (2019), *Justice for Some: Law and the Question of Palestine*, Stanford, CA: Stanford University Press.

Falk, R. (2017), *Palestine's Horizon: Towards a Just Peace*, London: Pluto Press.

Goodman, A. (2017), 'BDS Leader Omar Barghouti Dedicates His Gandhi Peace Award to Palestinian Prisoners on Hunger Strike', *Democracy Now*, 25 April.

Hager, M. (2016), 'Legislating against BDS: Israel's Current Blitz', *Foreign Policy Journal*, 26 February, https://www.foreignpolicyjournal.com/

2016/02/26/legislating-against-bds-israels-current-blitz/ (accessed 21 April 2017).

Handmaker, J. (2011), 'Beyond Exclusion: Assessing Palestinian Refugees' Struggle for Protection and Recognition and Their Potential Contribution to a Peace Settlement' in K. van der Borght, K. Byttebier and C. Mackenzie (eds), *Imagining a Shared Future: Perspectives on Law, Conflict and Economic Development in the Middle East*, London: Cameron May, pp. 197–222.

Handmaker, J. (2018), 'Liberal Israeli Human Rights Organizations Need to Learn How to Listen', *Mondoweiss*, 7 June, https://mondoweiss. net/2018/06/liberal-israeli-organizations/ (accessed 10 October 2019).

Handmaker, J. (2019), 'Researching Legal Mobilization and Lawfare', ISS Working Paper Series / General Series 641, pp. 1–19, http://hdl.handle. net/1765/115129 (accessed 9 May 2019).

Handmaker, J. and K. Arts (2019), *Mobilising International Law for 'Global Justice'*, Cambridge: Cambridge University Press.

Hauss, B. (2017), 'The Right to Boycott Is Under Threat', *ACLU*, 11 October, https://www.aclu.org/blog/free-speech/right-boycott-under-threat (accessed 26 June 2019).

Hoffman, F. (2003), 'Human Rights and Political Liberty', *International Legal Theory* 9 (1): 105–122.

IHRA (2016), 'Working Definition of Anti-Semitism', International Holocaust Remembrance Alliance website, https://www.holocaustremembrance. com/working-definition-antisemitism (accessed 9 May 2019).

International Court of Justice (2004), *Legal Consequences of the Construction of a Wall in the Occupied Palestinian Territory*, The Hague: ICJ.

Kearney, M. (2010), 'Lawfare, Legitimacy and Resistance: The Weak and the Law', in *Palestine Yearbook of International Law*, Vol. 16, Leiden: Brill, pp. 79–129.

Kretzmer, D. (1992), 'The New Basic Laws on Human Rights: A Mini-Revolution in Israeli Constitutional Law', *Israel Law Review* 26 (2): 238–246.

LaHood, M. (2016), 'Concerted Attempts to Silence Criticism of Israel in the U.S.', *Washington Report on Middle East Affairs*, May, https://www. wrmea.org/016-may/panel-3-concerted-attempts-to-silence-criticism-of-israel-in-the-u.s.html (accessed 26 June 2019).

Lazaroff, T. (2016), 'In Huge Blow to Israel, Netherlands Declares BDS "Free Speech"', *The Jerusalem Post*, 26 May, https://www.jpost.com/Israel-News/Politics-And-Diplomacy/In-huge-blow-to-Israel-Netherlands-declares-BDS-free-speech-455162 (accessed 26 June 2019).

Legal Insurrection (2018), website, https://legalinsurrection.com/ (accessed 9 May 2019).

Lis, J. (2011), 'Israel Passes Law Banning Calls for Boycott', *Haaretz*, 11 July, https://www.haaretz.com/1.5026309 (accessed 26 June 2019).

Mearsheimer, J. and S. Walt (2008), *The Israel Lobby and U.S. Foreign Policy*, New York: Farrar, Straus and Giroux.

Merry, S. (2006), 'Transnational Human Rights and Local Activism: Mapping the Middle', *American Anthropologist* 108 (1): 38–51.

OCHA (2016), *Fragmented Lives: Humanitarian Overview 2016*, East Jerusalem: United Nations Organization for the Coordination of Humanitarian Affairs, https://www.ochaopt.org/content/fragmented-lives-humanitarian-overview-2016 (accessed 26 June 2019).

Oltermann, P. (2019), 'German Parliament Declares Israel Boycott Campaign Antisemitic', *The Guardian*, 17 May, https://www.the guardian.com/world/2019/may/17/german-parliament-declares-israel-boycott-campaign-antisemitic (accessed 26 June 2019).

Oren, A. (2016), 'Israel Setting Up "Dirty Tricks" Unit to Find, Spread Dirt on BDS Groups', *Haaretz*, 20 June, https://www.haaretz.com/israel-news/.premium-israel-setting-up-dirty-tricks-unit-to-spread-dirt-on-bds-groups-1.5397740 (accessed 26 June 2019).

Palestine Legal (2019), 'American Studies Association Sued for Academic Boycott', 18 July 2018 (updated 6 February 2019), https://palestinelegal.org/case-studies/2018/3/8/american-studies-association-sued-for-boycott (accessed 9 May 2019).

Pappe, I. (2006), *The Ethnic Cleansing of Palestine*, Oxford: Oneworld.

Parker, B. (2016), *No Way to Treat a Child*, Ramallah: Defence for Children International Palestine, https://nwttac.dci-palestine.org/ (accessed 26 June 2019).

Reynolds, J. (2017), *Empire, Emergency and International Law*, Cambridge: Cambridge University Press.

Roy, S. (2012), 'Reconceptualizing the Israeli–Palestinian Conflict: Key Paradigm Shifts', *Journal of Palestine Studies* 41 (3): 71–91.

Russell Tribunal on Palestine (2011), 'Cape Town Session', 5–11 November, http://www.russelltribunalonpalestine.com/en/sessions/south-africa (accessed 9 May 2019).

Safi, M. and H. Davidson (2014), 'Israeli Legal Centre Abandons Lawsuit against Sydney Academic', *The Guardian*, 10 July, https://www.theguardian.com/world/2014/jul/10/israeli-legal-centre-abandons-lawsuit-against-sydney-academic (accessed 26 June 2019).

Samour, N. (2017), 'Palestine at Bandung' in L. Eslava, M. Fakhri and V. Nesiah (eds), *Bandung, Global History and International Law*, Cambridge: Cambridge University Press, pp. 595–616.

Shurat HaDin (2018), Website of the Israel Law Center, https://israellawcenter.org/ (accessed 9 May 2019).

Tamanaha, B. (2005), 'The Tension between Legal Instrumentalism and the Rule of Law', *Syracuse Journal of International Law and Commerce* 31 (1): 131–154.

Tonutti, A. (2013), *Feasting on the Occupation*, Ramallah: Al-Haq, http://www.alhaq.org/publications/Feasting-on-the-occupation.pdf (accessed 26 June 2019).

Tucker, J. and L. Brand (2019), 'Public Smear Campaign against Nadera Shalhoub-Kevorkian and Hebrew University's Failure to Protect Her', Committee on Academic Freedom of the Middle East Studies Association, 15 March, https://mesana.org/advocacy/committee-on-academic-freedom/2019/03/15/public-smear-campaign-against-nadera-shalhoub-kevorkian-and-hebrew-universitys-failure-to-protect-her (accessed 10 October 2019).

Tutu, D. (2012), 'Justice Requires Action to Stop Subjugation of Palestinians', *Tampa Bay Times*, 30 April, https://www.tampabay.com/opinion/columns/justice-requires-action-to-stop-subjugation-of-palestinians/1227722 (accessed 26 June 2019).

United Nations (1948), *Universal Declaration of Human Rights*, 10 December, General Assembly 217 A (III), https://www.refworld.org/docid/3ae6b3712c.html (accessed 9 May 2019).

United Nations (1949), *United Nations General Assembly Resolution 194 (III)*, 11 December, Article 11, https://www.hrw.org/legacy/campaigns/israel/return/un194-rtr.htm (accessed 26 June 2019).

United Nations (2017), *Israeli Practices towards the Palestinian People and the Question of Apartheid*, www.hlrn.org/img/documents/israeli-practices-palestinian-people-apartheid-occupation-executive-summary-english.pdf (accessed 26 June 2019).

Winstanley, A. (2017), 'Israeli "Law Center" Shurat HaDin Admits Mossad Ties', *Electronic Intifada*, 16 November, https://electronicintifada.net/blogs/asa-winstanley/israeli-law-center-shurat-hadin-admits-mossad-ties (accessed 26 June 2019).

Zonszein, M. (2016), 'In Israel, BDS Is Winning', *+972 Magazine*, 28 March, https://972mag.com/in-israel-bds-is-winning/118198/ (accessed 26 June 2019).

TEN | Rethinking academic Palestine advocacy and activism: academic freedom, human rights, and the universality of the emancipatory struggle

Jamil Khader

At the beginning of December 2018, I was invited to give one of three keynote addresses at a conference on mimesis, repetition, and change that was organized by the International Doctoral Program Mimesis at Ludwig-Maximilian University, Munich, Germany. My hosts asked me to talk about transnational women's writings, a talk that could be drawn from my book, *Cartographies of Transnationalism in Postcolonial Feminisms: Geography, Culture, Identity, Politics* (Khader 2013a). I thought I owed it to my hosts not simply to read from my book, but to critically revisit the issue of representation in light of theories of mimesis. I decided, therefore, to give a talk on mimesis and alterity in the political memoir, *My Home, My Prison* (1980), by the Palestinian journalist and political activist, Raymonda Tawil, in the context of larger debates about mimesis in Palestinian literary and cultural production. I planned to organize the talk into three sections, two of which were based on controversies in which I was involved since my return to Palestine/Israel from the US in 2013. These controversies stage the crisis of mimetic representation of Palestinian reality and the deadlocks in the articulation of mimesis and repetition in reimagining a genuinely egalitarian and emancipatory politics in Palestine/Israel.

I first planned to discuss debates about the Palestinian hip hop band DAM's music video, 'If I Could Go Back in Time', that leaves the Israeli occupation out of its representation of the socio-political and cultural realities in Palestine. After playing the music video, I performed a close reading of its postmodern techniques that problematize any notion of crude realism. I was driving home the point that any analysis of honour killing and (intra-familial) femicide must go beyond the reification of the colonial critique and examine the implications of the obfuscation of the global capitalist system in the analysis of violence against women around the world (Khader 2013b). This part of the talk went well.

I then proceeded to review theories of mimetic violence, especially in the work of René Girard, who was generally 'mimetically silent' about the Zionist settler colonial project, Israeli occupation, apartheid, and ethnic cleansing project in Palestine, what is known as the Ongoing Nakba (Girard 2009). At this point, I started noticing some fidgety and restless movements among audience members and conference participants, but I paid no heed. I explained that while Girard does not address the Ongoing Palestinian Nakba in any meaningful way, other Girardian scholars try to fill in this gap by applying his theory of mimetic violence to the Palestinian situation. I then used two disturbing examples of such analyses: first, I showed how Scott Atran reframes the Ongoing Nakba in the language of moral parity and concludes that Israelis and Palestinians are 'increasingly internalizing the worst of their anti-Other rhetoric'. Then, in a bizarre projective displacement, Atran's analysis of the 'mimetic reciprocity of mistrust, resentment, and rage' posits Israelis as Nazis and the Palestinians as imperialists (Atran 2015). Second, I referred to Mel Konner, another mimetic theory acolyte, who utilizes mimetic logic to decry what he refers to as the 'competing narratives of suffering' which both sides invoke to appeal to international public opinion and sympathies (Konner 2015).

At this point, all hell broke loose. A member of the conference organizing committee, who later claimed she was the one who invited me to speak at the conference (and I learnt later that she had just recently found out that she had Jewish roots), had an emotional meltdown and interrupted me, by saying that she would not listen to this anymore. I first did not understand where she was going with this; I assumed she was just outraged about the Nazi and imperialist analogy the way I was, but I soon discovered that she thought the opinions I was critiquing were my own personal opinions (even though I put the quote like all other quotes in a power point presentation and made that clear not only at the beginning of my talk but also by including an in-text citation for each quote). She then accused me of hate speech, while another member of the audience, who happened to be another invited speaker from Nuremberg, chimed in to accuse me of propaganda – that I used the gender analysis only as a front for my propaganda. Another conference participant, and I assume a graduate student in IDP mimesis, stated matter-of-factly, 'you cannot say these things in Germany' (Finkelde 2018). It was a miracle they did not play the antisemitic card, one of the most common ploys pro-Israeli critics use to silence academic Palestine advocacy and activism (Robinson and Griffin 2017; Salaita 2015).

I urged them to let me finish my talk, but the student who had officially invited me to speak at the conference approached me and said, 'this was not what we invited you here to speak about'. I quickly wrapped up my talk and answered a couple of questions about my book, before leaving the conference hall and hanging out in the lounge where I talked to three conference participants who were displeased with the way I was silenced by this McCarthyist suppression of academic freedom. Ironically, one of the main aims of my talk at the IDP mimesis conference was precisely to respond to mimetic theorists' analysis of the internalization of victimization in discourses of the Other and to chart a way out of the victimization impasse in which the ontic properties, or the particular content of Palestinian and Israeli or Jewish identities, are reduced to the status of the victim.

These same victimization discourses, I claim, also underlie some major arguments in the debate about the relationship between academic freedom and human rights discourses among academic Palestine advocacy activists and groups. In this chapter, I argue that framing the claims of academic Palestine advocacy groups about academic freedom in human rights discourses must be problematized and rethought. The fact that the European Union is considering action to make academic freedom a human right merely attests to the way in which the human-rights-based approach to academic freedom has become coopted and appropriated by hegemonic discourses and the language of the power structure (Scholars at Risk 2018). Drawing on the work of the Slovenian philosopher Slavoj Žižek, I propose to reconfigure academic freedom through a dialectical materialist theory of radical universality, what Žižek refers to after Hegel as concrete universality. Repositing the question of academic freedom in the language of concrete universality makes it possible not only to recognize the immanent universal dimension at the core of every particular identity, but also to ground the struggle for academic freedom in the universal emancipatory struggle (the class struggle, not struggles around identity politics).

Framing this discussion of academic freedom in the context of Žižek's political philosophy should not come as a surprise to anyone who is well-informed about Žižek's work and his consistently radical record on the Palestinian struggle for freedom. Žižek has been unwavering in his critique of Zionist genocidal ideology and its manifestations in Israeli politics and culture. He has written extensively about Zionist ethnic cleansing and settler terrorism, and how it pervades Israeli representations of the colonial occupation ('hamatzav'). He has even written about Zionist connections to Nazi Germany during the Second World War – a move which earned him the label 'antisemite' from Zionist and pro-Israel commentators and others (Žižek 2011). Yet Žižek is also critical of antisemitism not only in the Arab world, but in its Zionist and Christian Zionist manifestations as well. Unfortunately, recent journalistic and social media attacks have misrepresented his position on various related controversial issues, including his position on the refugees, Islam, and political correctness (Khader 2015, 2016; Kapoor 2018).

Engaging Žižek and examining the utility of his work in a collection that intervenes in the important topic of academic freedom could not be more appropriate. We have reached a point in this debate where misguided and unfounded claims about Žižek's allegedly retrograde positions should not go unchallenged anymore and where academics should not have to defend themselves for using Žižek. This is counter-productive for both academic freedom and the future of leftist politics specially, since in his work Žižek charts a solution to the impasse and predicament of identity politics: neither essentialism nor hybridity, neither particularity nor abstract universality, but concrete universality. Far from retrograde, these ideas hold the future of leftist politics and global egalitarian struggles.

Academic freedom and human rights

The relationship between academic freedom and human rights has emerged as a central locus of debates among academic Palestine advocacy groups over the last two decades. In their article on the relationship between academic freedom and human rights, for example, Omar Barghouti and Lisa Taraki criticize the Association of University Teachers (AUT) in

Britain for overturning their previous decision to boycott two Israeli universities in 2005. They contend that AUT holds as sacred the 'freedom to produce and exchange knowledge and ideas', regardless of oppressive contexts and unjust political conditions. They thus argue that AUT's 'privileging of academic freedom as a super-value above all other freedoms is in principle antithetical to the very foundation of human rights' (Barghouti and Taraki 2005). They thus conclude that 'the right to live, and freedom from subjugation and colonial rule, to name a few, must be of more import than academic freedom'. In case of a conflict between these two goods then, Barghouti and Taraki surmise, justice calls for prioritizing human rights over academic rights. Similarly, Rima Najjar Kapitan proposes that debates about academic freedom, especially with regard to Palestine/Israel, should be grounded in a human rights approach. A human rights approach to academic freedom, she contends, would problematize the application of terms such as objectivity and balance to these debates and place them in the 'broader societal context in which speech is promulgated' (Najjar Kapitan 2011, 269).

This valorization of human rights discourses over academic freedom clearly aims at carving a space for the rehumanization of the Palestinians in Western media and public discourses, in which Palestinians are not only represented as mindless Hamas zombie terrorists, but are also seen, in Robert Fisk's words, as 'a non-people' (Fisk 2018). Indeed, for the last two decades, Palestinian activists, international human rights organizations, and NGOs have sought to legitimize the Palestinian struggle for freedom, by incorporating Palestinians under the protections of universal human rights law (Allen 2013). While appeals to humanity and dehumanization are important as a strategy for combatting the denial of rights and protections to disposable out-groups that are conferred upon other people in liberal discourses, framing the Palestinian struggle for freedom in these terms is not enough.

Literature on the subject shows that the term 'humanity' is not a given, but a dynamic process in which the label human is shifting and reversible. As such, people can be denied humanity one day and granted human status another. Not only are humanization and dehumanization slippery terms that are subject to reversals, but also admission into cosmopolitan human rights law is not automatic. Palestinians can become truly human – that is, subject to the protections of international law, only when the UN and international human rights law confer upon them the status of humanity and afford them the rights and protections that other proper subjects of human rights law enjoy. As the philosopher Judith Butler argues, in her comment on Barghouti's and Taraki's article on academic freedom and human rights in the context of the occupation, the question of human rights must be considered in relation to 'the material and institutional foreclosures that make it impossible for certain historical subjects to lay claim to the discourse of rights itself' (Butler 2006). She correctly cautions that 'If academic freedom remains restrictively liberal, it will not be able to see that the subject who would exercise the rights of such a freedom must first be given rights to travel, be able to pass over borders unobstructed and unharassed' (Butler 2006).

Moreover, international law has been impotent in guaranteeing the protections and safety for Palestinians in the face of the thick Israeli record of human rights violations in the occupied territories and Gaza. Needless to mention, the US has been the major obstacle to actualizing this aspiration, even though the current Trump administration has coopted the same language of human rights and humanitarianism in imagining a solution for ameliorating the living conditions in the Gaza Strip. The Israeli newspaper *Haaretz* reported that Trump asked (read ordered)

Gulf countries to invest in Gaza's economy as a prelude to his attempt to pitch the 'deal of the century' to the world community. The problem is that humanitarian intervention ideologues do not take the term humanitarian seriously – they merely pay lip service to it or put it under erasure. As Žižek argues, humanitarian intervention is grounded in clear political motivations and presuppose an Absolute victim who is reduced to nothingness and incapable of defending itself (Žižek 2005, 115–131). Obviously, Palestinians have not met the preconditions to be worthy of all human rights goods.

Framing the struggle for freedom in these humanitarian terms, moreover, ultimately posits the struggle in non-political and cultural terms that have already been compromised by a long history of colonial and liberal notions of humanness. Tawil's political memoir, which recodifies the infrahumanity of the Palestinians in terms of the humanity of the Jews, the Western victim par excellence, offers an interesting example of the ways in which appeals to human rights discourses can end up reifying notions of victimization and victimhood that distort the universal nature of identity. While Tawil appropriates the traditional signifiers of Jewishness to replicate this content into the Palestinian Self, the more radical thing to do here is to recognize and actualize, as Žižek would have put it in his theory of radical universality, the immanent universal dimension that exists at the core of both Jewish and Palestinian identities.

The universal dimension of identity
In developing his theory of radical universality, Žižek reworks the Hegelian concept of 'concrete universality', the idea that there is no neutral or abstract universality and that every universality is coloured by a particular content. In Hegel, the universal coincides with the particular contents or concrete situations through which it

can be 'hegemonized', while at the same maintaining its universal frame in and through these concrete situations. Žižek thus maintains that for Hegel the particular content is not only a 'subspecies of the universality of the total process', it also hegemonizes this very universality, 'transmuting universality itself into a part of (or, rather, drawn into) the particular content' (Žižek 2001, 14). As such, the universal neither simply stands in opposition to some concrete content or particular feature of the totality nor is caught up in the antagonisms of particular life worlds or ways of life.

For Žižek, this Hegelian concrete universality constitutes the grounds for rethinking identity politics and the relationship between individual and collective identities as well as the meaning of belonging to the human genus. Žižek writes:

> 'Concrete universality' means that there is no abstract universality of rules, there are no 'typical' situations, all we are dealing with is exceptions; however, a concrete totality is the totality that regulates the concrete context of exceptions. We should thus, on account of our very fidelity to concrete analysis, reject any form of nominalism. To the nominalist claim that there is no pure neutral universality, that every universality is caught up in the conflict of particular ways of life, one should reply: 'No, today it's the particular ways of life that do not exist as autonomous modes of historical existence, the only actual reality is that of the universal capitalist system'. This is why, in contrast to identity politics, which focuses on how each (ethnic, religious, sexual) group should be able fully to assert its particular identity, *the much more difficult and radical task is to enable each group to access full universality*. This access to universality does not mean a recognition that one is also *part of the universal human genus*, or the *assertion of some ideological values that are considered universal*. Rather, *it means recognizing one's own universality, the way it is at work in the fractures of one's particular identity, as the 'work of the negative' that undermines every such identity*. (Žižek 2018; emphasis added)

For Žižek, universality manifests itself through the gaps, failures, and antagonisms at the heart of particular identities which not only destabilize identity from within, but also serve as the foundation for an authentic emancipatory universality (Žižek 2012, 361). Briefly, Žižek maintains that every identity is split from within and is coincident with a gap that exists immanently at its core. Žižek's crucial point here is that this split produces a gap or a destabilizing excess, 'the work of the negative', at the core of every identity, thwarting the possibility of forming any substantive particular content (identity). However, identities, which are misrecognized as self-enclosed and substantial, are prone to repress this universal dimension. Nonetheless, subjects should actualize the promise of this immanent universal dimension, by articulating and organizing the struggle for universal emancipation (the class struggle) 'through or at the site of *a thwarted particularity*' (Žižek 2012, 362).

Žižek uses the story of the slave army in the Haitian revolution as a primary example for this dialectical materialist understanding of universality. The former Haitian slaves rebelled against the limits of particular identities and opted, instead, to actualize the potential of their immanent universality. They thus redefined their identities by reinventing the European tradition and 'appropriating key elements of the "white" egalitarian-emancipatory tradition, ... obliterating the implicit qualifications which have *de facto* excluded Blacks from the egalitarian space' (Žižek 2009, 120). Nothing could have stunned and offended Leclerc's soldiers more than hearing the slave army sing *La Marseillaise*. This was not a gesture of assimilation to the hegemonic French colonial ideology, as Žižek correctly points out, but a resounding declaration that former Haitian slaves 'stand for the innermost consequences of [the French] revolutionary ideology, the very consequences [the French] were not able to assume' (Žižek 2009, 120). In this precise sense, they were more French than the French themselves, since they not only demystified the gaps and inconsistencies at the core of French identity, but more importantly, they showed that they were the true 'enfants de la patri', the ones who could fulfil its radical promise.

The point that needs to be emphasized here is that Westerners (Euro-Americans) have no monopoly over universality and Enlightenment ideals. They will always fail to fill it with a proper particular nationalistic (French or British or American) content. Similarly, advocates of identity politics assume that the particular content of any identity can easily fill in the empty space of universality. However, to paraphrase Žižek, the human subject will never succeed either in using any particular content to fill in this universality or in bringing the particular content into harmonious relations with the universal, because there is a fundamental contradiction between its 'singular subjective viewpoint', through which it perceives and colours reality, and its status as another object in that reality (Žižek 2012, 362).

The conclusion to be drawn here, specifically in the case of so-called postcolonial subjects, is that the truth of this subject, as Žižek provocatively argues, lies in its abstraction (incorporation into the global capitalist system) not in its concrete (cultural) content. Postcolonial critics, Žižek contends, assume that the truth of the postcolonial subject living in a globalized world is its cultural lifeworld, tradition, or way of life. Žižek refers to the Indian historian Dipesh Chakrabarty's example of the Indian software programmer who represents the truth of Indian lifeworld through his concrete (cultural) content such as rituals, etc. (Žižek 2011, 280–285). For Chakrabarty, this Indian programmer is a paradigmatic cipher of the unproblematic simultaneity or 'normalized coexistence of the universality of modernization and of particular lifeworlds'. Žižek , however, correctly notes that 'postmodernity is not the overcoming of modernity but its fulfilment: in the postmodern universe, premodern leftovers' are no longer experienced as obstacles to be overcome by progress towards a fully secularized modernization, but as something to be unproblematically incorporated into the multicultural global universe – all traditions survive, but in a mediated 'de-naturalized' form, that is, no longer as authentic ways of life, but as freely chosen 'life-styles'. In other words, within the totality of global capitalism, 'elements of pre-existing lifeworlds and economies (including money) are gradually re-articulated as its own moments, "exapted" with a different function' (Žižek 2011, 284).

Needless to mention, Žižek's critique of postcolonial discourses is very precise and targets the false neoliberal form of postcolonial struggles that coopts the real authentic egalitarian struggle in them. In other words, Žižek does not reject postcoloniality willy-nilly. Rather, he does not see the struggles of the postcolonial middle and upper classes in the global South or metropolitan centres to be as authentic as the struggles of the disposable communities in the countries or nations. In the case of India, for example, the Dalit not the Indian middle or upper classes are the truth of the injustice in the global capitalist system. As such, Žižek argues that only a commitment to the class struggle can differentiate the authentic struggle from its false bourgeoisified form.

In a different context, Žižek links this notion of concrete universality to the modern feminist movement, suggesting that feminism can live up to its radical potential only when it actualizes the language of possibility of this concrete universality. According to this model, feminists would not simply engage in inscribing a particular form of difference (i.e. gender or sexual difference) within the matrix of the dominant symbolic order; rather, they would interrogate and destabilize the universal framework within which a troubling excess is foreclosed:

This is what you must be conscious of, that when you fight for your position, *you at the same time fight for the universal frame of how your position will be perceived within this universal frame.* This is for me, as every good feminist will tell you, the greatness of modern feminism. It's not just we women want more. *It's we women want to redefine the very universality of what it means to be human.* This is for me this modern notion of political struggle. (Quoted in Pound 2008, 113; emphasis added)

The concern with particular sexual or gender difference in feminist discourses would embody the exception, as long as feminists seek not to single out this particular difference and elevate it to the level of the universal. The point is to instead appropriate the form of feminist particularity in order to interrogate and destabilize the very universal framework (i.e. multiculturalism and identity politics) within which this particular form of difference is posited. The concern here, in Fabio Vighi's words, is that the struggle for a particular form of difference (in Žižek's example above, sexual difference and human emancipation, respectively) becomes 'nothing but a content that is necessarily distorted by its own attempt to fulfill the demand of its abstract universal' (Vighi 2006, 108). What is crucial to keep in mind here is that the emphasis on the struggle against particular forms of oppression structured around secondary (visible) contradictions mystifies and displaces – even effaces – the fundamental antagonism, or the constitutive split, in the neocolonial global capitalist mode of production insofar as it constitutes the totality of social relations today. To this extent, the assertion of the concrete universality of specific forms of secondary contradictions can help distinguish the authentic emancipatory content of these struggles from its fake neoliberal form that will inevitably compromise it with the ideological logic of the hegemonic neoliberal regime. This is not to say that Žižek dismisses the important struggles that surround and accompany these secondary contradictions, but that he insists, above all, on the need to fully assume the repressed point of exclusion as 'the gap between the particular ... and the universal which destabilizes it from within', in order to reconfigure the very coordinates and terms of universality (Žižek 2012, 361).

This universal dimension inherent to identities is completely obfuscated in Tawil's autobiographical act (Khader 2013a, 121–152). Indeed, Tawil's political memoir is structured around a paradox: she inscribes Palestinian particular identity in a relation of mimetic identification with the archetypal image of the suffering Jew. Nonetheless, she inadvertently not only obfuscates the distinction between Israeli and Jewish identities, but also elevates Jewishness to a (pre)ontological position of victimhood. Tawil thus struggles with the main ethical conundrum of how to relate to the humanity of the Israeli as a persecutory Other. She was always reminded by her family members and friends that 'The Israeli with who you want to make dialogue is in uniform and carrying a gun' (Tawil 1980, 124). Moreover, people around her insisted that 'They are all Zionists, they all serve in the army – therefore they cannot be trusted' (Tawil 1980, 159). Nonetheless, Tawil questions such attitudes, writing:

> As long as [the Israeli soldier] was in uniform, he was an enemy – but inside the uniform, he remained a man nonetheless. Time and time again, I encountered the same conflict – how to relate to an enemy as a human being? How to relate to a human being as an enemy? (Tawil 1980, 149)

Instead of the monolithic demonization of the Zionists in Palestinian public discourse and the PLO national charter at the time, Tawil reconstructs this representation by splitting the Israelis into colonial Zionists and humanitarian, altruistic Jews. Tawil refuses to reify Jews and Israelis to the status of a symptom that displaces the immanent social contradictions of the Palestinian national liberation movement and Arab nations. Therefore, she narrates how some Israeli soldiers did assist dispossessed Palestinians, despite the military policies against collaboration with the enemy. For example, Tawil mentions how one soldier by the name of Hanoch was honoured by the Nablus mayor due to his tremendous help to the refugees in the Nablus areas (Tawil 1980, 14). In addition, she mentions how after the 1967 war, when the residents of Qalkilya were displaced from their town for the second time, an Israeli-Moroccan soldier defended those villagers against his troopers' sadistic humiliation of these helpless refugees. He angrily scolded them, adding: 'You people don't have a heart! Don't you have a home, a family? Is this Judaism? You ought to remember Auschwitz!' (Tawil 1980, 100).

There are several problems with such a strategy. First, this humanization of the soldiers has been central to Israel's efforts to whitewash the occupation and represent its military as the most moral army in the world. Nowhere is this strategy more obvious than in Israeli novels, films, and cultural production in which ideology appears in its opposite form, which Žižek calls non-ideology, whose strategy is to displace the realities of the occupation and to humanize the soldiers, by claiming inner life as a basis of common humanity (Žižek 2011, 56). The ultimate result here is that the occupation itself is blurred, while the inauthenticity of human intimacy in oppressive situations that lack any balance of power between oppressor and victim is celebrated and elevated as the sign of the humanity and the ordinariness of the Israeli soldiers, in particular, and Israeli society, in general. As Žižek writes,

> Such a 'humanization' thus serves to obfuscate the key question:
> the need for ruthless political analysis of what is being done in
> terms of political-military activity. Our politico-military struggles
> are precisely not an opaque History which brutally disrupts our
> intimate lives – they are a field in which we are always already
> engaged, even if it is in a mode of ignorance. (Žižek 2011, 58)

More importantly, and at the same time, Tawil appropriates
the most common signifiers of Jewishness to rehumanize the
Palestinians, by reframing the history of Palestinian suffering
and persecution in a mimetic identification with the archetypal
image of the suffering Jew. The slippage between Jew and Israeli
in her memoir notwithstanding, Tawil calls the Palestinians 'the
new Jews' (Tawil 1980, 77) and through the mass exodus of the
Palestinians in 1948 and 1967, 'the place of the Jewish refugees was
taken by the Palestinians' (Tawil 1980, 111). Speaking to Jewish
audiences on her book tour in the US, moreover, Tawil notes:

> Any person of conscience – Jew or Christian – should
> acknowledge this injustice, whereby the persecuted survivors
> of Nazi concentration camps were given a home by making
> the Palestinians homeless. 'We are like you', I told my Jewish
> listeners. *'We Palestinians are the Jews of the Arab world'*.
> (Tawil 1980, 201; emphasis added)

Through this mimetic identification, Tawil posits the Self as
Another, encoding Palestinianness in terms of the reproduction and repetition of the traditional signifiers of Jewish identity,
including the archetypal image of the suffering Jew, diaspora,
and genocide. While Tawil appropriates the traditional signifiers
of Jewishness to replicate this content into the Palestinian Self,
the more radical thing to do here is to recognize and actualize,
as Žižek would have put it in his theory of radical universality,
the immanent universal dimension that exists at the core of both
Jewish and Palestinian identities.

This is not simply about celebrating Edward Said as 'the last Jewish intellectual', the way some critics have done (Hochberg 2006), or to declare Arafat to be 'more Jewish than Jews', as Yitzhak Rabin did. Tawil's problem, it could be argued, is that she substitutes the universal dimension of Jewish identity for the particular content of the traditional signifiers of Jewishness. In his writings about antisemitism, for example, Žižek argues that there is a supplement produced about the Jews that makes Jewishness different from itself, and that recognizes, in Žižek's words, 'what is in Jew more than Jew' (Žižek 1989, 97). Tawil's mimetic attempt to pin down the precise meaning of Jewishness will necessarily leave something out. This remainder is, as Žižek points out, the Jewish embodiment of universality, which is not the result of 'the abstract-universal nature of their monotheism' but is the consequence of dis-identification with state power. Consequently, Tawil inadvertently elevates Jewishness to a transcendental signifier of victimization that in a way undermines her claims for Palestinian humanity. Judith Butler, for one, has correctly criticized Emmanuel Levinas for elevating Jewishness to a pre-ontological status of persecution and victimization, which led him to turn the alleged persecution of the Israeli state into a 'timeless Jewish essence' (Butler 2005, 93–94). Such a strategy, Butler shows, can only be predicated upon the displacement of the knowledge of the atrocities the Israelis have committed against the Palestinians. For Levinas, in short, one must take ethical responsibility and accountability for the face of the Other, as long as that Other is not Palestinian.

Towards a common struggle

This recognition of 'one's own universality' clears a space for envisioning a common struggle and destiny based on the experiences of those who have been excluded from the global capitalist system (Žižek and Daly 2004, 143–144). Going back to my IDP talk in Munich, my aim was also to demonstrate how Atran's mimetic theory obfuscates this common struggle in relation to the Real of global capitalism and the fundamental antagonism (class struggle), a point I was trying to relate back to my analysis of the music video. He writes:

> The first Jewish settlers in modern Palestine were poor Jews from the Pale who were suffering from the pogroms in Russia. They were seeking a life where they wouldn't have to suffer any more. Palestinians didn't have a title to any of the land; that was owned by bankers of the former Ottoman Empire, like the Sursuk family in Lebanon. The Jews came with titles that they paid their last *kopek* to acquire – some having walked 2,000 miles to get there. The Arab peasant said: 'I don't understand what this means; my ancestors have always cultivated this land'. So what happens? Both parties internalize themselves as victims, rather than face the problems. The Other became the '*cause*' of their victimhood. (Atran 2015)

In this simplistic analysis, Atran fails to link the struggles of poor Jews in Europe with the struggles of poor Palestinians under Ottoman domination, British imperialism, and Zionist settler-colonialism in a common struggle within the restructuring of the global capitalist economy throughout the nineteenth century. Instead of grounding this analysis in the structural and systematic causes of poverty, migration, colonialism, and genocide, in short, Atran opts to culturalize the question of violence and attribute its causes to subjective forms of violence perpetrated by some vague notion of the Other.

Conclusion

Academic Palestine advocacy and activism especially, on campuses around the world, is expected to confront many new challenges over the next few years. The radicalization of the political correctness culture, in which extreme claims to victimization and the attitude toward any form of Otherness as an intrusion into private space, coupled with the spread of antisemitic and Islamophobic hatred, requires reconfiguring the ideological premises and rhetorical moves underpinning academic Palestine advocacy and activism. The proper recognition of the universality of Palestinian identity, by realizing the universality that is immanent to every identity and assuming the point of exclusion in the global capitalist system, can clear a space for articulating a common emancipatory struggle for all.

References

Allen, L. (2013), *The Rise and Fall of Human Rights: Cynicism and Politics in Occupied Palestine*, Stanford, CA: Stanford University Press.

Atran, S. (2015), 'Peace Making in Practice and Theory: An Encounter with Rene Girard' in P. Antonello and P. Gifford (eds), *Can We Survive Our Origins? Readings in Renee Girard's Theory of Violence and the Sacred*, East Lansing, MI: Michigan State University Press, pp. 233–250.

Barghouti, O. and L. Taraki (2005), 'The AUT Boycott: Academic Freedom vs. Freedom', *The Electronic Intifada*, 31 May, https://electronicintifada. net/content/aut-boycott-freedom-vs-academic-freedom/5609 (accessed 17 December, 2018).

Butler, J. (2005), *Giving an Account of Oneself*, New York: Fordham University Press.

Butler, J. (2006), 'Israel/Palestine: The Paradoxes of Academic Freedom', *Radical Philosophy*, 135, https://www.radicalphilosophy.com/article/ israelpalestine-and-the-paradoxes-of-academic-freedom (accessed 17 December 2018).

Finkelde, D. (2018), 'The "Secret Code" of Honor: On Political Enjoyment and the Excrescence of Fantasy', *Culture, Theory, and Critique* 59 (3): 232–261.

Fisk, R. (2018), 'How Long after This Week's Gaza Massacre Are We Going to Continue Pretending that the Palestinians are Non-people?', *The Independent*, 17 May, https://www.independent.co.uk/voices/gaza-palestine-israel-conflict-us-embassy-jerusalem-jared-kushner-donald-trump-a8355631.html (accessed 17 December 2018).

Girard, R. (2009), *Battling to the End*, East Lansing, MI: Michigan State University Press.

Hochberg, G. (2006), 'Edward Said: "The Last Jewish Intellectual"': On Identity, Alterity, and the Politics of Memory', *Social Text* 24 (2): 47–65.

Kapoor, I. (2018), 'Žižek, Antagonism and Politics Now: Three Recent Controversies', *The International Journal of Žižek Studies* 12 (1): 1–31.

Khader, J. (2013a), *Cartographies of Transnationalism in Postcolonial Feminisms: Geography, Culture, Identity, Politics*, Lanham, MD: Lexington Books.

Khader, J. (2013b), 'The Invisible Link: Honor Killing and Global Capitalism', *Jadaliyya*, 21 January, http://www.jadaliyya.com/Details/ 27851/The-Invisible-Link-Honor-Killing-and-Global-Capitalism (accessed 17 December 2018).

Khader, J. (2015), 'Why Žižek's Critics Are Wrong: And Where They Could Have Gotten It Right', *In These Times*, 11 December, http:// inthesetimes.com/article/18683/why-zizeks-critics-are-wrong-and-where-they-could-have-gotten-it-right (accessed 24 September 2019).

Khader, J. (2016), 'Žižek Is Not a Racist Islamophobe', *Muftah*, 23 May, https://muftah.org/zizek-is-not-a-racist-islamophobe/#.XYpxRC4zbZ7 (accessed 24 September 2019).

Konner, M. (2015), 'Girardian Reflection on Israel and Palestine' in P. Antonello and P. Gifford (eds), *Can We Survive Our Origins? Readings in Renee Girard's Theory of Violence and the Sacred*, East Lansing, MI: Michigan State University Press, pp. 215–222.

Najjar Kapitan, R. (2011), 'Academic Freedom as a Fundamental Human Right in American Jurisprudence and the Imposition of "Balance" on Academic Discourses about the Palestinian–Israeli Conflict', *Arab Studies Quarterly* 33 (3–4): 268–281.

Pound, M. (2008), *Žižek: A (Very) Critical Introduction*, Grand Rapids, MI: William B. Eerdmans.

Robinson, W. I. and M. S. Griffin (eds) (2017), *We Will Not Be Silenced: The Academic Repression of Israel's Critics*, Chico, CA: AK Press.

Salaita, S. (2015), *Uncivil Rites: Palestine and the Limits of Academic Freedom*, Chicago, IL: Haymarket.

Scholars at Risk (2018), 'European Parliament Adopts Report that Resolves to Prioritize Academic Freedom in EU External Affairs', Scholars at Risk Network, 30 November, https://www.scholarsatrisk.org/2018/11/ european-parliament-adopts-report-academic-freedom/ (accessed 19 December 2018).

Tawil, R. (1980), *My Home, My Prison*, New York: Holt, Rinehart, and Winston.

Vighi, F. (2006), *Traumatic Encounters in Italian Films: Locating the Cinematic Unconscious*, Bristol: Intellect Books.

Žižek, S. (1989), *The Sublime Object of Ideology*, London: Verso.

Žižek, S. (2001), *The Fright of Real Tears: Krzysztof Kieślowski between Theory and Post-Theory*, London: British Film Institute.

Žižek, S. (2005), 'Against Human Rights', *New Left Review* 34: 115–131.

Žižek, S. (2009), *First as Tragedy, Then as a Farce*, London: Verso.

Žižek, S. (2011), *Living in the End Times*, London: Verso.

Žižek, S. (2012), *Less than Nothing: Hegel and the Shadow of Dialectical Materialism*, London: Verso.

Žižek, S. (2018), *Like a Thief in Broad Daylight: Power in the Era of Post-Humanity*, London: Allen Lane.

Žižek, S. and G. Daly (2004), *Conversations with Žižek*, Cambridge: Polity.

ELEVEN

Against academic freedom:
'terrorism', settler colonialism, and
Palestinian liberation[1]

C. Heike Schotten

> Academic freedom and aiding and abetting terrorism are
> mutually inconsistent.
>> President Judy Genshaft and Provost David Stamps,
>> University of South Florida (2003, 73)

> As chancellor, it is my responsibility to ensure that all
> perspectives are welcome and that our discourse, regardless of
> subject matter or viewpoint, allows new concepts and differing
> points of view to be discussed in and outside the classroom in a
> scholarly, civil and productive manner.
>> Chancellor Phyllis Wise, University of Illinois
>> Urbana-Champaign (Wilson 2014)

However remote, maudlin, or tendentious it may seem, I want to begin this chapter by noting that the work of academic boycott against Israel takes place in what is, still, a distinctively post-9/11 era. This is especially true in the US, the geopolitical location of my own work; however, given the outsized impact of US policy on the rest of the world, it is an observation that bears repeating. The short political memories of the American people, combined with the carnival-esque grotesqueries of the current presidential administration, lend themselves to a kind of amnesiac Trump exceptionalism that disregards the precedent-setting (and therefore Trump-enabling) atrocities of the George W. Bush administration. Yet the fact remains that the US – and, consequently, the rest of the world – remains steeped in a specific political and historical period significantly indebted to that administration, a twenty-first-century chapter of US empire known more popularly as the War on Terror.

Of course, Palestinians' struggle for liberation and self-determination has been interwoven with the rubric of 'terrorism' since well before the twenty-first century, to the point that 'terrorist' has become virtually interchangeable with 'Palestinian' or is understood always to somehow name or intimate the fact of Palestinian-ness (Naber, Desouky and Baroudi 2006). That this specific identification has become broadened in the War on Terror era, however, into a catchall designation for Muslims, Arabs, and anyone deemed by parochial American eyes to 'look like' them is both an indication that we remain stuck in a post-9/11 moment and also, I will suggest, a cipher into how and why, exactly, this particular episode of US empire seems to be so resilient.[2]

In this chapter, I situate academic boycott work in the US in the context of the War on Terror in order to better understand the signature ways that academic boycott in particular and the Boycott, Divestment and Sanctions (BDS) movement in general are targeted, disciplined, and punished on US campuses. In the first section, I examine the firings of two tenured Palestinian-American professors – Sami Al-Arian and Steven Salaita – in order to argue that administrators' rationalization of these firings as protections of academic freedom reveals the moralistic, settler colonial investments at work in the very notion of academic freedom itself, which therefore explains why it cannot protect academic boycott proponents, much less Palestinian and indigenous scholars, from the punitive machinations of settler colonial eliminationism. In the second section, I offer a potted history of the category of 'terrorism' as it has been deployed in the War on Terror, showing its continuity with settler colonial ideological imaginings of the 'savage' and, therefore, the reproduction of settler colonial eliminationist tactics within the anti-'terrorism' policing and punishment of BDS on US campuses. I conclude by questioning the usefulness of academic freedom as a protective recourse for academic boycott advocates, suggesting instead that its valorization may be per se harmful insofar as it is bound up with the ideological and material project of settler colonialism.

Academic freedom and/as settler colonialism

This chapter's two epigraphs, chronologically separated by more than a decade, provide an unwitting map of the cultural and political coordinates of our post-9/11 era. The first, from 2003, was offered by the administrators responsible for firing tenured Computer Science Professor Sami Al-Arian from the University of South Florida. Palestinian-American, a long-time community organizer, and a civil rights activist, Al-Arian first came to his university's attention after being interviewed on FOX News by the now-disgraced Bill O'Reilly. Throughout the highly contentious interview, O'Reilly cast aspersions on Al-Arian's honesty and repeatedly linked him to terrorism, a line of questioning that culminated with O'Reilly airing a more-than-decade-old audio recording of Al-Arian saying 'Jihad is our path. Victory to Islam. Death to Israel' at a rally for Palestine in Cleveland, Ohio. O'Reilly concluded the interview by saying to Al-Arian, 'if I was the CIA, I'd follow you wherever you went. I'd follow you 24 hours ... I'd be your shadow, Doctor' (Transcript, 2003).[3] Shortly after the show aired, Al-Arian was placed on paid administrative leave by USF administrators and barred from campus due to 'security' concerns. Thence proceeded a protracted struggle between USF administration and Al-Arian, USF faculty, national academic professional organizations, and free speech advocates over Al-Arian's tenure. At first, following an investigation by the American Association of University Professors (AAUP) into

USF's handling of the case, administrators seemed to backpedal, suggesting they would not fire Al-Arian after all. But his later, 2003 indictment on federal terrorism charges – 17 counts in all under the USA Patriot Act – was eventually cited as the ultimate reason for his termination from the university. Acquitted on eight counts, the jury deadlocked on the remaining nine, with Al-Arian finally agreeing to a plea deal with prosecutors. He was deported from the US in 2015.[4]

Genshaft and Stamps' (2003) comment on the Al-Arian case presents a frank, binary opposition between 'terrorism', on the one hand, and academic freedom, on the other. An echo of then-President Bush's dictum that 'Either you are with us, or you are with the terrorists', Genshaft and Stamps make clear that standing with 'us' and preserving academic freedom are one and the same, wholly necessary rejections of 'terrorism' if the safety and sanctity of the university is to be preserved. Their firing of Al-Arian, then, is an uncontroversially rational act of choosing 'us' and 'freedom' over 'them', the 'terrorists'. By contrast, Chancellor Phyllis Wise's comment, offered more than ten years later in explanation of her firing of tenured English and Indigenous Studies Professor Steven Salaita, seems less stark. Salaita, also Palestinian-American as well as an active proponent of the BDS movement against Israel, was dismissed before he could assume his newly-contracted position as a tenured professor at the University of Illinois Urbana-Champaign (UIUC) because of his 'uncivil' tweets regarding Israel's 2014 mass slaughter of Palestinians in the Gaza Strip. Assuming the mantle of dialogue and inclusion, openly disclaiming any intention of punishing anyone for their political viewpoints, and by no means calling him a 'terrorist', Chancellor Wise explained that the university simply cannot tolerate non-scholarly, non-civil, or non-productive *expressions* of political viewpoints. As she says earlier in this same statement,

'The decision regarding Prof Salaita was not influenced in any way by his positions on the conflict in the Middle East nor his criticism of Israel'. Thus, it is not Salaita's *views* regarding Israel that were the cause of his termination, much less his involvement with 'terrorism', but rather the uncivil and unproductive *expression* of his views regarding Israel that prevented him from assuming his contracted position.[5]

There is much to be said about each of these cases and many continuities and connections to be drawn between them. For the purposes of this chapter, however, I want to zero in on the seemingly unlikely shift from 'terrorism', in 2003, to 'incivility', in 2014, as the intolerable enemy of academic freedom offered by university administrators to justify terminating tenured, Palestinian-American faculty. While the domain of political violence would seem far removed from that of the more bourgeois norms of polite discourse, my suggestion here is that there is rather more continuity between 'terrorism' and 'incivility' than may at first seem evident, and that this rhetorical shift reflects, but cannot be entirely explained by, the increasing neoliberalization of the American university.[6] What links 'terrorism' to 'incivility', I want to suggest, is instead (or also) a distinctly settler colonial moralism that lies at the heart of US order and has been re-animated in the post-9/11 moment.

Settler colonialism is a distinct form of domination that seeks the '*dispossession* of Indigenous peoples of their lands and self-determining authority' (Coulthard 2014, 7). It is, therefore, better understood as a specific *structure of power* that conditions all social, ethical, and political relations within the polity, rather than a single act of conquest or one-time event (Coulthard 2014). Patrick Wolfe has suggested that the specific logic of settler colonial domination is *elimination*: settler colonialism aims to eradicate indigenous people(s) and societies in order to construct a new, settler society atop the land expropriated from them, with the ultimate goal of indigenizing colonizers as 'natives' themselves (Wolfe 2006). My own contribution to thinking through this form of domination has been to focus on the *moralism* of settler colonial eliminationist *ideology*. As I have argued elsewhere (Schotten 2018), settler colonialism is a *biopolitical* project that does not exceptionalize certain forms of bare life (Agamben 1998; Svirsky and Bignall 2012) so much as constitute life 'itself' as inherently valuable and worthy of normative futurity. Commonly troped as 'innocent', this unmarked 'life itself' is a privileged object of value and rationality within settler colonialism, that which is impossible to refuse without being abjected as backward, 'savage', irrational, or abominable. This discourse is essential to settler colonial regimes and distinctly self-serving, even as it is consistently veiled via the guise of ostensibly self-evident truths about the rationality of self-preservation, the purity of children, or the inherent value of human life. However, by refusing to mark these positions on life *as* positions at all, settler colonial ideology smuggles a highly normative value system into the polity, whereby only settler life qualifies or is properly recognizable *as* life 'itself', and thus the only life considered valuable, worthy, innocent, rational, or worthy of protection.[7]

This unmarked yet highly moralized ideology of life and its value also necessarily produces its 'opposite', that which refuses 'life' in an unthinkable or utterly unconscionable manner. This is the 'death' of this bio/necropolitics, although anyone who rejects the seemingly commonsensical value of 'life itself' quickly becomes a symbol or harbinger of that death. This is the work done by the term 'savage', and understanding settler colonial biopolitics as specifically *moralizing* explains its distinctly derogatory character and wholesale condemnation of entire peoples and ways of life as 'uncivilized'. Indeed, insofar as indigenous peoples reject settler sovereignty, they not only refuse conquest (i.e. they refuse to be dominated), but they become *enemies*: abjected within a settler colonial ideology that frames them as simultaneously absurd and hostile, irrational and unthinkable enemies of life 'itself'. Their existence is more than mere fodder for killing or letting die, as a more familiar biopolitical analysis might have it. Rather, indigenous existence is a mortal threat to the coherence, meaning, stability, and persistence of the settler state (Simpson 2011). This is why native peoples must be actively eliminated: not because they are a remnant of what has been exceptionalized from politics, but rather because their continued (and thus dissident) existence embodies an out-and-out menace to the polity as such. Genocide of indigenous peoples, then, insofar as they flout or refuse the imposition of settler sovereignty, is fully compatible with a moralizing valuation of 'life itself', and is the material reality of the more formal theoretical claim that biopolitics is also and always a necropolitics.[8]

In today's moment, those irrational, unthinkable figures of death inevitably produced by settler colonialism's moralizing, eliminationist ideology are less associated with native people(s) than with Muslims and the now pervasive and toxic Islamophobia that is one prominent site and residuum of the War on Terror. However, my suggestion is that the 'terrorist' is the contemporary, imperial version of the 'savage' of yesterday, whose existence and perseverance threatens the coherence and hegemony of US settler sovereignty (Byrd 2011; Daulatzai 2016; Schotten 2018). If this is right, then expressing 'uncivil' views *is* in some sense equivalent to 'terrorism' insofar as it issues the same sort of threat to the US settler state and its knowledge production: the threat of total delegitimation, incoherence, and annihilation. Indeed, 'civility' was the master term of Salaita's firing and a bitterly ironic synopsis of his alleged failings, an irony that was lost on neither Salaita himself nor on commentators who quickly made the connection between 'civility' and 'civilization' (Salaita 2015, 2016; J. Singh 2014). Hired to teach in an Indigenous Studies Department, Salaita was fired because he both represented and advocated for the existence and resistance of native peoples (Palestinian or otherwise), and it is precisely *this* representation and advocacy that is unthinkable within the given terms of the War on Terror.

'Civility' is thus not divorced from the problem of 'terrorism', but is rather a clue that 'terrorism' is in fact a contemporary form of 'savagery' (Daulatzai 2016), insofar as both threaten the continuity of life and meaning as 'we' know it (Schotten 2018). Salaita, in refusing to speak in the reasoned tones of liberal rationality when discussing – or, really, just simply naming – Israeli state-sponsored genocide as such, marked himself out as a 'savage', as someone unwilling to conform to the dictates of academic and civil society that circumscribe the domain of the rational. That Salaita's firing was justified in the reasonable, liberal terms of civility and civil discourse therefore represents neither an innovation in administrative parlance nor a post-imperial, emergently neoliberal order in academia. Rather (or also), it is an evocative sign that the travesties and conceits of settler colonialism continue to animate both contemporary American foreign policy and domestic US institutional infrastructure.

Importantly, the university administrators who fired both Al-Arian and Salaita openly affirmed their commitment to academic freedom, insisting that firing tenured faculty was not a limitation of academic freedom but rather its preservation. In my view, this is not a case of administrative doublespeak. Rather, it is an indicative sign that academic freedom is caught up in the same moralizing discourse of settler colonial eliminationism that circumscribes what is and is not thinkable in the era of the War on Terror, a discourse that – as these cases demonstrate – is thoughtlessly replicated when it comes to the issue of Palestinian liberation. The transparent targeting of tenured faculty on the basis of their race, ethnicity, and anti-Zionist/anti-colonial politics was understood by university administrators in each case as a means of protecting the university from hostile enemy threats, threats whose persistence would only have invited further harm, chaos, and destruction to their campuses. This is a mimetic reproduction of the eliminationist logic that demands that 'savages', 'terrorists', and all other existential threats to the settler order be purged so it can survive. We should therefore be wary of using one of the academy's signature values, 'academic freedom', to defend or protect academic boycott advocates. Not only will such an endeavour ultimately fail, but it will shore up the moralized settler colonial power relations the boycott otherwise seeks to dismantle.

'Terrorism' as Nazism

Attacks on campus Palestine advocates are not limited to the firing of tenured faculty, of course. They run the gamut from monitoring and surveillance of known BDS supporters (students and faculty alike); cancellation of speakers, cultural events, and classes considered to be anti-Israel; sanctions from university administrators; and lawsuits by outside organizations. All this is documented in *The Palestine Exception to Free Speech*, a groundbreaking report issued by Palestine Legal and the Center for Constitutional Rights (2015). From a wealth of noteworthy data, two themes stand out. The first is that the overwhelming majority of attacks on pro-Palestine students and faculty took the (sometimes simultaneous) form of accusations of antisemitism and/or connections to 'terrorism'. The second is that universities repeatedly couched their discipline of Palestine advocates in the language of civility. It is important to be clear that neither the form of these accusations nor the terms of their accompanying discipline and punishment are accidental. They are not accidental not only because attacks on campus Palestine advocates are well-funded, highly orchestrated campaigns conducted by a cache of pro-Israel organizations and foundations, often in collaboration with the Israeli government, to counter BDS and criticism of Israel on college campuses.[9] They are also not accidental because these forms of attack, discipline, and punishment are symptomatic of the underlying settler colonial politics of the current War on Terror chapter of American empire. The discourses of both 'terrorism' and antisemitism are crucial to this politics, and the fact that their discipline and punishment are doled out in terms of 'civility' is not (simply) ironic but also evidence that the War on Terror is merely the latest episode in America's ever-unfolding ideological disqualification of indigenous, anti-colonial political commitment in general and Palestinian liberation in particular as immoral, unthinkable, or a form of nihilism and evil.

Understanding how and why this is so requires a genealogical detour into the development of the category 'terrorism', a term whose recent history explains the otherwise mystifying ideological rigour with which it is applied in the United States only to the behaviour of Arabs, Muslims, and those who 'look like' them (and not, say, to the activity of white supremacists, the police, or the US government[10]). Since the mid-1970s, 'terrorism' has been deliberately produced as both an identity category and a moral epithet. In both cases, its definitional distinctness is its evil: a 'terrorist' is an evil person and 'terrorism' is an evil act. As George W. Bush made rhetorically clear throughout the eight long years of his presidency, the distinguishing hallmark of 'terrorism' is its evil, and contemporary US and Israeli 'terrorism' discourse repeatedly construes this evil as specifically Islamic, with 'Islamic terrorism', or sometimes 'radical Islamic terrorism', or sometimes just Muslims/Islam in general being seen as identical to or inter-changeable with 'terrorism' as such (Khan 2005; Stampnitzky 2013).[11] As a result of this decades-long development, 'terrorism' has come to name a peculiarly abominable form of political vio-lence, a violence that is evil not because it is committed by a spe-cific actor (e.g. the state, or a non-state group or cell) or because it is a specific type of violence (e.g. it targets civilians or uses human shields), but rather because it targets and threatens people and places that otherwise ought rightfully to be protected, those defined and decided-upon in advance to be 'innocent'.

This development was by no means inevitable; moreover, it is not as radically new as Bush's moral Manicheanism might suggest. As Nadine Naber argues with regard to Arab American history, in a point that is also apposite to the problem of 'terrorism', 9/11 did not constitute 'an essential break or rupture' with a prior unmarked past but is, rather, better understood 'as an extension if not an intensification of a post-Cold War US expansion in the Middle East' (2012, 61; see also Mamdani 2004). I explore this history in greater detail elsewhere (Schotten 2018), but a few points can be made here. First, 'terrorism' becomes internationally significant in the era of decolonization. At this time, passionate debates were unfolding at the United Nations regarding the status of political violence, with Western nations seeking to condemn the violence of national liberation movements as 'terrorism' and the Soviet and unaligned states seeking to reframe the violence of colonial powers as the real 'terrorism' (Brulin 2011).

Less well-known is the important role played by Israeli Prime Minister Benjamin Netanyahu in the development of the 'terrorism' discourse, a man who has built his longstanding political career in part on the dogged promotion of an anti-'terrorism' platform (Said 2001 [1984]; Zulaika 2003). In 1979 and again in 1984, Netanyahu convened two international conferences that did enormous ideological work to solidify 'terrorism' as a specific phenomenon in international discourse (Beinin 2003; Brulin 2015). These conferences were attended primarily by Israelis and Americans, many of the latter of whom we now recognize as the 'first wave' of neoconservatives (or their institutional avatars).[12] The most significant outcomes of these two influential conferences were as follows:

(1) 'terrorism' becomes a morally overloaded term naming unthinkable, irrational, and annihilatory violence against 'innocents';

(2) 'terrorism' becomes inextricably associated with Islam, the Arab world, and, in particular, Palestinian resistance in the form of the PLO and other 'terrorist' organizations;[13] and

(3) Israel becomes linked with the US as part of a free and democratic West, the innocent and undeserving victim of 'terrorist' violence whose members must create 'an anti-terror alliance that all the democracies of the West must join' to defeat (Netanyahu 1981).

The upshot of these conferences, then, was not simply that 'terrorism' is evil. It was also that 'evil' means anti-civilizational violence committed by Muslim, Arab, and anti-democratic beings who do not value life – either their own or, more importantly, that of 'innocent' Westerners.

Israel's significant role in formulating and defining 'terrorism' in this particular, highly moralized way, ensured that its targets are not simply the West and the innocent, freedom-loving people within it, but also more specifically Jews and Jewish people, at least insofar as Israel defines itself as a Jewish state. The good-versus-evil paradigm established by these 'terrorism' conferences, then, established Israel and Jewish Israelis firmly alongside

Christian and Jewish Americans on the 'good' side as democratic, modern, Western, and civilized, leaving Arabs, Muslims, and Palestinians on the 'evil' side along with 'terrorism', irrationality, backwardness, and savagery. Moreover, the frequent invocations of Nazism at these conferences – as the origin of 'terrorism', as the prior historical phase in the development of 'terrorism', or even as less evil in comparison with the newly emergent threat of 'terrorism' – meant that 'terrorism' was fashioned by Israelis and US neoconservatives into the new Nazi threat – to Europe, to America, to Jews, and indeed to the entirety of the West and its civilization. This 'terrorism'-as-Nazism discourse subsumed Israel and, consequently, Jewish people, into the West as part and parcel of its civilizational and imperial project via the enterprise of fighting 'terrorism'. This enterprise helped consolidate the US–Israeli alliance as part of a shared democratic and Western civilization that is equally menaced by the same threat, Arab/Muslim/Palestinian evil. As Netanyahu rather brilliantly summed up,

> The antagonism of Islamic and Arab radicalism to the West is frequently misunderstood. It is sometimes explained as deriving from American support for Israel. But the hostility to the West preceded the creation of Israel by centuries, and much of the terrorists' animus is directed against targets and issues that have nothing to do with Israel. Indeed, the relationship is most often the other way around. Middle Eastern radicals did not develop their hatred for the West because of Israel; they hated Israel from its inception *because it is an organic part of the West*. That is, because Israel represents for them precisely the incarnation of those very traditions and values, foremost of which is democracy, which they hate and fear. (Netanyahu 1986, 62–63; original emphasis)

It is not, then, that 'terrorists' are responding to or resisting US empire and Israeli colonialism. It is rather that 'terrorists' hate

Israel because it is '*an organic part of the West*'; that is, because it is democratic and civilized. And terrorists hate democracy and civilization because, as we have seen, they are evil. Indeed, this is what evil effectively means. 'Terrorism' becomes another word for savagery and nihilism, for the negation of Jewishness and the West and everything that alliance ostensibly stands for: freedom, democracy, and the American way.[14]

Against academic freedom

Recall that the majority of attacks on student and faculty advocates of Palestinian liberation took the form of accusations of anti-semitism and/or support for 'terrorism'. The deep co-implication of these two accusations, their mutual necessity even, should by now be clear. It is similarly unsurprising that a primary term of discipline and punishment of Palestine advocates is 'civility', given that 'terrorism' names the 'savagery' of anti-civilizational people(s) and activities. Finally, however, the extreme gravity and sanctimony of antisemitism and 'terrorism' charges should now make more sense, along with these terms' application only to advocates of decolonization, Palestinian liberation, and most viciously to those who themselves seem to embody the 'savage' – that is, Palestinians, Arabs, and Muslims.[15]

All this should make us sceptical of the notion that 'academic freedom' could effectively counter the formidable, moralizing, 'terrorism'-as-Nazism discourse or defend advocates of Palestinian liberation from persecution within the academy, for a couple of reasons. First, it should reveal 'terrorism' and antisemitism charges for the imperial and settler agendas they actually are, rather than face-value accusations of which its targets could ever actually be acquitted. Second, and consequently, it should make clear that debates about the nature, definition, or limitations of academic freedom function to veil rather than expose the settler agendas driving the crackdown on Palestinian liberation to begin with. As we saw, in the cases of Al-Arian and Salaita, university administrators claimed to be defending academic freedom by firing tenured faculty. They did this without any seeming cognitive dissonance not because they were deluded about the true meaning of academic freedom, but rather because upholding academic freedom in the post-9/11 academy really does require the elimination of 'terrorist', 'savage', and other 'uncivil' threats to the sanctity of the settler university. Like the War on Terror, in other words, academic freedom is a discourse and strategy of settler colonialism. These administrators are not wrong, therefore, and the correctness of their positions should be taken seriously as exposing the uselessness of academic freedom as a tool for liberation, whether we are talking about the Palestinian freedom struggle or the individual cases of student and faculty repression that litter its path.

To be sure, it may be strategic to mobilize academic freedom in particular moments. The rubric of academic freedom proved extremely useful in the wake of Salaita's firing, for example: hundreds of faculty, many in no way anti-Zionist, saw in this case a dangerous overreach of administrative power and fundamental breach of faculty academic freedom and agreed to boycott UIUC on this basis. Nevertheless, academic freedom understood as a faculty member's right to speak her views and opinions free from administrative punishment simply fails to account for the historical legacies and structural relations of power that determine not just what can and can't be said, but also whose speech is considered intelligible, rational, and 'civil' and whose is not.[16] Indeed, the effectivity of the 'terrorism'-as-Nazism discourse is its profoundly *moralizing* character. Moralism operates not primarily by expressing itself as a point of view, but rather by disguising itself as something commonsensical or self-evidently true, an irrefutable premise without which the entire academic (or moral, political, cultural, etc.) edifice would collapse. The incontestability of its perspective is what allows it to sanction and invalidate opposing views as not views at all, but rather immoral and unthinkable forms of annihilationism, if not the very end of the world as such.[17] In this sense, university administrators and other defenders of the current order are not wrong to call defenders of Palestinian liberation 'terrorists'. If anything, they are right, since for them decolonization *really is* 'terrorism' – that is, the end of the world as they know it.[18] The response to such moralism cannot be to plant our own flag on the ground of 'free speech', casting decolonization as one opinion among many that any 'reasonable' person might support. This in no way alters the imperial conditions of the settler university; moreover, it admits decolonization into the marketplace of ideas as one choice among many, no better or worse than, say, colonialism, capitalism, Zionism, or American exceptionalism. Our defence of liberation would therefore simply sidestep – and thus enable if not perpetuate – the very thing we are fighting against. By ignoring the disciplinary moralism at work in defining *whose* freedom matters and *whose* voices are able to be heard and/or worthy of protection, academic freedom becomes another way of ignoring settler colonialism while simultaneously propping it up.

Many have pointed out that the struggle for Palestinian liberation has become a defining political issue in academia, one that simultaneously compresses and stands in for a host of struggles over university democratization: resistance to privatization, faculty demands for shared governance, fights over curricular control, contestations regarding 'hate speech' and acceptable discourse on campus, etc. (Maira 2018). That Palestine could coalesce or stand in for these seemingly disparate struggles suggests not that it is a lightning rod but rather a tuning fork, clarifying the singular note at the heart of these struggles: the inter-related issues and problems of settler colonialism (e.g. racism, nationalism, dispossession, capitalism, and neoliberalism) (Collins 2011). This may be why the academic boycott remains so controversial within the US academy: because it raises fundamental questions about the settler state itself. As Sunaina Maira writes,

> The boycott interrupts a liberal multicultural discourse in the settler university about cross-cultural 'dialogue' between Palestinians and Israelis, Jews and Muslims, which elides Zionism and anti-Palestinian racism. Doing so raises the spectre of Palestinians gone missing – dead, encaged, displaced, or fighting – and forces us to confront US settler-colonial mythologies and ongoing imperial violence in the darker regions of the world. (2015, 89)

In other words, advocacy of Palestinian liberation – in particular when it takes the form of academic boycott or other explicit challenges to Zionism itself (rather than to discrimination, occupation, or settlements *simply*) – goes to the root of the problem by calling into question the legitimacy of both the US and Israel *as settler states*. It is for this reason that Palestine advocacy is moralizingly characterized as unthinkable, intolerable, and a form of nihilism – whether that takes the form of aiding and abetting 'terrorists' or of speaking in an 'uncivil' manner.[19]

To adequately defend not simply the cause of Palestinian freedom, then, but also the students and faculty who advocate it, we must go beyond the political parameters of settler-empire that define the War on Terror and, therefore, the narrow liberal frame of academic freedom. As Roderick Ferguson and Jodi Melamed (2013) write, 'freedom struggles don't arise out of the same history as academic freedom, precisely because that latter history, a legal tradition based on claims to safeguard liberal individualism, touts freedom in the abstract but allows for water cannons, death threats, vandalism, and bullets to be unleashed on nonviolent protesters'. In other words, there is no incompatibility between academic freedom and the elimination of 'savagery' and 'incivility'; indeed, the latter may be the very work of the former.

Thus, when confronted with settler ultimatums that demand choosing between 'us' and the 'terrorists', or between 'civility' and 'incivility', we must remember that all languages and visions of decolonization are unspeakable and unimaginable within the colonial terms of academic freedom, and show up, if at all, only as 'savage', anti-civilizational, or 'terrorist' threats to the academy as it currently exists. The settler moralization of 'terrorism' explains both how and why supporters of Palestinian liberation are the primary targets of concerted right-wing attack simultaneously as it renders the academy incapable of either advocating or realizing liberatory, decolonizing agendas (Lloyd and Schueller 2013; cf. Ferguson and Melamed 2013). As Kandice Chuh writes,

> We may refuse the liberal framework of academic freedom and the dictates of professionalism that ask us to consider the civility of speech, to ask instead, who gets to express themselves with incivility – through state-sanctioned violence and/or racist, sexually violent, and white supremacist discourse and activities, say – and for whom is incivil speech impermissible? In fact, we know that it is speech emergent outside the powerfully structured domain of civility that is a practice of freedom – of the freedom that is before and beyond the academy, civil society, or broadly, the liberal order. It is the freedom that is not given or ever taken but is already and has always been ours, the freedom that inheres in existence. (2018, 166)

As Palestinians are known to insist, that existence is a form of resistance, and precisely because the structure of domination they face is the purposeful attempt at their elimination. Salaita's and Al-Arian's *sumud* – their steadfastness – in the face of eliminatory violence, not to mention their bravery in challenging that eliminatory violence, are what got them fired in the name of academic freedom. Surely our strategies of defending academic boycott, then, should not be complicit with this violence. Rather than accommodate ourselves to the 'civil' confines of academic freedom, we might instead learn from Al-Arian, Salaita, and the steadfastness of Palestinians everywhere in the face of their targeted elimination, and choose the only option clearly off the table in today's post-9/11 era, the side of the 'terrorists'. This is the abject and degraded meaning of Palestinian existence and resistance in a US settler-imperial context. It is, therefore, the vital and very necessary site of our solidarity.

Notes

1 I am grateful to Leila Farsakh, William Clare Roberts, the editors of this volume, and the volume reviewer for their critical readings of and constructive feedback on previous versions of this chapter. All remaining errors, oversights, and arguments are my own.

2 On the conflation of 'terrorism' with Islam, see Naber (2008); Rana (2016). On the US racialization of 'the terrorist' as a conglomeration of 'persons who appear "Middle Eastern, Arab, or Muslim"', see Volpp (2002). On the globalization of 'the Muslim' as a racialized figure of savagery via the discourse of 'terrorism', see Daulatzai (2016); Daulatzai and Rana (2018).

3 For the crucial role played by FOX News in what the Center for American Progress (CAP) calls the Islamophobia Network in America, see Ali et al. (2011). For a trenchant critique of the CAP report's failure to grasp the deeply racialized and ideological character of Islamophobia in the US, see Sheehi (2018).

4 Hatem Bazian (2018) argues that Al-Arian's case is the both the epitome of and defining precedent for the harassment and silencing of Palestine advocates in US academia. To my knowledge, however, no centralized repository of information exists that details Al-Arian's many and extensive struggles to, for example, attain US citizenship, fight the use of secret

evidence against suspects in federal courts, and surmount the massive forces arrayed against him – up to and including the federal government – to keep his job at USF. His ultimately unsuccessful struggle to defeat trumped-up federal terrorism charges is detailed in the 2007 documentary film *USA vs. Al-Arian*; meanwhile, his daughter, Laila Al-Arian, has written extensively about her father's prosecution and persecution. The website www.freesamialarian.com, however, no longer appears functional. More complete documentation of Al-Arian's extraordinary life and the racist persecution he faced in the US is important in its own right as well as to the multiple histories of US immigration, post-9/11 'terrorism' panic, Islamophobia, and Zionism, not to mention academic freedom, about which Wikipedia (the only existing collation of information about Al-Arian that I can find) declares: 'His professorship became the most significant academic freedom case since Angela Davis in the 1960s'. That Al-Arian is relatively unknown in comparison with Davis, even in left circles, suggests the urgency of documenting his life and struggle for social justice movement work as well.

5   Similarly, despite the vast amount of internet ink spilled over Salaita's case, to my knowledge there exists no single repository of information documenting Salaita's struggle with UIUC or the formidable forces arrayed against him, which may not have included federal terrorism charges but certainly did include elected officials, prominent donors, and, potentially, international Zionist advocates and organizations (Ali Abunimah's blog at *Electronic Intifada* is the most comprehensive source on these details I have found). Additionally, to my knowledge, no one has yet elaborated the many important connections to be made between Salaita's case and Al-Arian's. Both of these are important tasks for scholars of academic freedom, US racisms, the War on Terror, Islamophobia, and US Zionism to take up in the future, not to mention the US justice for Palestine movement. For Salaita's own reflections on his struggle, see Salaita (2015).

6   But see Tithi Bhattacharya and Bill Mullen's excellent essay (2015) on the convergence of neoliberalism with Zionism in the US academy.

7   Key to the production of this innocent and valuable life is the institution of settler temporality as *futurist*, or incessantly future-oriented in its aspiration to eliminate the native entirely and thereby erase itself *as* settler colonial (see Schotten 2018; Strakosch and Macoun 2012; Veracini 2011).

8   Elsewhere (Schotten 2018), I make the case more fully for a biopolitics of settler sovereignty that is irreducible to the operation of race and racism as defined by Foucault (2003), but which retains his analysis

of the necessary connection between biopolitics and necropolitics that is mandated by the invocation of the 'defence of society'. Although Mbembe (2003) offers an important corrective to Foucault in establishing the openly necropolitical operation of colonial regimes, he does not connect necropolitics to biopolitics in any necessary way, nor does he consider the role of the discourse of social defence in relation to either colonialism or necropolitics.

9   For a concise, encyclopaedic account of the development of a sustained, coordinated attack on 'critical thought about the Middle East' in the US academy, see Beinin (2006). For an in-depth account of the foundations that fund the Zionist organizations, think tanks, and 'news' sites attacking the BDS movement in the US, both on campus and off, see the International Jewish Anti-Zionist Network (2015). For recent documentation of the funders behind the highly secretive Canary Mission website and campus anti-divestment campaigns, see Josh Nathan-Kazis (2018a, 2018b) as well as the previously-censored four-part *Al Jazeera* documentary, *The Lobby – USA* (available for viewing at ElectronicIntifada.net).

10 This remains true, notwithstanding the Department of Homeland Security's recent decision to start taking 'white supremacist terrorism' seriously; on this striking pattern, see Schotten (2015). I should emphasize that my interest in this chapter concerns 'terrorism's' specifically twenty-first-century deployment in the War on Terror, and my detailing of the emergence of this particular usage should not be taken as an exhaustive history or account of the term 'terrorism' as such, which obviously well predates this historical moment. For a genealogy of 'terrorism' that traces the term to at least the French Revolution, see Erlenbusch-Anderson (2018).

11 Arun Kundnani (2012) has persuasively argued that the War on Terror has entered a new phase, wherein the pure 'evil' of the otherwise inexplicable 'terrorist' actor has been overtaken by the notion of 'radicalization', which allows for (previously taboo) explanation of 'terrorist' activity, albeit solely in the guise of ideological indoctrination – for which the destructive teachings of Islam is still responsible. This development explains the domesticization of foreign policy counterterrorism measures in the form of Preventing Violence Extremism (PVE) and Countering Violent Extremism (CVE) programmes and policies (see Kundnani and Hayes 2018).

12 In 1979: Henry Jackson, George Will, Norman Podhoretz, and Midge Decter; in 1984: George Schultz, Paul Johnson, Jeane Kirkpatrick,

Bernard Lewis, Charles Krauthammer, Walter Berns, and Midge Decter again. For more on neoconservatism, see Ehrman (1995).

13 A lurking if unstated reference point for Netanyahu at these conferences was also the Iranian revolution which, along with the many explicit references to the PLO, helped solidify the connection between anti-imperial, anti-colonial political violence and Islam, which comes to function as another name, cause, and explanation for such violence and, ultimately, for 'terrorism' itself. I am grateful to Leila Farsakh for this point.

14 An important missing piece of this narrative is the role that 'totalitarianism' discourse played in the development of 'terrorism', a discourse that first linked Communism with Nazism and then transformed this unlikely amalgamation into 'terrorism', a new form of inexcusable leftist politics necessarily implicated with genocidal or other murderous political practices (cf. Bush's famous fake phenomenon 'Islamo-fascism'). The bizarre Orientalist underpinnings of anti-totalitarianism provide an additional point of origin for the racialization of Arabs and Muslims specifically; see Pietz (1988); Schotten (2018); N. P. Singh (2003).

15 This use of 'terrorism' as an epithet to manage, control, stifle, quash, and punish resistance to empire and settler colonialism is not unknown with regard to indigenous North American people(s) either, however. In 2016, indigenous and allied water protectors were surveilled, policed, and brutalized by state and private security forces as they fought the installation of the Dakota Access Pipeline on tribal lands in North Dakota. The activities of this entirely non-violent movement were characterized as 'terrorism' and 'jihadism' by security forces and dealt with using anti-'terrorism' weaponry, tactics, and strategies (see Brown, Parrish and Speri 2017).

16 This point gets overlooked when it is taken for granted that academics generally have 'epistemic advantages over non-academics' and, thus, 'greater power over public discourses' (see Arianne Shahvisi, this volume). Clearly, of course, it depends significantly on which academics (and which public discourses) we're talking about.

17 Previous attempts by academic boycott supporters to marshal academic freedom in their defence neglect this point, ultimately remaining within a liberal framework that preserves existing structures of power rather than targeting or undermining them directly; see, e.g., Judith Butler's widely-celebrated essay, 'Israel/Palestine and the Paradoxes of Academic Freedom' (2006).

18 On the necessity of concreteness in naming and advocating for decolonization, see Tuck and Yang (2012).

19 Shahvisi attempts to salvage civility as an academic norm by having it
    mean respect for people's dignity (rather than limitations on the tone
    or emotion of people's speech) and making a distinction between per-
    sons and institutions, arguing that Salaita's speech criticized the insti-
    tution of Israeli settler colonialism but not any Israeli or Jewish person
    as such, and is therefore civil ('Privilege, Platforms, and Power', this
    volume). Yet I am not persuaded that these definitional distinctions
    can address the problems of moralizing, settler colonial overdetermina-
    tion I've outlined here. For example, what happens when Jewish stu-
    dents claim that an anti-Zionist professor's tweets are attacks on their
    dignity? What happens when Jewish students – or Jewish colleagues –
    claim that a professor's support of academic boycott harms or humili-
    ates them? Salaita actually addresses this in a public talk he gave at
    Brooklyn College in November 2014, noting that negative response to
    his tweets was often rooted in feelings of personal rejection and/or feel-
    ing 'unsafe' (for discussion, see Schotten 2018, Chapter 5). Regardless,
    it's not clear how or why a civility re-packaged as dignity that also
    distinguishes between persons and institutions could have protected
    Salaita (much less his speech) from being fired, given not simply the
    hegemonic Zionist conflation of Jews with Israel, but also the racist,
    settler colonial disqualification of Salaita as someone entitled to speak on
    such matters at all, PhD or no PhD (i.e. he had no epistemic advantage
    to marshal, despite being a published researcher, and in fact is epistem-
    ically *dis*qualified just because of who he is, not only because of what
    he said). To use other examples from Shahvisi's argument, it's even less
    clear how these definitional distinctions could effectively sanction rac-
    ist or transphobic academic work as *un*civil. Couldn't a transphobic
    feminist claim she is critiquing the institution of patriarchy when she
    argues that trans women are not women? Couldn't a racist declare he is
    criticizing the institution of political correctness by talking about the
    virtues of European colonialism? The fact of the matter is, pervasive
    systems of structural inequality and exploitation determine not simply
    what is and is not civil, but also who is and is not a person (both per
    se, as well as who is a person rather than an institution), not to mention
    who is qualified to make such distinctions in the first place. Indeed, in
    Shahvisi's own words, wherever we encounter the emptiness of liber-
    alism's platitudes, 'power fills that void' (this volume, Chapter 12). If
    we do not name and dismantle that power directly, but instead leave
    it intact and merely adjust the parameters of its institutional tools, we
    remain stuck tinkering within (and thereby repairing and sustaining)

that system of power rather than uprooting it. My suggestion, then, is that any retention of 'civility', no matter how carefully re-thought, retains its place and function in the liberal-colonial order, necessarily reproducing the systems of violence from which it emerges.

References

Agamben, G. (1998), *Homo Sacer: Sovereign Power and Bare Life* (D. Heller-Roazen trans), Stanford, CA: Stanford University Press.

Ali, W., E. Clifton, M. Duss, L. Fang, S. Keyes and F. Shakir (2011), *Fear, Inc.: The Roots of the Islamophobia Network in America*, August, Washington, DC: Center for American Progress.

Bazian, H. (2018), 'Sami Al-Arian and Silencing Palestine' in S. Daulatzai and J. Rana (eds), *With Stones in Our Hands: Writings on Muslims, Racism, and Empire*, Minneapolis, MN: University of Minnesota Press, pp. 306–325.

Beinin, J. (2003), 'Is Terrorism a Useful Term in Understanding the Middle East and the Palestinian–Israeli Conflict?', *Radical History Review* Special Issue: Terror and History, 85 (Winter): 12–23.

Beinin, J. (2006), 'The New McCarthyism: Policing Thought about the Middle East' in B. Doumani (ed.), *Academic Freedom after September 11*, Brooklyn, NY: Zone, pp. 237–268.

Bhattacharya, T. and B. Mullen (2015), 'Steven Salaita's Firing Shows Where Zionism Meets Neoliberalism on University Campuses' in A. Dawson and B. Mullen (eds), *Against Apartheid: The Case for Boycotting Israeli Universities*, Chicago, IL: Haymarket, pp. 201–204.

Brown, A., W. Parrish and A. Speri (2017), 'Leaked Documents Reveal Counterterrorism Tactics Used at Standing Rock to "Defeat Pipeline Insurgencies"', *TheIntercept*, 27 May, https://theintercept.com/2017/05/27/leaked-documents-reveal-security-firms-counterterrorism-tactics-at-standing-rock-to-defeat-pipeline-insurgencies/ (accessed 13 March 2019).

Brulin, R. (2011), 'Defining "Terrorism": The 1972 General Assembly Debates on "International Terrorism" and Their Coverage by the *New York Times*' in B. Baybars-Hawks and L. Baruh (eds), *If It Was Not for Terrorism: Crisis, Compromise, and Elite Discourse in the Age of War on Terror*, Newcastle upon Tyne: Cambridge Scholars, pp. 12–30.

Brulin, R. (2015), 'Compartmentalization, Contexts of Speech and the Israeli Origins of the American Discourse on "Terrorism"', *Dialectical Anthropology* 39 (1): 69–118.

Butler, J. (2006), 'Israel/Palestine and the Paradoxes of Academic Freedom', *Radical Philosophy* 135 (8), https://www.radicalphilosophyarchive.com/article/israelpalestine-and-the-paradoxes-of-academic-freedom (accessed 13 March 2019).

Byrd, J. (2011), *The Transit of Empire: Indigenous Critiques of Colonialism*, Minneapolis, MN: University of Minnesota Press.

Chuh, K. (2018), 'Pedagogies of Dissent', *American Quarterly* 17 (2): 155–172.

Collins, J. (2011), *Global Palestine*, London: Hurst & Co.

Coulthard, G. (2014), *Red Skin White Masks: Rejecting the Colonial Politics of Recognition*, Minneapolis, MN: University of Minnesota Press.

Daulatzai, S. (2016), 'The 9/11 Present: Perpetual War and Permanent Unrest' in *Fifty Years of the Battle of Algiers: Past as Prologue*, Minneapolis, MN: University of Minnesota Press, pp. 65–80.

Daulatzai, S. and J. Rana(2018), 'Writing the Muslim Left: An Introduction to Throwing Stones' in S. Daulatzai and J. Rana (eds), *With Stones in Our Hands: Writings on Muslims, Race, and Empire*, Minneapolis, MN: University of Minnesota Press.

Ehrman, J. (1995), *The Rise of Neoconservatism: Intellectuals and Foreign Affairs 1945–1994*, New Haven, CT: Yale University Press.

Erlenbusch-Anderson, V. (2018), *Genealogies of Terrorism: Revolution, State Violence, Empire*, New York: Columbia University Press.

Ferguson, R. and J. Melamed (2013), 'Academic Freedom with Violence', *AAUP Journal of Academic Freedom* 4, https://www.aaup.org/sites/default/files/Response-FergusonMelamed.pdf (accessed 13 March 2019).

Foucault, M. (2003), *'Society Must Be Defended': Lectures at the Collège de France 1975–1976* (D. Macey trans), New York: Picador.

Genshaft, J. and D. Stamps (2003), 'Addendum: Comments from President Judy Genshaft and Provost David Stamps on Draft Report' appended to 'Academic Freedom and Tenure: University of South Florida', *Academe*, 89 (3): 59–73.

International Jewish Anti-Zionist Network (2015), *The Business of Backlash: The Attack on the Palestinian Movement and Other Movements for Justice*, March, http://www.ijan.org/wp-content/uploads/2015/04/IJAN-Business-of-Backlash-full-report-web.pdf (accessed 13 March 2019).

Khan, L. A. (2005), 'The Essentialist Terrorist', *Washburn Law Journal* 45 (Fall): 47–88.

Kundnani, A. (2012), 'Radicalisation: The Journey of a Concept', *Race and Class* 54 (2): 3–25.

Kundnani, A. and B. Hayes (2018), 'The Globalisation of Countering Violent Extremism Policies: Undermining Human Rights, Instrumentalising Civil Society', Amsterdam: The Transnational Institute, https://www.tni.org/files/publication-downloads/cve_web.pdf (accessed 13 March 2019).

Lloyd, D. and M. J. Schueller (2013), 'The Israeli State of Exception and the Case for Academic Boycott', *AAUP Journal of Academic Freedom* 4, https://www.aaup.org/sites/default/files/LloydSchueller.pdf (accessed 13 March 2019).

Maira, S. (2015), 'The Ghosts That Haunt Us: USACBI and the Settler University' in A. Dawson and B. Mullen (eds), *Against Apartheid: The Case for Boycotting Israeli Universities*, Chicago, IL: Haymarket, pp. 81–90.

Maira, S. (2018), *Boycott! The Academy and Justice for Palestine*, Oakland, CA: University of California Press.

Mamdani, M. (2004), *Good Muslim, Bad Muslim: America, the Cold War, and the Roots of Terror*, New York: Pantheon.

Mbembe, A. (2003), 'Necropolitics', *Public Culture* 15 (1): 11–40.

Naber, N. (2008), '"Look, Mohammed the Terrorist Is Coming!" Cultural Racism, Nation-Based Racism, and the Intersectionality of Oppressions after 9/11' in A. Jamal and N. Naber (eds), *Race and Arab Americans before and after 9/11: From Invisible Citizens to Visible Subjects*, Syracuse, NY: Syracuse University Press, pp. 276–304.

Naber, N. (2012), *Arab America: Gender, Cultural Politics, and Activism*, New York: NYU Press.

Naber, N., E. Desouky and L. Baroudi (2006), 'The Forgotten "-ism": An Arab American Women's Perspective on Zionism, Racism, and Sexism' in INCITE! Women of Color Against Violence (eds), *Color of Violence: The INCITE! Anthology*, Cambridge, MA: South End Press, pp. 97–112.

Nathan-Kazis, J. (2018a), 'A New Wave of Hardline Anti-BDS Tactics Are Targeting Students, and No One Knows Who's Behind It', *The Forward*, 2 August, https://forward.com/news/407127/a-new-wave-of-hardline-anti-bds-tactics-are-targeting-students-and-no-one/ (accessed 13 March 2019).

Nathan-Kazis, J. (2018b), 'Revealed: Canary Mission Blacklist Is Secretly Bankrolled by Major Jewish Federation', *The Forward*, 3 October, https://forward.com/news/national/411355/revealed-canary-mission-blacklist-is-secretly-bankrolled-by-major-jewish/ (accessed 13 March 2019).

Netanyahu, B. (1981), Foreword to B. Netanyahu (ed.), *International Terrorism: Challenge and Response*, New Brunswick, NJ: Transaction.

Netanyahu, B. (1986), 'Terrorism and the Islamic World' in B. Netanyahu (ed.), *Terrorism: How the West Can Win*, Baltimore, MD: Johns Hopkins University Press.

Palestine Legal and the Center for Constitutional Rights (2015), *The Palestine Exception to Free Speech: A Movement Under Attack in the US*, September, https://ccrjustice.org/sites/default/files/attach/2015/09/Palestine%20Exception%20Report%20Final.pdf (accessed 13 March, 2019).

Pietz, W. (1988), 'The "Post-Colonialism" of Cold War Discourse', *Social Text*, 19/20 (Autumn): 55–75.

Rana, J. (2016), 'The Racial Infrastructure of the Terror-Industrial Complex', *Social Text* 32 (4): 111–138.

Said, E. (2001 [1984]), 'The Essential Terrorist' in E. Said and C. Hitchens (eds), *Blaming the Victims: Spurious Scholarship and the Palestinian Question*, London: Verso, pp. 149–158.

Salaita, S. (2015), *Uncivil Rites: Palestine and the Limits of Academic Freedom*, Chicago, IL: Haymarket Books.

Salaita, S. (2016), *Inter/Nationalism: Decolonizing Native America and Palestine*, Minneapolis, MN: University of Minnesota Press.

Schotten, C. H. (2015), 'Why the Charleston Massacre Isn't Terrorism, and Palestinian Resistance Always Will Be', *Mondoweiss*, 11 July, https://mondoweiss.net/2015/07/charleston-palestinian-resistance/ (accessed 13 March 2019).

Schotten, C. H. (2018), *Queer Terror: Life, Death, and Desire in the Settler Colony*, New York: Columbia University Press.

Sheehi, S. (2018), 'Duplicity and Fear: Toward a Race and Class Critique of Islamophobia' in S. Daulatzai and J. Rana (eds), *With Stones in Our Hands: Writings on Muslims, Race, and Empire*, Minneapolis, MN: University of Minnesota Press.

Simpson, A. (2011), 'Settlement's Secret', *Cultural Anthropology* 26 (2): 205–217.

Singh, J. (2014), 'Why Aren't We Talking about Racism and Colonialism in the Salaita Affair?' *Electronic Intifada*, 9 September, https://electronicintifada.net/content/why-arent-we-talking-about-racism-and-colonialism-salaita-affair/13842 (accessed 13 March 2019).

Singh, N. P. (2003), 'Cold War Redux: On the "New Totalitarianism"', *Radical History Review* Special Issue: Terror and History , 85(Winter): 171–181.

Stampnitzky, L. (2013), *Disciplining Terror: How Experts Invented 'Terrorism'*, Cambridge: Cambridge University Press.

Strakosch, E. and A. Macoun (2012), 'The Vanishing Endpoint of Settler Colonialism', *Arena* 37/38: 40–62.

Svirsky, M. and S. Bignall (eds) (2012), *Agamben and Colonialism*, Edinburgh: Edinburgh University Press.

Transcript: O'Reilly Interviews Al-Arian in September 2001 (2003), 20 February, https://www.foxnews.com/story/transcript-oreilly-interviews-Al-Arian-in-september-2001 (accessed 13 March 2019).

Tuck, E. and K. W. Yang (2012), 'Decolonization Is Not a Metaphor', *Decolonization: Indigeneity, Education and Society* 1 (1): 1–40.

USA vs. Al-Arian (2007), dir. Line Halvorsen, 102 minutes, http://www.usavsalarian.com/ (accessed 13 March 2019).

Veracini, L. (2011), 'Introducing *Settler Colonial Studies*', *Settler Colonial Studies* 1 (1): 1–12.

Volpp, L. (2002), 'The Citizen and the Terrorist', *UCLA Law Review* 49 (June): 1575–1599.

Wikipedia (2019), 'Sami Al-Arian', https://en.wikipedia.org/wiki/Sami_Al-Arian#cite_ref-47 (accessed 13 March 2019).

Wilson, J. K. (2014), 'Chancellor Phyllis Wise Explains the Firing of Steven Salaita', *Academe Blog: The Blog of Academe Magazine*, 22 August, https://academeblog.org/2014/08/22/chancellor-phyllis-wise-explains-the-firing-of-steven-salaita/ (accessed 13 March 2019).

Wolfe, P. (2006), 'Settler Colonialism and the Elimination of the Native', *Journal of Genocide Research* 8 (4): 387–409.

Zulaika, J. (2003), 'The Self-Fulfilling Prophecies of Counterterrorism', *Radical History Review* Special Issue: Terror and History , 85 (Winter): 191–199.

TWELVE | Privilege, platforms, and power: uses and abuses of academic freedom

Arianne Shahvisi

Introduction: unpacking civility

Academic freedom is widely regarded as critical to the operation of academia. Limitations to scholarly enquiry threaten to restrict and determine the course and content of knowledge production, which would be anathema to free enquiry. Yet just as the broader notion of free speech is never unlimited, the speech of academics must have its bounds. Speech can cause harm, a fact which is recognized by hate speech legislation. Academics have epistemic advantages over non-academics, amounting to greater power over mainstream discourses. This is partly because they are considered – as a matter of definition – to be more credible in their areas of expertise than non-academics, and partly because they have tremendous 'platform privilege', in that they can easily access many platforms from which their views can be espoused (Shahvisi 2018). These epistemic privileges amplify the extent to which academics can cause harm through their speech. Thus conservative controversialist Jordan Peterson's damaging and misleading misogyny, transphobia, and climate-change denial are bolstered by the platforms and credibility his academic post affords him (Earle 2018; Sanneh 2018).

If academics are capable of greater harm through their public speech than non-academics, it stands to reason that their public speech should be subject to additional constraints. What might such constraints look like? One operational constraint on the speech of academics is that of 'civility'. Inside and outside the classroom and campus, the public speech of academics is expected to be 'civil'. Those who invoke this demand rarely define the term or defend what it includes and forbids. Power fills that void, and recent years have seen 'civility' become a placeholder for senior administrators looking to protect the university's marketability in an increasingly financialized sector. While in the previous chapter, Schotten questions the value of academic freedom and resists 'civility' or any concomitant constraint on acceptable speech, here I argue that justice requires attention to the harms and possibilities of our utterances, and suggest some ideas for a more justifiable set of constraints on academic freedom.

Even with its definition indeterminate, 'civility' is a problematic word. It is the deportment of those who are 'civilized', the emblem of the contested term 'Western civilization', the virtue that colonial 'civilizing missions' sought to enforce. In its vagueness, being 'uncivil' is liable to revert to these forms and assume the role of determining who belongs, of casting out those whose way of being is unpalatable, ugly, uncomfortable. Its ephemeral quality, and its ability to determine who is Other, makes marginalized groups more liable to be targeted by civility as an exclusion criterion. It is unsurprising therefore to note that those who have been targeted most vociferously by the civility discourse are people of colour. Once cast as uncivil, a person is particularly harmed in her ability to operate as an academic, since her credibility is undermined by her outsider status. To be uncivil is to be unsophisticated, impolite, a barbarian.[1] Using the word 'civility' sanitizes the morally repugnant associations it so often codes:

> It's not politically correct to call your enemies 'barbarians'
> anymore! But to tell someone they need to be more 'civil' sounds
> ... well, more civil. (Lê Espiritu and Puar 2015, 70)

While these concerns are significant, one might opt to bracket them and be charitable about the function of a reclaimed version of civility (or an equivalent concept) in securing necessary constraints on academic freedom. One important objective of civility, or something like it, is sharing discursive spaces in the face of disagreement. Accordingly, civility might be defined through its relationship to 'civic virtue', which pertains to the qualities each person must inculcate in herself in order to contribute to a successful community. Civility might then be described as the 'disposition that makes political life possible because it allows those with different and conflicting views of the good to live peacefully side-by-side' (Boyd 2006, 865).

Yet this definition raises new difficulties, since assuming that those with 'conflicting views' will be able to live 'peacefully side-by-side' if only they adopt the correct 'disposition' rests on several questionable presuppositions. First, it assumes that the views that people hold will never or rarely translate into concomitant behaviours or actions which preclude the option of living peacefully side-by-side. Further, powerful social institutions and groups are generally able to enforce their view of the good, subjecting less powerful groups to structural, if not direct, violence. Ought we to lionize civility and peace in these cases, and if so, to what end? Such an expectation is redolent of the 'white moderate who is more devoted to "order" than to justice; who prefers a negative peace which is the absence of tension to a positive peace which is the presence of justice' (King, Jr 1963).

Second, standard definitions of civility imply that 'different and conflicting views of the good' should always be permitted to coexist. This assumes a world in which neutrality or pluralism is generally germane in the consideration of ethical and political problems. Again, this is precluded by the uneven distribution of power. Rather, the definition seems relevant only to a world characterized by idealized, contained, and impersonal 'trolley problem'-style dilemmas (Foot 1967), in which two individuals can reasonably argue for diametrically opposite positions without either contributing to any more serious or long-term harm. While civility may be apt to facilitate tactful disagreement on topics within abstract areas of academia, where the disagreement instead pertains to people's lives and identities, it is not so obvious that there *can* be coexistence of conflicting views of the good without considerations of civility receding to irrelevance as people reprioritize securing or protecting their existence or dignity. Accordingly, the demand for civility must be correlated with the stakes of a particular topic of discussion, the discursive forum, and the context in space and time. This sentiment was recently summarized by a social media user: 'We can disagree and still love each other unless your disagreement is rooted in my oppression and denial of my humanity and right to exist' (Son of Baldwin 2015).

Civility is often understood as a constraint on the manner of speech rather than the content (the case studies in the next section demonstrate this point). In other words, civility aims not to limit freedom of speech, but stipulates that the *manner* in which one deploys that freedom is critical to the social acceptability of the utterance. Again, several problems arise. Are the content and tone of speech so easily separate? When a person's manner is deemed to be inappropriate, it is often her choice of words that is deemed to be at fault. It seems reasonable to limit freedom of speech by outlawing words that are harmful by virtue of being pejorative or oppressive, but that then becomes a constraint on *content* not *manner*. Yet it is more common in practice for a person to be declared uncivil for being inappropriately emotional, most commonly for being 'too angry'. Imposing this constraint is often described by critics as 'tone policing'. The targets of tone policing tend to be women and people of colour, who in light of racist and sexist stereotypes are readily cast as overly emotional (Poland 2016). The effect of tone policing is to dispute the content of a view by discrediting the manner in which the content was delivered, which again blurs the boundary between the two. If civility is used to set limits on speech via the tone of that speech, it is more likely to punish those who are personally (and therefore emotionally) affected by live political issues, which is to say, those who belong to marginalized groups.

Tone policing, or any tone-based civility constraint, treats emotional content as unhelpful or damaging to productive discussion. Yet this claim is far from self-evident. A good deal can be learned from the incidence and nature of a discernible emotional tenor within a discussion of moral or political views. Anger, in particular, may be read as a measure of the effects of a particular moral position on the wellbeing of a particular person or group. Where anger is repetitive among members of a particular social group and not among others, rather than inferring their 'incivility', one could instead infer that they are disproportionately negatively affected by a particular action or speech act, which might point to another person or group's 'incivility'.

The confusion around civility is not helped by the fact that it is most often deployed by those with the power to enforce the consequences of incivility, and is accordingly propagated along the contours of robust power dipoles. The unremitting derision of Islam and Muslims by the cartoonists at *Charlie Hebdo* is rarely described as 'uncivil', rather it is more often seen by mainstream commentators as an archetypal and even admirable exercise of free speech (Lê Espiritu and Puar 2015). Yet consider that in 2009 *Charlie Hebdo* fired a writer for a statement that was viewed by some as antisemitic (he later challenged the magazine for unfair dismissal and won the case) (Greenwald 2015). Evidently the magazine *does* enforce constraints on the freedom of speech of its writers, it just doesn't extend that 'civility' to Muslims. Further, the constraint is on content, rather than tone (which is unfalteringly snide). It is interesting to note that the magazine's much vaunted 'bravery' and 'independence of thought' so closely mirrors the political interests of France (and the West more generally) in its devaluation of Muslim lives.

Civility is sometimes deployed from the opposite political direction, as a complaint against the public utterances of a powerful person like US President Donald Trump, for example. Yet even here, the focus on manner or tone rather than content becomes troubling. Critics complain that Trump's manner is not 'statesmanlike', that he lacks a certain professionalism in his public engagement. While these lines of critique may seem explicable and accurate to any observer, they are only marginally less troubling than critique of Trump that fixates on his body shape or hair style. While Trump's public utterances are certainly made more harmful by his abrasive manner, the content of his speech ought to be the focus of our moral concern. Otherwise we commit ourselves to the result that an abrasive, rough-mannered politician instead forcefully advocating for the rights of marginalized groups would also be unacceptable, which seems off-key. Trump is 'uncivil' because his worldview, as evidenced by the content of his speech, is anathema to justice for marginalized groups. While his aggressive, discourteous manner is likely a symptom of this worldview, alone it is not enough to carry critique of his speech.

Civility weaponized

Over seven weeks in the summer of 2014, 2,251 people were killed in the Gaza Strip under Israel's 51-day military assault 'Operation Protective Edge' (United Nations Office for the Coordination of Humanitarian Affairs 2015). Among the many commentators who observed the killing on social media with horror and indignation was Indigenous Studies scholar Steven Salaita, whose tweets angrily denounced Israel's actions as the actions of a violent colonial power acting with an impunity which has been manufactured, at least in part, by the deliberate conflation of critique of Israeli state violence with antisemitism (Mackey 2014). Salaita's impassioned tweets used strong language in places, named Israel as a colonial power, criticized the equation by defenders of Israeli state violence of anti-Zionism with antisemitism, expressed the wish that West Bank settlers would 'go missing', and suggested that Netanyahu's violent military incursions had gone so far that his wearing a 'necklace made from the teeth of Palestinian children' would surprise nobody. Importantly, Salaita refused to understand the onslaught as deriving from 'Jewish–Arab acrimony', noting that he was 'in solidarity with many Jews and in disagreement with many Arabs' (Mackey 2014).

Salaita's tweets came to the attention of major donors to the University of Illinois at Urbana-Champaign, who complained to then-chancellor Phyllis Wise. Some grievances related to the tone of the tweets, others to the claim that they were antisemitic. Salaita's new academic post at the University of Illinois, which he was due to begin that autumn, was withdrawn and he was not hired. Wise released a statement which attempted to explain the decision in the face of widespread indignation:

> The decision regarding Prof Salaita was not influenced in any way by his positions on the conflict in the Middle East nor his criticism of Israel.
>
> ...
>
> What we cannot and will not tolerate at the University of Illinois are personal and disrespectful words or actions that demean and abuse either viewpoints themselves or those who express them. We have a particular duty to our students

to ensure that they live in a community of scholarship that challenges their assumptions about the world but that also respects their rights as individuals. (Wise 2014)[2]

Elsewhere in the same statement, Wise urged that discussions be conducted in a 'scholarly, *civil* and productive manner' and a '*civil*, thoughtful and mutually respectful manner' (my italics). She also asserted that academics have a responsibility to uphold 'traditions of scholarship and *civility*'.

Salaita's case gave the notion of civility in academia its break-through role, and Wise's statement serves to highlight even more of its tribulations and contradictions. I do not have space to explore all of these here, but I will note that the fact that Wise's actions were driven by pressure from donors points to the chilling impact that the financialization of the higher education sector is having on freedom of speech (see e.g. Giroux 2015).

It is important to set aside the charge that Salaita's tweets were factually inaccurate or antisemitic. Salaita is a scholar of Indigenous Studies. His trade is the careful examination of long histories of the oppression and genocide of indigenous people and the theft and destruction of indigenous land. Recognizing and naming Israel as a settler colonial state is a matter of profes-sional duty; frustration at the widespread mischaracterization of Israel as a terrorized democracy an occupational risk. Further, as a scholar of Indigenous Studies, it is important that we recog-nize Salaita's epistemic authority in his characterization of Israel's actions, in just the same way that we trust cosmologists when they tell us about the first moments of the universe. This is not to say that we should always take things on trust and defer to authority, or that non-scholars cannot also be experts, but that the appro-priate course of action if we doubt an expert's challenge to the mainstream perspective is to engage with their more rigorously defended work, rather than flatly deny their authority. Interested readers may find Salaita's arguments spelled out in detail and fully-referenced (2006, 2011, 2016). This is particularly important in Salaita's case because the credibility of people of colour is so often undermined. It is also important in the case of work which explores the experiences of a marginalized group such as the Palestinians, since the hegemony of the mainstream position is liable to make us prima facie distrustful of those who challenge it.

The actions of the Israeli state are clearly the target of Salaita's critique, which makes no direct or indirect reference to Jews except the aforementioned proclamation of solidarity. The strategic uses of 'antisemitism' to protect the actions of the Israeli state from critique are damaging to those doing the careful work of challenging the real and terrifying force of genuine antisemitism,[3] and are therefore contrary to the aims of anti-racism and should not be tolerated. These have been well documented and rebutted elsewhere (Jewish Voice for Peace 2017).

In her statement Wise claimed that Salaita's firing had nothing to do with 'his positions on the conflict in the Middle East nor his criticism of Israel'. It is difficult to believe that this statement could be true since documents were released which indicated that donors were troubled by Salaita's views, and it is obvious that those donors influenced Wise's decision. Had Salaita used the same tone to deride a sports team, it seems implausible that it could have cost him his job. Words are only 'disrespectful' when they express particular content. Again, it is plain that tone and content are not separable.

Yet even taking Wise at her word leads to confusion and contradiction. The decision to revoke Salaita's job was apparently the result of his use of 'personal and disrespectful words' that 'demean and abuse either viewpoints themselves or those who express them'. Can one abuse viewpoints? Surely that is just a melodramatic description of disagreement? The absurdity of this statement has been widely noted (Moshman and Edler 2015). It seems to imply that 'you can politely disagree with the Ku Klux Klan, but be careful not to demean any of their viewpoints' (Moshman and Edler 2015, 2).

Salaita's tweets were undeniably emotionally charged. His anger was palpable. His tweets responded directly to the vastly disproportionate violence of a powerful state against a relatively powerless population under long-term siege. Gaza was under bombardment; Salaita was responding live to that reality. How was one supposed to talk about Palestine that summer? How is one supposed to talk about Palestine full stop? Are we required to be dispassionate, and if so, who does that serve? Performing civility for the pleasure of global North donors will not save the limbs of Gazan children. How can it be that the right of Palestinians not to be slaughtered, and the right or responsibility of scholars to challenge that violence, are secondary to US students' 'rights as individuals'? If Wise saw critique of Israeli violence as an affront to Jewish students – as this seems to imply, and which raises its own issues – what does the silencing of that critique mean for Palestinian students? Wise's 'civility' is selective and inconsistent: it is shaped by realpolitik rather than the non-excludable public good it ought to be.

Less than a year after Salaita's job was revoked, another scholar of colour also faced rebuke for her social media use. Saida Grundy, an incoming Black sociologist at Boston University, tweeted a series of critical statements relating to the inheritance of slave status and the culture of white male privilege in US universities (Shahvisi 2015). A vicious, racially motivated backlash ensued among conservative student groups that accused Grundy of sexism against men and racism against white people (Grundy 2017). Rather than allow the sociologist herself to capitalize on this teachable moment to explain why reverse oppressions do not exist, or extend support to a scholar undertaking bold educative work in the unpaid public sphere, Boston University president Robert A. Brown – whose training is in engineering, not sociology – kowtowed to Grundy's critics. Grundy was not fired, but Brown's public letter undermined the value of her social commentary and bolstered her critics:

> I understand there is a broader context to Dr. Grundy's tweets and that, as a scholar, she has the right to pursue her research, formulate her views, and challenge the rest of us to think differently about race relations. But we also must recognize that words have power and the words in her Twitter feed were powerful in the way they stereotyped and condemned other people.
>
> Too often conversations about race quickly become inflamed and divisive. We must resolve to find a vocabulary for these conversations that allows us to seek answers without intemperance, rancor, or unnecessary divisiveness. (Coker 2015)

Civility makes no direct appearance here, but the critique of Grundy's words as being inappropriately 'powerful', and as characterized by 'intemperance', 'rancor', and 'unnecessary divisiveness' bears all the hallmarks of a demand for civility in Wise's sense. The Grundy case bears important similarities to Salaita's.[4] Both stand accused of *producing* division, disrespect, and intemperance, rather than *responding* to these features as they encounter them in the world. Their critics and bosses were – wilfully or unconsciously – insensitive to the influence of power in the topics they discussed, and therefore inclined to see their interventions as the first violation of an imagined neutrality and egalitarianism in the context of which 'civility' would be an appropriate constraint.

The medium of expression is critical to this discussion. Many academics, myself included, use social media in something closer to the way in which one sounds off to friends about political matters, rather than the highly ritualized, sterilized form required for academic writing. While we have been trained to avoid emotion in our academic expression, and while the gatekeeping processes of academic publishing ensure that emotion is censored, this does not mean that academics do not have emotional responses. Social media then become 'a platform for the expression of political outrage that is censored elsewhere ... Twitter, and social media more generally, should be embraced for the risky expression it engenders, not subjected to the normativizing standards of forms long known to us' (Lê Espiritu and Puar 2015, 66). Indeed, some of us are more liable to respond with emotion than others, because the topics in which we are experts involve real-world moral content (compare Grundy's scholarship on race to Brown's scholarship on chemical engineering), and some of us are liable to have a still more emotional response because a particular issue bears on our personal positionality. Scholars of colour such as Salaita and Grundy often fall into this last category.

Dignity and dissent

Salaita's and Grundy's cases demonstrate the ways in which 'civility' has been used by university administrators to appease donors, placate powerful student groups, and protect the reputation of the university in relation to national and regional political hegemonies. Yet even if this instantiation of civility is imprecise and unjust, clearly there must be limits to academic freedom to prevent academics deploying their epistemic privilege in ways that produce or increase harm, particularly towards marginalized groups.

Another standard definition describes civility as:

> a variety of norms about language, tone, and attitude governing
> an exchange of words and ideas: for example, showing respect
> for the other person or persons with whom one is conversing;
> avoiding insulting, demeaning or derisive language (or gestures);
> and genuinely listening to (and trying to make good sense of)
> what the other person says. (Leiter 2012)

Accordingly, civility, or the constraint on speech that facilitates social living, is rooted in some unspecified notion of respect. To be civil is to be respectful; to fail to show respect is to be uncivil. If that is correct, then acquiring a more precise and useful definition of civility requires a clear definition of what respect is, and who or what its object is. Respect has been discussed extensively within moral and political philosophy (Dillon 2018), and distinctions have been made between its different forms. Synthesizing some of that literature, one can distil three varieties of respect that are useful in sharpening the concept of civility: *dignity* respect, *appraisal* respect, and *institutional* respect.

Dignity respect (which has its roots in the work of Immanuel Kant) is the idea that each person is entitled to be treated as an end in herself, as a person with equal moral status to other persons, whose needs and preferences are automatically accounted for within any moral calculations. *Appraisal* respect, or evaluative respect, is an attitude of reverence or praise that is not automatic but is instead earned by virtue of some kind of distinction, whether moral or otherwise (Darwall 1977; Hudson 1980). I might respect a person's courage, or their decision not to consume animal products. *Institutional* respect (Hudson 1980) is an attitude that is adopted towards particular institutions by virtue of obeying rules and adhering to or observing particular rituals or practices. Institutions are 'a complex of positions, roles, norms and values lodged in particular types of social structures and organizing relatively stable patterns of human activity' (Turner 1997). They are formal or informal sites of social power such as organizations, practices, or beliefs that are powerfully and sometimes violently enacted or upheld, and the demand for and practice of institutional respect fortifies institutions. Examples of institutional respect include obeying the law, wearing a poppy in the UK around Remembrance Day, or the use of honorifics when addressing particular people.

A more rigorous analysis of civility can be generated by considering which of these notions of respect may be used to pose legitimate constraints on freedom of speech. Dignity respect is uncontroversial. It constrains freedom of speech by requiring that we do not engage in speech that causes indignity to others. This means that speech which causes harm or humiliation to others or threatens their existence should not be accepted. By contrast, institutional respect should *not* be conferred unconditionally, and should be withdrawn where the institution in question does not uphold the dignity respect of particular individuals or groups. In other words, institutional respect should be conferred only as a form of *appraisal* respect, with dignity as the unit of appraisal.[5] This means that laws which do not uphold the dignity of people should not be honoured, or that one need not use honorifics where they replicate gender roles or binaries that insult the dignity of those who they do not represent or entrench the low social status of others. Or, to put the point more strongly, perhaps one ought to *actively* disrespect laws, customs, codes of conduct where they undermine the dignity of some people. Importantly, dignity respect cannot be subject to the same conditionality: one must respect the dignity of others regardless of one's appraisal of them.

These constraints apply to all of us, but given the aforementioned privileges held by academics, ensuring that these restrictions are upheld is particularly important. If an academic publicly claims that women are unfit to be scientists, that transwomen are not women, or that people of colour are less intelligent, that is a much more serious matter than if the same views are expressed by my neighbour, who is a pest control specialist. Academics are more likely to be heard and are more likely to be believed. But there are additional reasons for expecting academics to meet a more stringent standard in their speech. Academics are responsible for the learning of their students, and dignity is critical to learning. Further, withdrawing or withholding respect for institutions in accordance with their appraised value is essential to research.

Academics' speech determines the learning environment experienced by students. One can paraphrase the constraints imposed by dignity respect with the requirement that academics create 'safe spaces' in their classrooms. Safe spaces are often ill-defined and are widely aspersed. In other work, I describe two senses of 'safety' within a discursive space: first, excluding particular people (generally those with a specified form of social privilege) in order to facilitate a specialist or sensitive discussion; second, excluding particular language or behaviours which are deemed to be marginalizing (Shahvisi 2018). This second sense is important in educational environments.

Creating a safe space is strongly contingent on the way in which academics set up the direct classroom environment, but it is also contingent on what else is known about the teacher. The views of a teacher with a known public social media presence may affect the possibility of a safe space within their classroom, even despite efforts to that effect: e.g. a teacher who has expressed transphobic views on a public social media account may struggle to produce a learning environment within which trans and other students feel comfortable. But what counts as 'safety'? Callan draws a distinction between 'intellectual safety' and 'dignity safety' (2016). Dignity safety is achieved when each person is confident that in a particular space she will not be treated by others as having an 'inferior social rank'. Intellectual safety, by contrast, obtains when there is no culture of antagonism, when deeply held views and beliefs are not challenged. Callan argues that we should strive towards dignity safety while struggling against intellectual safety. Likewise, we should reject intellectual safety in our research, but be mindful of the way in which the credibility of our scholarship renders it more liable to endanger the dignity safety of others. Researchers must challenge particular institutions in order to minimize the effect of biases on their research design and analysis.[6]

This points us to a new distinction. Unacceptable, 'uncivil' speech violates the dignity of certain people or groups. Acceptable, 'civil' speech upholds the dignity of all people and groups, but may refuse to respect institutions, particularly if those institutions violate the dignity of certain people or groups. These obligations may clash where individuals are (representatives of) an institution, so that their dignity may appear to be violated by condemnation of the institution to which they belong or which they represent. Political and religious leaders are people and institutions at once; Israeli settlers are representative of the settler colonialism they enact, an institution which violates the dignity of Palestinians and many others globally.

How does this distinction apply to the cases in the previous section? Salaita spoke out for the dignity respect of Palestinians by refusing to abide by the unspoken rule that the institution of the State of Israel and its illegal settlers should be respected. Grundy challenged the institutions of white supremacy and male supremacy. In so doing, they publicly underscored their commitment to justice, and produced a backdrop against which students from marginalized groups (and indeed, all students) could feel assured of dignity safety within their classrooms, while students from privileged groups, which is to say, students whose identities are associated with powerful institutions, could expect to have their intellectual safety challenged. As such, they upheld their duties towards students. Their words were powerful, but they were not oppressive (and ipso facto, not threatening to anyone's dignity) but rather underscored their performative disrespect for the institutions they criticized. They were both recognizably angry. While anger in the context of a violation of dignity respect might be seen as contributing to or constituting violence, theirs instead served as a signifier of urgency and intensity in relation to the dignity at stake.

Conclusion: civility by another name

Steven Salaita should now be a professor at the University of Illinois, teaching his students to speak truth to power and to challenge institutions with whatever tone suits the gravity of the harms they incur. There are many other academics who thrive on insulting the dignity of particular social groups and who are enjoying long careers.[7] The tone they adopt is often 'civil' in Wise's sense, but the content of their work, including its methodology and attention to appropriate context, is 'uncivil' according to mine, and I worry for the students they teach and the harmful influence they have on public discourse.

Dignity respect is essential; institutional respect should be handed out gingerly, and challenged often. Academics should be held to account more readily than non-academics, but the *content* of their speech should be adjudicated, not its tone. A world without emotional responses to moral shortcomings is an impoverished one in which only the most privileged people can find a home. If an academic speaks in the service of dignity, let her speak however she wishes. There is a unique momentum and urgency that comes of anger, and our collective losses will be great if we snub it out.

Let me finish with Katherine Franke's words, which demonstrate the farcicality of 'civility' in its conventional sense:

> Let me say one thing emphatically. Whatever else civility may be, it is not an academic norm. Rigor is an academic norm. Making arguments backed by evidence is an academic norm. A willingness to re-examine our settled premises in the service of understanding a problem more fully and more carefully is an academic norm. Civility ... undermines the very values we hold dear in the academy. Civility has the air of something that is taught in finishing schools. (Weiss 2014)

Notes

1 These points are explored in greater depth in Schotten, this volume.
2 This is an extract from the same statement quoted in Schotten, this volume.
3 Eleven Jewish worshippers were shot dead in their synagogue in Pittsburgh, Pennsylvania, in the course of writing this chapter (Schwartz 2018).
4 Other examples of civility, or some placeholder notion being used to discipline academics, abound (Moshman and Edler 2015).
5 A similar point is made by Dillon (1992, n. 12).
6 Consider the multitude of flawed studies which attempt to discover biological bases for social differences between races and genders (Dennis 1995; Fairchild 1991; Tattersall and DeSalle 2011; Vidal 2012).
7 To name just a few: Jordan Peterson, for his views on gender roles (Sanneh 2018); Niall Ferguson (Ahmed 2016; Mishra 2011), Nigel Biggar (Adams 2017), and Bruce Gilley (Patel 2018), for their defences of colonialism (see Reynolds in this volume); Kathleen Stock, for her transphobia (Jaffe 2018).

References

Adams, R. (2017), 'Oxford University Accused of Backing Apologists of British Colonialism', *The Guardian*, 22 December, https://www.theguardian.com/education/2017/dec/22/oxford-university-accused-of-backing-apologists-of-british-colonialism (accessed 8 March 2019).

Ahmed, Y. (2016), 'So Brits Are Proud of Colonialism? Clearly They Need Some Lessons about the Reality of the British Empire', *The Independent*, 21 January, http://www.independent.co.uk/voices/so-brits-are-proud-of-colonialism-clearly-they-need-some-lessons-about-the-reality-of-the-british-a6825666.html (accessed 8 March 2019).

Boyd, R. (2006), 'The Value of Civility?', *Urban Studies* 43 (5–6): 863–878.

Callan, E. (2016), 'Education in Safe and Unsafe Spaces', *Philosophical Inquiry in Education* 24 (1): 64–78.

Coker, H. C. (2015), 'Boston University President Responds to Saida Grundy Controversy', *Jezebel*, 12 May, https://jezebel.com/boston-university-president-responds-to-saida-grundy-co-1704004301 (accessed 12 November 2018).

Darwall, S. L. (1977), 'Two Kinds of Respect', *Ethics* 88 (1): 36–49.

Dennis, R. M. (1995), 'Social Darwinism, Scientific Racism, and the Metaphysics of Race', *The Journal of Negro Education* 64 (3): 243–252.

Dillon, R. S. (1992), 'Respect and Care: Toward Moral Integration', *Canadian Journal of Philosophy* 22 (1): 105–131.

Dillon, R. S. (2018), 'Respect', *Stanford Encyclopedia of Philosophy*, https://plato.stanford.edu/entries/respect/ (accessed 26 June 2019).

Earle, S. (2018), 'Outselling the Bible', *London Review of Books Blog*, March, https://master-7rqtwti-i7feq5lebr6se.eu-2.platformsh.site/blog/2018/march/outselling-the-bible (accessed 8 March 2019).

Fairchild, H. H. (1991), 'Scientific Racism: The Cloak of Objectivity', *Journal of Social Issues* 47 (3): 101–115.

Foot, P. (1967), 'The Problem of Abortion and the Doctrine of Double Effect', *Oxford Review* 5.

Giroux, H. A. (2015), 'Democracy in Crisis, the Specter of Authoritarianism, and the Future of Higher Education', *Journal of Critical Scholarship on Higher Education and Student Affairs* 1 (1): 7.

Greenwald, G. (2015), 'In Solidarity with a Free Press: Some More Blasphemous Cartoons', *The Intercept* 9.

Grundy, S. (2017), 'A History of White Violence Tells Us Attacks on Black Academics Are Not Ending (I Know Because It Happened to Me)', *Ethnic and Racial Studies* 40 (11): 1864–1871.

Hudson, S. D. (1980), 'The Nature of Respect', *Social Theory and Practice* 6 (1): 69–90.

Jaffe, A. (2018), 'Cis Fears and Transphobia: How Not to Debate Gender', *Verso Blog*, https://www.versobooks.com/blogs/3868-cis-fears-and-transphobia-how-not-to-debate-gender (accessed 8 March 2019).

Jewish Voice for Peace (2017), *On Antisemitism: Solidarity and the Struggle for Justice*, Chicago, IL: Haymarket.

King, Jr, M. L. (1963), 'Letter from a Birmingham Jail [King, Jr.]', https://www.africa.upenn.edu/Articles_Gen/Letter_Birmingham.html (accessed 13 November 2018).

Lê Espiritu, E. and J. K. Puar (2015), 'Civility, Academic Freedom, and the Project of Decolonization: A Conversation with Steven Salaita', *Qui Parle: Critical Humanities and Social Sciences* 24 (1): 63–88.

Leiter, B. (2012), 'The Circumstances of Civility' in C. W. Clayton and R. Elgar (eds), *Civility and Democracy in America: A Reasonable Understanding*, Pullman, WA: Washington State University Press, pp. 124–128.

Mackey, R. (2014), 'Professor's Angry Tweets on Gaza Cost Him a Job', *The New York Times*, 12 September, https://www.nytimes.com/2014/09/13/world/middleeast/professors-angry-tweets-on-gaza-cost-him-a-job.html (accessed 1 November 2018).

Mishra, P. (2011), 'Watch This Man', *London Review of Books* 33 (21): 10–12.

Moshman, D. and F. Edler(2015), 'Civility and Academic Freedom after Salaita', *AAUP Journal of Academic Freedom* 6: 1–13.

Patel, V. (2018), 'Last Fall This Scholar Defended Colonialism, Now He's Defending Himself', *The Chronicle of Higher Education*, 21 March, https://www.chronicle.com/article/Last-Fall-This-Scholar/242880 (accessed 8 March 2019).

Poland, B. (2016), *Haters: Harassment, Abuse, and Violence Online*, Lincoln, NE: University of Nebraska Press.

Salaita, S. (2006), *The Holy Land in Transit: Colonialism and the Quest for Canaan*, Syracuse, NY: Syracuse University Press.

Salaita, S. (2011), *Israel's Dead Soul*, Philadelphia, PA: Temple University Press.

Salaita, S. (2016), *Inter/Nationalism: Decolonizing Native America and Palestine*, Minneapolis, MN: University of Minnesota Press.

Sanneh, K. (2018), 'Jordan Peterson's Gospel of Masculinity', *The New Yorker*, 26 February, https://www.newyorker.com/magazine/2018/03/05/jordan-petersons-gospel-of-masculinity (accessed 8 March 2019).

Schwartz, A. (2018), 'The Tree of Life Shooting and the Return of Anti-Semitism to American Life', *The New Yorker*, 27 October, https://www.newyorker.com/news/daily-comment/the-tree-of-life-shooting-and-the-return-of-anti-semitism-to-american-life (accessed 8 March 2019).

Shahvisi, A. (2015), 'Epistemic Injustice in the Academy: An Analysis of the Saida Grundy Witch-Hunt', *Academe Blog*, 20 May, https://academeblog.org/2015/05/20/epistemic-injustice-in-the-academy-an-analysis-of-the-saida-grundy-witch-hunt/ (accessed 12 November 2018).

Shahvisi, A. (2018), 'From Academic Freedom to Academic Responsibility: Privileges and Responsibilities Regarding Speech on Campus', in D. A. Downs and C. W. Surprenant (eds), *The Value and Limits of Academic Speech: Philosophical, Political, and Legal Perspectives*, New York: Routledge, pp. 266–284.

Son of Baldwin (2015), *Twitter*, 18 August, https://twitter.com/sonofbaldwin/status/633644373423562753?lang=en.

Tattersall, I. and R. DeSalle (2011), *Race?: Debunking a Scientific Myth*, College Station, TX: Texas A&M University Press.

Turner, J. H. (1997), *The Institutional Order: Economy, Kinship, Religion, Polity, Law, and Education in Evolutionary and Comparative Perspective*, Harlow: Longman.

United Nations Office for the Coordination of Humanitarian Affairs (2015), 'Key Figures on the 2014 Hostilities', United Nations Office for the Coordination of Humanitarian Affairs – Occupied Palestinian Territory, https://www.ochaopt.org/content/key-figures-2014-hostilities (accessed 29 March 2019).

Vidal, C. (2012), 'The Sexed Brain: Between Science and Ideology', *Neuroethics* 5 (3): 295–303.

Weiss, P. (2014), '"Civility" Is for Dancing Classes, Not Universities, and Is Tool of Pro-Israel Political Operatives – Franke', *Mondoweiss*, 24 September, https://mondoweiss.net/2014/09/universities-political-operatives/ (accessed 12 November 2018).

Wise, P. M. (2014), 'Illinois | The Principles on Which We Stand | Illinois', https://web.archive.org/web/20160415002934/https://illinois.edu/blog/view/1109/115906 (accessed 1 November 2018).

Index